LOOK BOTH WAYS

Look Both Ways

Katharine Coles

A Double Journey
Along My Grandmother's
Far-Flung Path

TURTLE POINT PRESS
Brooklyn, New York

Kathleen Jamie, excerpt from "Moon"
from *The Overhaul*. Copyright © 2012
by Kathleen Jamie. Reprinted with
the permission of The Permissions
Company, Inc. on behalf of Graywolf
Press, Minneapolis, Minnesota,
www.graywolfpress.org.

Excerpt from "Postcard from a
Destination" is from Dangerous Goods
by Sean Hill (Minneapolis: Milkweed
Editions, 2013). Copyright © 2013 by
Sean Hill. Reprinted with permission
from Milkweed Editions. milkweed.org.

Excerpt from "Landscape" from *Poems:
1962-2012* by Louise Glück. Copyright
© 2013 by Louise Glück. Reprinted
by permission of Farrar, Straus and
Giroux. All rights reserved.

Requests for permission to make
copies of any part of the work should
be sent to:
Turtle Point Press
info@turtlepointpress.com

Library of Congress Cataloging-in-
Publication Data is available from
the publisher upon request

Design by Zab Design & Typography

ISBN: 978-1-885983-58-9
Ebook ISBN: 978-1-885983-65-7

Printed in the United States of
America

For my mother, Joan Link Coles; her brothers, Peter and Andy Link; and Joan's and Peter's other children, Jeff Coles, Peter Coles, Bennett Link, and Hillary Link (in memory). Love and thanks to all of you.

Moon,
I said, *we're both scarred now.*

Are they quite beyond you,
the simple words of love? Say them.
You are not my mother;
with my mother, I waited unto death.

— KATHLEEN JAMIE, "Moon"

I'll miss you when you're here.

— SEAN HILL, "Postcard from a Destination"

CONTENTS

A NOTE ON THE WORK

THIS WORK BEGAN in family lore, in my grandmother's stories, and in the many hundreds of pages of letters and journals left to me. Part of my goal here has been to give my grandparents voice, and in service of this I have as often as possible allowed their words, even when I have questioned their truthfulness, to represent them directly. Their quotes are distinguished from my own text by italics. For my text, I have used underlines for emphasis. As I worked, the book also came to be about my own journey through both their words and the places where I followed them. I have consolidated and elided events in their lives and in mine, and have also used my imagination to fill in details that are missing.

In excerpted material, I have left my grandparents' vocabularies as I found them, including atypical spellings and usages as well as sometimes derogatory terms that were common in their day but have fortunately passed out of use, and that I would never choose to use myself. I have also let spellings considered standard at the time, such as the old Dutch spellings of Indonesian names and place-names, stand; to avoid confusion, I have also used these spellings in my own text.

The sketches of Walter's field expeditions were done by professional artists who accompanied the expeditions. Of the three sketchbooks we have, only one, by H.W.T. Mulle, is signed by the artist. The artists for the other two books, which I believe are by different hands, are unknown.

xiii

LOOK BOTH WAYS

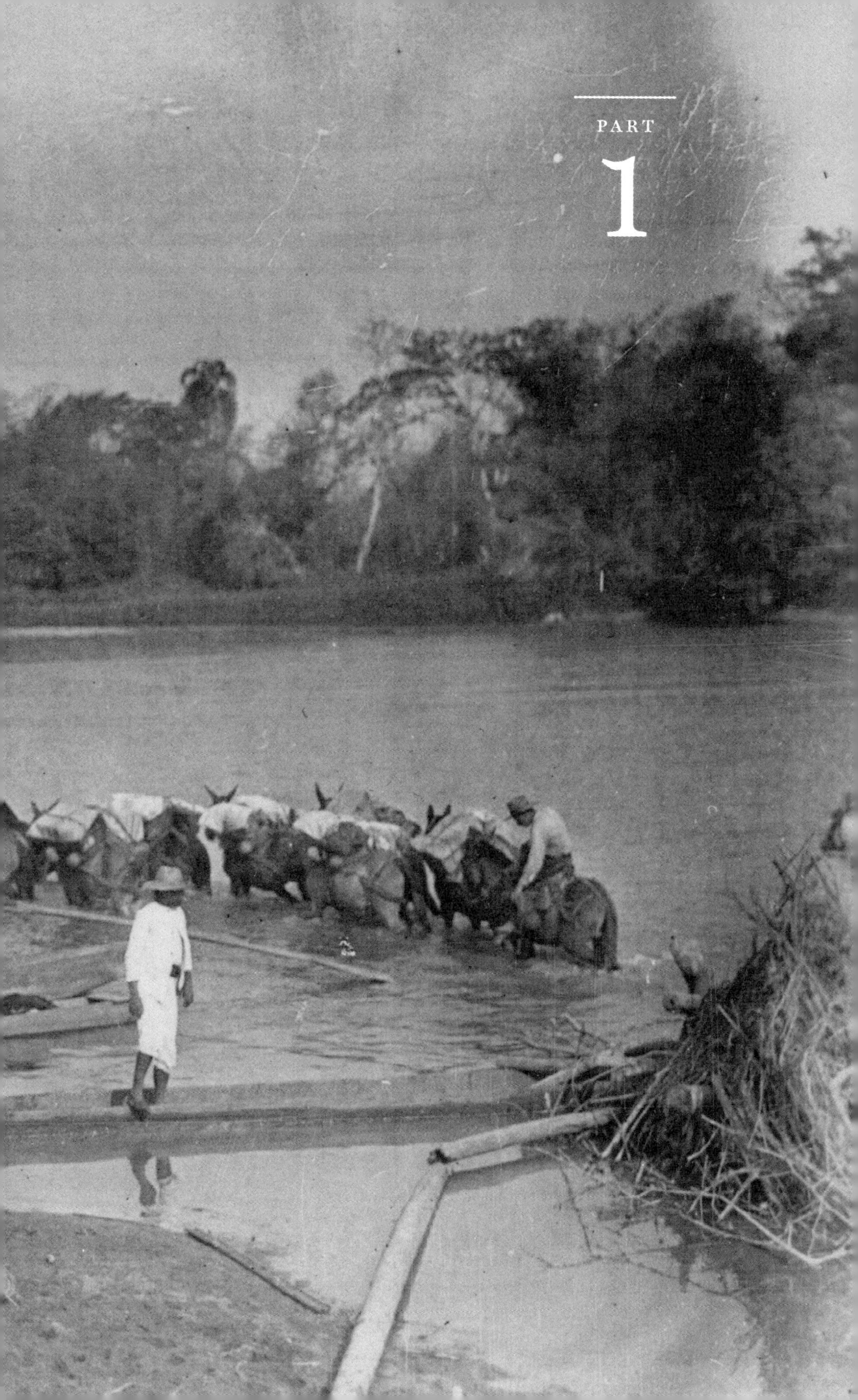

PART 1

CHAPTER 1

A SELF DIVIDED

To speak is also to be.

ISABELLE ALLENDE

WALTER LINK is absolutely a man!
It's a passing reference in my grandmother's diary, but I make a note. In fall of 1923, Miriam Magdalen Wollaeger was a sixteen-year-old freshman at the University of Wisconsin. She'd met the man in question, who would become my grandfather, at the Lutheran church supper. About Tom, my grandfather's first rival, she wrote, *There is someone who feels like I do, to whom I can tell my strange ideas and have them appreciated.* And, *He wants to read my poems,* a line we've all heard. In spring of '24, about Al: *He has a dandy blue canoe, with all the equipment one could think of, including cooking utensils.* Not to mention *a little flivver,* small like her, and dashing, blue to match her eyes. He loved that she drove like a man, much too fast.

Sensibility. Gear. Manhood. Her words are my window and my mirror. Packing for my flight to Wisconsin, my first trip in their footsteps (*archives*, I say to my husband, Chris, who likes to know where I am going and why), I imagine the girl who will become my grandmother looking for a combustion engine and a full tank, for someone to pick her up and move her, for transport.

Walter, five years older, I see less clearly. After the church supper, he lingered on Barnard Hall's front porch until it was time for her to sign in. Already careful of her, he watched the clock. The next day, he took her for a walk in the snow, a date he could afford.

Frugality. Discipline. Family virtues, I've been led to believe, that made him a successful explorer and made her think she should love him. The linear head of a scientist; the lean physique of a cross-country runner. Tall and brooding, he had the long nose that came through my mother to me and impossibly big feet that would torment him on journeys seeking oil in the tropics. If Miriam by virtue of sex and class could flit from English to music to French to zoology, Walter stayed focused, determined to thrive. *I think he is very sensitive, and considers himself inferior in some ways—dear little (?) dumbbell!* Miriam could afford to view education as class ornament, but, like me, Walter's father earned his meager living, until he lost the power of speech and could no longer deliver his sermons, from the word.

Among his children: an attorney, a botanist. Karl Paul, chemist and inventor of warfarin, twice won the Lasker Award and was rumored to have been short-listed for the Nobel. Two petroleum geologists. Margie and Helene had orchids named for them; Ruth was a milliner. Ten children survived. Like most of them, like me, Walter became an atheist, hard headed and willing to rely on himself in everything but love. He was, I think looking back, as American as oil, absolutely of his time.

Then Al began to woo her, and, though Walter promised to take her canoeing (*I hope he does!*) as soon as the lake ice melted, he had no boat to match that blue canoe, much less a fast piece of sky on wheels.

And Miriam: what was she? Eighty years later, I find among her papers a poem penciled in a bluebook, returned ungraded because she was supposed to turn in an essay. In just this way, I troubled my college French professor by translating Baudelaire in place of grammar exercises. I imagine her lying on her dorm-room bed, wondering what it would be like to bushwhack through jungles and gaze from mountaintops over wild landscapes.

> To plough the foaming waters of the boundless Spanish main,
> To plunge amid the swelter of a pelting tropic rain,
> To wade thigh-deep against the racing waters of a stream—
> All these would be fulfillment of my highest, golden dream.

It's formally predictable, but not bad, I think, for sixteen. Embodying desire, she spins through a Wisconsin blizzard on lamplight and white sheets, piloting her own boat. I follow her onto the water, our keel slicing the waves, moving us forward through active and vivid images:

> To hear the billows swishing as they're riven by the bow,
> With their crests like smoke a-flying, lighting dark green
> depths below,
> To feel the rush and smother of a million airy bubbles—

Here, at the end of the second stanza, comes the moment when the poem moves from its sustained provisional infinitive—*to plow, to plunge, to feel*—and into the present, where the journey becomes embodied, or so I expect, in <u>her</u>—

> O, the dash and vigorous joy of life make a fellow lose his troubles!

Did this line trouble her as it does me? Sixteen-year-old Miriam, pining for adventure as I did, enters her dream—in a boy's skin. I remember this: when I was growing up, too, all the heroes were boys, except the intrepid Nancy Drew, who had Ned. Miriam had to take some trouble to accomplish her split, shifting from *me* in the last line of the opening stanza to the third-person *fellow* in the last line of the second. Did it occur to her that this shift stops

21

"I Hunt Black Gold"

LINK (*left*) mapped out 160,000 unexplored square miles in South America. His team

D ON'T let anybody give you any baloney about how glamorous it is to hunt for oil in the jungle. There's no glamor in the hot stink of a dead thing. Or the ticks that worry the hell out of you. There's no glamor in not seeing a woman, any kind of woman, for a couple of years. Or watching a sick burro lie down on the trail and blow up like a balloon. Or walking into an Indian village and finding it in the final stage of a smallpox epidemic. Maybe that jungle looks pretty in technicolor but it's murder when you've got to cut a path through it. And, brother, don't let anybody tell you there's anything romantic about a poisoned arrow sticking in your gut, or a fever that rots your body and turns your blood black. . . ."

He leaned back a minute, his eyes traveling to the huge maps that completely covered the walls of his office. "But I will say this," he added slowly, "there *is something*. Not any phony glamor or romance—but there is a fascination, a complete excitement. . . ."

This is Walter Link, a hard, big-shouldered

six-footer, still in his forties, chief geologist for Standard Oil of New Jersey, the man largely responsible for the discovery of millions of barrels of black gold all over the world, the man known to the head-hunting Dyaks of Borneo as Toean (Master) Goddam.

It takes a special kind of man to be a Toean Goddam. For most new geologists in foreign field work, the bloom wears off quickly. After a couple of months in the middle of nowhere, seven out of ten blow up, say the hell with it, and want to come home. It isn't just the fear of being shipped home in a wooden box (as some are); it's the loneliness, the overworked imaginations, the tensions that pile up and pile up until a man finds himself going home in a nice, tight strait jacket. To stick with this job and flourish in it and hunger for more, takes a special kind of man. It takes a Toean Goddam.

"This fascination I was talking about," Link continued. "You get a guy who's really truly a geologist, and he doesn't get too excited about New York or Paris. But stick him out in the

34 ARGOSY

Walter Link is absolutely a <u>man</u>!

the poem short, disturbing both its rhythm and its logic? Did she even consider "the dash and vigorous joy of life make me lose my troubles"? If she were my student now, I would tell her, look there, into the poem's flaw, for its key. If she were myself, oh, I could have taken her in hand.

Asail on that bed, plowing through the night, she can't hear me. *What more could any man desire?* Her spirit calls, but she can't follow. In the final stanza, when her speaker separates from that *fellow* and they go their separate ways, she has to stay home.

A square of window, whited out. *I want to break away as did 'Desmond', dress as a man and fight my way.* Movies and novels and her own poem notwithstanding, her will was weaker than her desire. She wouldn't step into those britches she'd stitched from words and go. I have always envied her life's romance and, yes, adventure. Now, I watch her begin it daunted, already divided. She imagined motion, imagined the vast unknown, imagined moving through a world that never existed. She called her poem "Adventuring." What she couldn't imagine: herself.

Absolutely a man. An American of his time. She couldn't become him.

Instead, with her mother's help, she would marry him.

But why could she not become him? To my mother Joan, even Miriam's accomplishments represented her failure to live up to her gifts. She read Latin and spoke fluent German, French, Dutch, Spanish, and Malay as well as English; she was a student of violin and voice whose music teacher urged her to drop everything but her *fiddle*; she was a championship swimmer, diver, horseback rider, polo player; at barely twenty she received a degree in geology from the University of Wisconsin; she had the largest working vocabulary of anyone my mother, who herself earned PhDs in geology and psychology, has ever known; she traveled around the world twice before the advent of passenger flight; she lived in Colombia, Java, Sumatra, Costa Rica, and Cuba.

23

I have always been amazed that she managed all this as a woman in her time, even if her travels were made not on her own sweaty nickel but on that of her husband, my grandfather. Behind my eyes, Miriam touches the hem of my wedding dress, its lace hand-pearled for her own marriage sixty-two years before mine; in her filthy Sarasota kitchen, still missing Havana, she makes me paella from the contents of a box, three cans, and Florida tap water; at eighty-five, she sets down her beer and tilts her head, wattles trembling, to pour a raw oyster into her red-lipsticked mouth; she skids her Pontiac into the supermarket parking lot, tires screeching. Even in her Florida old age, where she looks like any other pensioner, I admire and envy the romance of Miriam's life, all the things she told me that she never told my mother, her entitlement. I even admire her driving, her heavy foot, her muttered curses and refusal to give up her keys. She made her own way in a world still deeply unfriendly to women. She loved her children and resented being a mother. Like her mother and mine, like anyone, she succeeded and she failed.

By twenty-two, Miriam had traveled every hemisphere, a goal I wouldn't accomplish until I was in my forties. There are worse reasons to marry. In her place, her time, could I have been braver? With all my freedoms, can I now?

Still, I have to consider the possibility that she should have done everything differently. Wherever she lived, she left her children with servants to play bridge, polo, tennis; she went out dancing; she flirted, and more, with aviators and deputy consuls. Oh, my mother remembers, Miriam was glamorous, bolero-jacketed, sequined. Chanel No. 5 lingered in every room she left.

She should have become an explorer like Walter, persuading the oil companies (her mother, her husband, herself) that she, too, could cut her way through the jungle with a machete while her *precious brats* stayed—where?

She should never have had children. She should have stayed home. She should never have married. She should have married somebody else.

24

She should have given more to her children or taken more for herself. She should not have been angry at what she'd given up. She should have given up nothing.

She should have been the exception. She should have done it all and done it alone.

She should have been everything she was and more, should have been ordinary. She should have been something else altogether.

I begin to imagine what flights I might undertake myself. Her flaws notwithstanding, to me she glitters. She is not only romance, but history.

She wasn't even sufficiently herself. *I don't know what I want or think or feel.* Miriam's own mother, Mandy Gettelman Wollaeger, daughter of a brewer and married to a furniture business until it failed, was famous in Milwaukee for charm and hospitality, especially toward men, and in her family also for cruelty, which she taught to her daughter in exquisite lessons. Four foot ten, dictatorial, willful, she managed her children with deft rigor. With her husband, Louis, she had less success.

Even as a small girl, Miriam cooked for her spoiled older brother, Louis Jr., and younger sister, Tony, saw them off, then delivered breakfast to her mother in bed before hurrying to school herself. Female and thus fatally flawed, she became her mother's petted companion and reviled servant. *My Darling Petty*, Mandy addressed letters all her life, and *Mother's Dearest Blessing. Mommy Darlingest*, Miriam wrote, until she was nearly forty. *Baby*, she called my mother, over Joan's furious protests, until she died.

Mandy, having watched her dull brother get the education she longed for, made sure both daughters went to the University of Wisconsin, just as my mother left no doubt that I would go to college and probably graduate school. *I am merely fulfilling her own dreams.* Still, in 1923 as in the 1890s—as, indeed, in the 1950s, even the 1970s—there were few clear paths for a woman seeking a life beyond that of wife and mother. Like Mandy before

Miriam, Lakeside, Wisconsin, 1925

her and my mother after, Miriam chafed against her restraints but couldn't overturn them or sidestep them. Instead, she created loopholes. To imagine herself in action, Miriam thought herself divided. Through beating men at sports, through conversation, through charm, she became the exception: honorary member of the male sex, object of men's desire, so lively they mistook her for beautiful.

I count Miriam's admirers at school: Edgar, Skeex, Ets, Leo, George, Tom Lake, both Link brothers. When I suggest Miriam got around, my mother defends her. Things were different then: a whirl was what a girl lived in; being seen too much with one boy was what she had to avoid. *Fellows do make better friends when they are real friends than girls.*

In November 1924, Walter took Miriam to watch the northern lights play over Lake Mendota. She saw four movies a week, emotion flickering in the darkness, but nothing could equal the aurora for taking her out of herself. They sang "Stille Nacht," Miriam's mezzo soaring above Walter's bass and over the water.

As you say the German songs are always a font of understanding. Miriam sent Mandy his photograph—*He looks like a very nice fellow*—then took him home for Thanksgiving.

What passed between Walter and Miriam that weekend? Between Walter and Mandy? *I think he is the kind you can respect and admire.* As he walked in the front door, Mandy took his arm—her head barely cleared his elbow—and led him off to her sitting room to apply her wit. *The kind of work he does will keep him wholesome and clean inside and out.* She adopted his nickname, Brutus. *Friendships such as his will have a good influence over you.* And she adopted his pet name for Miriam, *his Muckie.*

It was Miriam who couldn't decide. *He's a dandy* kid, she wrote to her mother. But her dreams were shaped by the stories she already knew. To her journal: *I will be a solitary girl—until someday the man of my dreams wakes me, and then I can do anything. Oh, I will love him (if only I don't make any mistakes first. God please guide me!).*

The world tells her to give over, to keep herself in check, to slumber. Through time, I see myself in her—small, straight-bodied, self-absorbed, often frustrated, uncertain, reckless, secretive, her head easily turned by novelty, by beautiful clothes, by men. I want her to be wise. *I'm destined to be forever in doubt as to which man of several I like best. It is a sad weakness.* Over ninety years have passed. *I would not want to have missed it.* She has had some glimmerings, but she is not wise yet, and neither am I.

I remember ice skating on Lake Mendota during the year we spent in Madison; trying not to draw my grandmother's eye, or her temper, by getting underfoot in Milwaukee; picking wild, intensely sweet blueberries with my brothers on the windswept shores of Lake Superior, running as wild as they did, getting lost. I don't remember Mandy, who held me only once not long before she died, already descended far enough into her dementia not to know me any more than I could know her. Now, looking into a more distant past, I rummage in the Wisconsin Historical Society archives for newspapers advertising dresses Miriam might have bought and movies she might have seen; I walk downtown, identifying buildings that would have been here when she was young, trying to picture still-unpaved roads gone muddy after rain.

On campus, I buy an ice cream at the old Babcock Hall Dairy Store, which my parents would have patronized in the fifties. I tour Barnard Hall with its visible ductwork, tall windows, and original radiators, still crisply new when Miriam wrote her poems and letters there, now advertised as historic.

January 1925: a new diary. *D'you suppose I'm falling in love with Brutus?* There was a line, invisible and moving, she was always about to cross, had just crossed. Miriam, at seventeen often late like my mother, like me running to catch up with herself, strewing ribbons and buttons and torn stockings in her path, tried when he arrived to come down *promptly (notice!) hair up and everything.*

They went to see *North of 36* at the Strand. *His touch thrills me.* After the film, they met his elegant brother Karl Paul at the Chocolate Shoppe. *K.P. and I had a battle of wits. But Brutus squelched him, saying, "She goes with the man, not the clothes."* Little did he know. She loved play, dance, immanence and its delicate timing.

Absolutely a man. She didn't stop to wonder what that meant.

The scene as I play it begins with the pair not touching. *I wonder if he really loves me?* He steps into her; she backs away, foot mirroring foot, shoulder-to-shoulder, pushed before him as if by a magnet's negative force. Leading, he steps back. *He has no money.* Breast, hip, thigh: he draws her forward, the space between them neither opening nor closing. At last, the distance narrows. When he pulls her into his arms and whirls her into the night, I sigh.

But Walter would never really learn to dance. She had to learn to make it look like she was following. *I wanted so to have him kiss me goodnight, but unless I act rather lingering, he seems to lack the courage.*

If I could speak to them, what would I say? He didn't take her into his arms. At *The Thief of Bagdad*, Miriam thought not of Walter beside her but about a distant land, a man returning to claim his beloved on a magic carpet. *The old discontent and restlessness and wanderlust stronger than ever.* She was miles away. She felt distracted, introspective. *If only I had enough character to know what I wanted!*

I find a Chocolate Shoppe in Madison, founded in the sixties, long after their time. There is no dance floor. Though the Orpheum Theater, built in 1926, still stands on State Street, its iconic sign competing with the capitol dome for attention, the Strand was demolished in 1990 to make way for a parking lot, its façade hauled off and tucked into storage in some Historical Society warehouse, awaiting a future that wants to see it again.

My mother's cousin Tom lives in the house Karl Paul built in the 1930s on a hill outside town. He and I sit on the terrace drinking

Miriam, Lakeside, Wisconsin, 1925

wine, looking down the long lawn where as a child I chased fireflies through the grass. Though Karl spent the northern winters locked in depression behind his study door, I knew his summer self, my mother's favorite and also mine among the great aunts and uncles; his gentle-humored wife Elizabeth a progressive and lovely anti-Miriam, unpainted, hair smoothed into a simple bun, who channeled her own brilliance without apparent resentment into her children and courteous but passionate activism. Tom, who has her bones, is bemused, as I was, to learn that his father, whom we both knew as a white-maned and gently ironic man of science, possessed a shadow self, a devil in wit and on the dance floor too.

In February, during Walter's second visit, Mandy was exercising her temper on her husband, who, when she wouldn't give him money, borrowed from friends he never repaid. *I'd never marry if I thought there'd be such unpleasantness.*

Used to real hardship, Walter fitted himself in, working puzzles, praising Miriam's cooking, helping Lou work on the Ford. Sitting alone, he listened to Bach and Beethoven on the Victrola, each note a little miracle only money could buy.

When they got back to Madison, the closeness of the visit held, just long enough. *I told my beloved that I love him.* In love with the dance. For the moment, she was right there, under his hand.

Two weeks earlier, K.P. had *confessed his love*, the second man that day. *If Brutus weren't so much in love*—like her, he was a tease, light and brittle and quick, happy to watch himself woo. His mouth to her ear, the brasses scorching the air—she was his feather, his Ferris wheel gone wrong, his reckless schooner: I, too, have imagined myself free yet utterly mastered. *If only Brutus isn't hurt and martyrish.* She laid her head back and laughed. *I'm not going to tell Brutus at all.* When she put it that way—but what could she do? And why did he refuse to see?

In May, Miriam rode horse drills in the big parade. Major was ten times her weight, the ground wet and slick, the horse's hooves slipping. She was leading, in control, but all Walter saw was how small she looked, back straight, thighs straining to grip the horse's body. He was a flicker on the edge of her mind. *I am almost afraid that he is cramping my style.*

Mandy had forbidden her to go out with Walter more than two nights a week. Had she expected Miriam to resist, to make of this obstacle a stronger bond between herself and her lover? *Are you getting tired of the boy? Be careful what and how you say and do things.*

What did Miriam long for? Her lover. Her mother. Sometimes she confused them. Every night they didn't see each other, Walter called to tell her what time to go to bed. *He believes he's been appointed regent in your absence.* She wanted privacy of mind and to be understood. She wanted love and freedom. I know how this is, though I came of age in a different time, with different risks, different protections, buying and carrying condoms long before I ever planned to use them, in the years immediately following *Roe v. Wade. Perhaps my letters are, as you say, shorter and dumber.* How could she say what she felt or wanted to the tiny woman with the stinging slap? She didn't know herself. She looked at Walter awash in sweet longing. She never wanted to see him again. In her journal, she *asked for a big handsome man with a rich car to take me riding in my cute new clothes, and he would take me places!* A means to an end. *O, I know it's wicked and ungrateful.* Love. Liberty. For either, she would have to give up something she hadn't tasted. She dreamed she could go back, that she and Mandy could be close as lovers again, and she wouldn't have to choose. *Then my Mommy and I will go bummin' together and have a gorgeous time afterwards in a nice little house by the sea.*

One Saturday evening, she and Walter went to the pump house, which sits at the lake's edge, the water that feeds its intakes lapping beneath the foundation. Among the hydraulic equipment, the smell of the lake rising from beneath their feet, she felt shy and young and itchy. *My goodness, Brutus was bold.* Pressing back, backing away. *I guess I haven't been strict enough.* After he left her at the dorm, she lay awake, flushed and disturbed. *He's getting a bit too passionate and I mustn't let him.*

It's summer when I visit, and the building, now housing laboratories, is cool and quiet. With its modernized interior, it floats in layered history. Not far from here my parents would meet at a Hoofers Club party, my father lying on the floor plucking his mandolin until my mother stepped on him. Did she really break it, or is that my invention? She was majoring in geology to prove to her father she was worth as much as any boy. My parents, too, would marry in Milwaukee, stepping off Miriam's porch into new lives. I would marry in my own hometown, where I now live with Chris, from the Ladies Literary Club. Like Walter, like Chris, my father was in love, I presume, and hopeful. My mother, as always, was dazzling and angry. Was she also, like me, in love?

On Sunday, Miriam waited for Walter to phone, but he left her to herself. *It'd be just my luck to fall in love with him when I can't have him.* Only then?

The next day was a Monday, *a perfectly gorgeous night,* one of the evenings they weren't to see each other. When he called, she was already half carried away. *I simply had to go out for a walk with him, and so we went up on top of the ski-slide. Across the lake there were just one or two lonely lights, while the stars were so big and bright they looked as if they were on fire.*

A child. Why should she have seen how ill-suited they were? Not love, the idea—

When I told him he was naughty and asked him if he thought he'd ever get to heaven, he said he was as close as anyone could get right then.

Filigree of leaves against bright sky and water. Night air soft and close, fired with starlight. Soft pine duff underfoot; clothes rubbed thin at knees and thighs. That June, Walter came to the Wollaegers' summer house on the shore of Lake Superior as a member of the family, as far as Mandy was concerned. At Lakeside,

33

Miriam had always been free as her brother to ramble, to swim and dive, canoe and sail, wade and scramble up rock faces. As I was also taught to do, she went her own way, in trousers.

Walter imagined a life that might include both of them within one frame. If he couldn't lead on the dance floor, he could in the woods. He bounded on his long legs up any hillside, leaned down to offer his hand. She required not help, but the very mastery she would resent. Though she loved to win at any sport, she couldn't long tolerate a man she could beat. Still, here in the woods, she could take his offered hand. They could admire each other.

During the long northern evenings, the family sat on the screened porch and listened to the whine of mosquitoes pressing the mesh. They played cards, or Miriam strummed her uke while everybody sang along. Mandy folded Walter in so easily he almost felt he belonged.

At summer's end, he would board a boat bound for South America, where Standard Oil was sending him for two years while Miriam stayed behind. *My spirit of Adventure.* He found himself a hundred times a day looking at Miriam, trying to memorize her face or capture a turn of phrase, one of those lines of poetry she was always dropping, an attitude of body. He had bought a used camera with his waiter's wages, and he photographed her plying her paddle in the front of the canoe; lowering herself down a cliff face, rapt in concentration; wading into the lake; diving, laid out over the water—photos I thumb through, edges worn ragged. To me, they become documents of an obsession they can't explain. Barely out of adolescence, at rest she is dreamy if not moody; in her sailor's blouse or tank swimsuit she looks disheveled and a little dumpy.

Like me, he was trying to capture but also to decode. This life had made her, but into what? In the mornings, he awakened to the distant sound of her singing as she took an early walk along the shore.

At last, the days of rest ended. Walter was leaving for Venezuela; Miriam would head north on a field trip, having decided that she, too, like my mother and uncles after them, would become a geologist. On their last rambles, they talked of living in the wilderness as partners, looking together for oil to light cities, to drive civilization.

As Mandy stands on her toes to kiss her little girl goodbye, I feel something ending before it's quite begun, while something else gains force and momentum just over the horizon. It was hard to say goodbye to Walter, but this farewell also sent a tremor of excitement through her. He would go forth in their stead and return with spoils and tales to tell. He had promised to write, and Mandy to reply. She had long since given up dreaming of her own journeys. She looked forward to following him in words.

Though she knew the cottage would be quiet, Mandy wasn't prepared for the emptiness she felt as the screen door slapped shut. Tony and Lou were both out. Louis knew to stay out of her way. As she sat over her unread book on the porch, she mulled over her loose-endedness. Like any girl being wooed, she mustn't write Walter until he had written her, but in the morning, she settled herself outside in the shade and began her letter to Miriam.

Last night when you left it almost seemed to me as though Brutus wanted to kiss me too—or was I mistaken? I should have been glad to if I had thought he really wanted me to....

CHAPTER 2

INTERLUDE:
WHAT I HAVE OF HER

FROM SARASOTA, SHE SENDS ME an embroidered shawl. A kimono. Velvet evening purses; suede gloves, elbow-length, the color of our eyes or the aquamarine in her last wedding set, the stone huge on my hand. Mandy's Burmese sapphire and diamond ring mailed loose in an envelope. A batik, wayang figures intricate on a deep blue ground—

Something my mother wanted for herself, as perhaps she wanted all of it. Now in her eighties, Joan tells me her jewelry will come to me, every piece, and not her granddaughters; I will have the choice of everything, as she did not, as I never thought to give her—

Miriam's wedding dress, which would not have fit my mother, who inherited Walter's height. She sends them all while she is still alive, while she can see me in them, in the body like hers even smaller than it looks because it is straight and solid and broad shouldered, its blue gaze a reflection of her own. Having her eyes means not that I see like her, but that I look like her.

Having at last gotten Miriam's permission to clear out the Sarasota house, my mother throws away pots with broken handles, bathing caps festooned with rotting rubber flowers, empty jars, every check Miriam's mother Mandy, dead by then for thirty-five years, ever wrote. She boxes magazines and blenders with burned-out motors for Goodwill, but before my uncles can load them into the car my grandmother is hauling them back inside. At night, my mother lies in bed waiting for Miriam to shut off her lamp then rises to cram papers into trash bags and sneak them out to the curb, with no regard for history, reading nothing. In the morning, she finds Miriam in her nightgown on the front lawn, the papers strewn around her.

My mother saves for me Chinese rice bowls, hand-painted china, crystal cordial glasses the size of thimbles I am too thirsty to use. I am interested in how the past persists into the present. I'll hang onto these things for anyone who might want them later.

I ask about the boxes of photographs. Women in long dresses and button boots picnicking beside a lake; men in twenties bathing suits, arrayed around my young grandmother, drinking champagne at a poolside shaded with palm trees. Visit after visit, I asked Miriam to label them. I might see a smile cross her face as she shuffled through the box and obediently applied her pencil to the backs of the snapshots, naming people, places I want to visit. She rarely answered my real question: who and what were they to her? One night, she showed me a ring—a square of jade set simply in gold, brought back from Batavia, now Jakarta. The photos' ghosts had brought something to mind. She didn't say what.

So many stories, so few told. Miriam had wanted to be a writer. For years, she sent me poems written in her youth, laden with flowers and turbulent skies and hints of romance, veiling as much as they revealed, poems I didn't know how to read. There must be more. On the phone, listening to my mother describe a tea set she concedes is not my style, I think about my grandmother's

Miriam, Lakeside, Wisconsin, 1925

daydreaming, shuttered face. I say I want those poems, letters, journals, the old photos with names spidered in pencil on their backs: everything paper.

There is a pause on the line. My mother says, "I think we've thrown most of it away."

Another pause, while I collect myself.

"Save what's left," I say. "If it's okay with Grandmama."

I imagine my grandmother looking out the sliding glass doors into her backyard toward the canal that travels to an ocean we have both crossed more than once. Her chin tilts up, her faded eyes seeing not this green Florida day but some distant morning streaming with sun, in which her own eyes are as brilliant as the tropical sky. Sixty years before, she wrote, *There is always the chance that a diary might fall into hostile hands, before one's death. Might not children or family be disillusioned if they read some of its pages?* She always wanted to be read, though on her terms. The papers my mother tossed, Miriam recovered. A lifetime.

"I'll have to ask her permission," my mother says.

I have my permission. Miriam has known for years what I will do. Not now, but someday, when she is long gone. Even then, I will take my time.

My mother, she warns: "I fell in love a few times, you know." And that is that.

CHAPTER 3

THE VENEZUELA TRIANGLE: A COURTSHIP IN THREE (OR SO) VOICES

WALTER UNHINGED HIS LEGS and stretched them into the aisle of the tour bus, watching Liberty lift her torch, the ferry slipping toward Bedloe's Island. The city I have paced from downtown to midtown, where I have run the park and along the river, read my poems in dive bars and fancy auditoriums, and dined in company and alone, rises over the city he sees, not quite erasing it. Now, sitting quietly in my seat, I strain to listen to the guide.

He had two ambitions: to make a name for himself at Standard Oil, and to make Miriam his wife. He had two years to succeed or let her go. Simple, except he couldn't keep her attention when he was standing in front of her, and now he was gone.

Wall Street, Broadway. As my bus stalls in traffic I try to imagine how midtown looked when the elevator was only beginning to transform it. With him, I shift my eyes from concrete to words and back, scan lists of the equipment he needs. Log books. Plane table. A Brunton compass with a mirror in its cover; pocket transom; camera; alidade; barometer. He couldn't have too many socks, though he didn't yet know it, or too much tobacco. His father's old shotgun for hunting; the revolver from army surplus. When he wasn't shopping, he wrote Mandy, he would hang around the office making sure the big dogs saw him. He was going to do something to remember.

Who was he? Containing, I wonder, what romance, what forms of violence? His shirt pocket held those photos of Miriam at Lakeside in her bathing suit, laughing, her round hip cocked. Cradled in the branches of a tree, about to start singing. Launching off the pier in a twisting one-hand stand, the body wheeling around its axis, force a solid thing. Silhouetted against the brilliance of the water, her poise seems impossible. Looking at these beside the shots of him gazing always pensive and unsmiling at the camera, I remember that he was the beautiful one, whatever the family myth—the one who gave my mother her cheekbones and long-lashed eyes as well as her height. What, I wonder, made Miriam so vivid in person, so hard to turn away from? The photos can't tell me; they can only hint.

He is being carried into his future. She is in flight. Ninety years later: she has fallen, gone to water and air; he is gone with their letters, almost all of them, in which words turned to ash, as fragile and temporary in the end as the text arriving from Chris on my iPhone. Where they crossed, I am left. In his eye, she balances on one hand, uncontainable. Yet, he caught her. The proof is in my hand.

Oil: slippery, evasive, mysterious as time, pooled underfoot, surfacing in a seep, rainbow-slicking a pond, blue flame on water; or exploding like the held breath of a whale, the flesh of whose ancestors it renders: plankton, algae, anything that floated and died eons ago. To become fossil then fuel, it must be sedimented over and cooked under pressure; must migrate, buoyant, through permeable rock until it encounters an opening it cannot escape, a trap, a pocket created through structure, stratigraphy, hydrography. A dome, an anticline, a fault, or a fold; unconformity, lens, reef, difference in water pressure, a tilt in the hydrocarbon-water contact. Following his lead, I read disturbing history, evidence the earth below us never was solid: even rock transfigures. Where there was once an ancient seabed, riverbed, lakebed, coral reef, water where things lived, there is now a peak, a basin, a jungle, a desert.

The company starts him in Venezuela's Maracaibo Basin because he's green and oil is everywhere, structure legible on the surface. In more challenging geographies, he'll need intuition to follow structure underground; he will descend pits into the earth or drill down and bring a core up. Here, if he can't find oil, he's in the wrong job.

His mind is precise, I know, the mind of the scientist I own. I think as I begin that it's without lyricism, without the will to transform, though he turns out to be as inventive in his way as any poet. The map he makes is a thumbprint or an echo; it has whorls and arrows. It won't show you a town, a road, or a house, won't take you to the nearest mall or tell you where a star snugs into constellation. It shows which fractures occurred in the Paleocene, the Eocene, the Oligocene; shows cleats and upthrows and sediment transport—space and time, what happened when. It is the after-the-fact report of catastrophe still in progress, which you follow to a conclusion: drill here.

I first met him when I was seven or eight, after he outran the Brazilian army and returned to the States. He and my mother reconnected, more or less, and every summer we visited La Porte's swankiest neighborhood, the elegant house with a pool that he bought to prove to the town of his impoverished childhood he'd succeeded. Though he wasn't any more interested in her children than he had been in his own, he organized cribbage tournaments for me and my brothers, his films flickering like memory on the screen in his vast study full of artifacts, including the ebony elephant family that now sits on the étagère in my living room, minus tiny ivory tusks.

Now, his letters to Mandy are in my hands. Unlike my grandmother, he would not have foreseen this, his words working their way into the contours of my mind, going subterranean. *He writes of what he sees and does and thinks thereby keeping his friends acquainted and in touch with him.* Mandy was right: before Walter set foot on the SS *Carabobo*, Miriam could have papered a wall with his inscrutable hand. *If we do the same there will never be the strangeness and aloofness that so often develops when people are separated by long distances and unlike conditions.* Letters arrived in thick bundles. Read one a day, Mandy commanded, and answer it; then she'd have a nice stack to send every Friday.

But Miriam didn't follow him, not even in words, as I do. There was too much to fill her time. Whiff of apples and wood smoke. A trail under bare trees, a lively two-year-old who loved to run and Harry's horse pounding at her heels, not quite able to catch her. She would see Harry again that night, staying out past the 9:00 p.m. bedtime Walter had appointed with Mandy's blessing. *I won't have it. The next man you go out with as often as that you will be engaged to.* She'd thought the time without Walter would pass slowly, but days ripped by as if a hard wind tore at them.

Dear Brutus. What could she write? Today, six dates, two with Harry. Mandy's whisper in her ear. *Remember that you are building your future in* character, health, *and* intellect. But what girl wants to be a work in progress? She wanted to come into herself magically, as when the horse surged beneath her or she leapt from the diving board into perfect suspension: each choice committed her to something, but her body chose for her. Thinking got in the way.

Eighteen: like me, shutting the door on one boy and opening

it to another, she couldn't give up on anything. Was the fault in the self she knew, or that she didn't know herself? Was there a difference?

Maracaibo now is urban sprawl, hotels and condos, blue lake bristling with oil rigs. Then, the town was small, isolated by water, the basin wild. In the wilderness, they had open-sided tents for cooking and eating, two more to house the white men, Walter Link, junior geologist reading comics sent by his sweetheart's mother, and his boss, Krug, his nose in *Green Mansions*, that imperial romantic tragedy, which had been circulating the camps. Twenty-five Venezuelan *peons* lived under five small tents. *Combination Spanish, Indian, Negro, and American*, they were, according to Walter, *an awful mess*.

Even here, white men didn't cook. Pots clattered; the smell of whatever meat Walter had bagged—rabbit, turkey, deer—filled the air. After snuffing the light, he lay in his hammock under his mosquito bar, protection against malaria, and drifted off wondering where her letters were. *My Dear Mrs. Wollaeger, I wanted to write last nite, but I had rather a depressive feeling.* Mail from the U.S. might get stuck in customs or lie dumped and forgotten in some dockside warehouse. The little wind-up Victrola he'd ordered might be anywhere. *I wrote to Muckie cause I always do that.* During the rains mail had to come by burro through thick cactus forest. Too often no letters meant Miriam hadn't written. He wrote to her every day. Mandy he wrote as often as an ordinarily ardent suitor.

I imagine him then, as Mandy did, among Indians, Spaniards, more recently arrived Americans, Dutch, and English—each jostling for advantage in a land cash poor but rich in resources, especially oil, new to the politics of capitalism, primed for development. El Benemérito, the Worthy One; El Bagre, the Catfish: President Juan Vicente Gómez had complete power. The oilmen, American and European, offered cash then condemned corruption; they bought politicians, women, laborers, and treated them with contempt.

I see all this through the lens of his letters and very different politics, my imperfect hindsight on a history that hadn't yet unfolded. By the time I consider following him to Venezuela and Colombia, Indian attacks have been replaced by guerilla raids and cartel murders; civil war rages in Colombia; kidnapping in both countries has become a thriving for-profit business. One article, "How to Keep Your Ignorant Ass from Getting Kidnapped in Colombia," boils its advice down to "avoid Colombia." The president of my university at the time, a former Bush State Department official, assures Chris that if I am kidnapped in Indonesia he'll get me out, thus adding kidnapping to Chris's list of worries. About Venezuela and Colombia, he declines to promise.

For now, not capitulating so much as sensible, I make no plans. But anything can change. Even the ground moves.

And Walter? *The Americans down here are disgusting in every way*—gambling, whoring, trading coin for pleasure. To him, their failure was domestic, in responsibility to their own families and ideals, not Venezuela or its people.

Lifting his letter to my nose, I can almost smell green damp, mud, and salt. *Now that I have finished a letter to every one that I owe one to—perhaps I can slip one to you while the rest are not looking.* Walter understood what I am learning: Mandy, tiny and formidable, like her daughter, like me, was a coquette, prepared to be charmed. She looked forward to his news of malaria and thieves and Indian raids next to complaints about socks or tobacco lost in the mail. She liked to be courted and teased. He told her about the six-foot rattler he'd beheaded, its skin now *dried and tucked away.* He gave mileage and coordinates. She knew more about his whereabouts than her daughter's.

When she was done writing Walter, she wrote to Miriam. *Precious Blessing.* She'd had no letter from her daughter in three weeks. *If I don't hear from you tomorrow I'll hit you.* She was worried about Harry. *And Blessing—if you will be as fine and big as Brutus and I know you are, everything else will take care of itself, and no one need worry.*

Krug got the flu, then malaria. They loaded him onto a mule, and there was Walter, *in the sticks, alone with 25 peons and a damned poor knowledge of Spanish.* Every day, he cut trail with the laborers, slashing at fica with his machete, competing to set the pace, developing endurance for which he would become famous.

When they found a spot, he set up his plane table. On good days, they might get clear space for some long shots, a half or even three-quarters of a mile. Walter liked plotting points, feet and tenths of feet, and drawing lines to join them, everything extraneous vanishing. This was his chance. The big dogs were coming soon, and he was determined that his map, by a junior geologist working alone, would be better than any by the nearby teams. *I am my own boss.* At night he cleaned his pistol and counted bullets, tins of food, even pencils. Nothing would disappear on his watch. Then, he wrote letters.

Does he know yet his love is measured, increasing with distance? Will he ever?

Mandy sent the *Saturday Evening Post* with its article on Venezuela. A cake, tobacco, good socks. Walter kept telling her where he was. Native trails and jungle became roads and drilling sites. He imagined how it must have looked to the first geologists. *I guess you can't kill em. If they couldn't lick that kind of work they wouldn't be geologists.*

To Walter, she wrote, *Tell me what is in your mind.* He told her so much already; couldn't she guess the rest?

Like her, I read my way in. Thumb-worn photographs. An earth in flux.

He proposed first to Mandy, who could make things happen. *I'm in love with her,* Walter said to his candle's flickering light while the cook crooned a song in Spanish. *And she with me.* Her letter beneath his elbow said so. With her journals before me, trying to follow the plot, I have my doubts. The force between them flickering. Everything could vanish. *An engagement, not to be announced, but for you, and Mr. Wollaeger, Muckie and myself.*

Now, he had better write to his girl.

Burro. Boat. Warehouse. Train. From the age of instant messaging, I count the time with him: up to four weeks for the letters to reach Milwaukee and Madison. As few as two. The same for a reply, if Miriam answered right away. When had she ever?

Week 1

Snow fell in the woods where Miriam's skis and those of the young men chasing her made the only sounds under the wind. The wind swept her onto the frozen lake, her iceboat's runners whispering *s*'s and *k*'s. Like Mandy, I search her letters for mention of Walter— the weekly calendar, even edited so Harry's name appears only twice, took pages. Then there were the lists of needed clothes: blouses, stockings, another evening gown. *Mommy, could I have a green one?* She showed no sign of knowing the future was closing around her. Walter may have been strong, stalwart, romantic (those scorching letters!), quick for her. He was absent.

And Miriam knew what Mandy wanted to hear. *Ooh! Oh! Oh!!! I got five letters and a postal card from Brutus! Maybe I wasn't floating around on air!*

There was nothing so perfect as their courtship.

Week 2

I wonder if you would mind if I got her a Hope Chest? She can sit on it and wander away a little farther ahead. Walter dreaming Miriam dreaming of him. As if she ever stayed still. The dark cloud of her head resting on hope. Stille Nacht.

Week 3

Two days after Christmas, his letter came. Miriam was still home, but Mandy read it twice before waking her. *Tell me.*

I am in love with Muckie and she with me. How could Miriam argue? She had felt the lure of the imagined figure alone under candlelight, tested the words, written them. While she cried, Mandy held her, told her *everything will be jake.*

Week 4

The day passed, a week. She returned to Madison. What would it take, to move herself to <u>I will</u>, from the present to the future? Barely nineteen. At her age, I was always, an old friend reminds me, trailing young men. And, she adds, I was oblivious. Still, in an age devoted to one-at-a-time, I'd had more serious beaux than she, and had tried them farther; I would get through as many again before the last. I had the freedom to make up my own mind, a well-equipped handbag, and time to choose. I was free even to choose none at all.

Mandy: I think we should put Brutus out of his uncertainty.

Miriam: *Your letter was so cute.* She couldn't win. She spent two days in bed, until Mandy, determined, sent the cable. *Loving good wishes, dear son.*

Is that satisfactory? If it isn't I'll spank you—I still can and will. Mandy's virtuosity, her fingers on every string, violently pulling. Her vicarious life, everything she had missed.

I have a particularly bad case of nostalgia—(see Webster)—as well as one of downright lonesomeness, and it is enough to make me weep buckets, or even barrels.

From <u>I do</u> to <u>I will</u> to <u>I miss</u>. Did she miss Walter or herself? *Absolutely a <u>man</u>.*

In a way I was sorry when I read your letter—sorry that you should suffer so, and then on the other hand I was glad because it really means that you love Brutus. Willful misreading, which I sometimes engage in myself. Before Miriam, a month of waiting for every year of her life. *You have the nice little job of training his*

"Muckie" *to be the very best kind of a wife and mother.* What would a hope chest mean to her, with her single option? *You can tell Brutus one nice new perfectly good settlement cookbook is already waiting.* Later, Miriam disliked cooking so much she learned to hate to eat.

What would a hope chest, the idea of it, mean to Walter? A gift not to her but to himself, the first of many. Mandy wondered if he was safe, too cold or too warm, wet or dry, if the candlelight strained his eyes. *I will be glad when I have had an answer to the cable.*

Both writing to Walter, to each other, weaving the web of letters. *Have you ever thought that you can say* next year *we are going to meet him in New York if all goes well?* Two heads bent under separate lamps, one the head of a woman enthralled by love. She will keep his letters until she dies.

Week 5

The last envelope from New York held Mandy's cable. *Dear Mrs. Wollaeger.* No. *Dear Mandy.* Again. *Dear Mother.* Two weeks to reach him. *I will do the best I can to make myself fit for your little girl. I will do all things that are right for your sake.* His heart, the beating of cicadas. *Hers and mine too.* He fell in love with rattlesnakes, mosquitoes, *the gallant little mule* who'd carried his thin slip of paper.

So be it. At school, Miriam's room was her own, and her head, if not her hand. And she was working outside, surrounded by men, an exception. *Now that you have taken up his line of work, you'll be his companion in that too.* On weekend field trips surveying in the country north of Madison, at Devil's Lake reading layers and signs and fossils in boulders scoured by glaciers from the earth, she felt body and mind come together and focus nervy energy into ambition. My mother took the same courses in 1952, also driven by the need to prove herself. After them, I scale cliffs and examine

49

outcrops, as if my untrained eyes will ever read rock; as if I will want to. Not even, I remind myself, quite the same rocks.

Miriam carried tripods, bent over her plane table. She let herself imagine working with Walter side by side, and he encouraged her. *We all know that in many ways women are just as or more capable than men.* But he didn't think she might seek knowledge for her own use. *There are so many women now that don't even care what their husbands are doing.*

The engagement was secret; nobody was to know. She only needed to be steady, while Harry and the other young geologists jostled to partner with her in the field.

At last Walter had received his Victrola and the Christmas box with its records. *I could not have bought a better selection to suit my taste.* Or his memory. Mandy had taken Miriam downtown to a studio and recorded her singing German songs he knew, songs in French he didn't, serenading him through a disc and needle.

He worked to distract himself. He adopted a monkey and a fawn that followed him like a dog, nuzzling his hand. He took photographs. *When we sit down after dinner to have a cigar and even a glass of beer we feel much like a bunch of highbrows and millionaires.*

This is where I imagine myself as he imagined her: in the wilderness, but only so wild. Cheerful around camp, she did wifely chores. In the field, like Rima from *Green Mansions*, she followed him invisibly through the jungle, singing from the shadows of the towering Vochysia trees. Anyone could have guessed from her first appearance that Rima—female, alone, living in the forest— was doomed to be prey, though she was the ablest character in the book. *I guess when we are married I can take her to most any place that is reasonable, and be sure that she is enjoying every bit of it.*

I know what is the matter—you are changing from a girl into a woman and therefore the fears and the uncertainties. I went through the same ordeal myself. That passage, the dark study where Mandy's father had said he was sending her dull brother to college, but for her finishing school would do. *It seems so much simpler and easier to stay as one was.* She remembered girlhood dances as the inside of a kaleidoscope moving fast.

What had she seen in Louis Wollaeger? A dreamer, so handsome, his letters all in German. *I think of men I could have married for their beauty, the ones who wanted to take care of me—how many times a box I was happy to carry or a tool I was ready to use was simply lifted out of my hands, leaving them with nothing to do.* For Mandy as for Miriam, marriage was an end for women, more than a beginning. They had no alternative. When Mandy's clock ran down, Louis was there.

Even Walter wrote that he wanted Miriam to have dresses and dances to wear them to while she could. *For a geologist is not always in places where there is even a slight amount of social life.* Wishful thinking. *I have always sort of dodged that part of life, and now I see that it should not be done.*

He didn't yet know what I know, what Mandy surely suspected. *He's a darned unselfish man.*

He was only trying to keep her. Soon he would vanish into the unmapped borderlands between Venezuela and Colombia, where I will cross his shadow. The rivers were nearly dry. Boats went aground on sand bars. Strange whistles pierced the jungle; flocks of parrots flashed their wings over the river. At night, his tent was lit like a target. *Reading, I am listening so hard I hear the sloths breathing.* One evening, a rustle, a rush of air—an arrow thudded into one of the kitchen crates, its shaft still trembling when he got there, the cook on his knees. Walter pulled it from the soft wood, keeping the poison tip away from his hands. He felt alert and free. *I don't blame them.* The bowman had targeted not the Americans but the Venezuelan who worked for them. It was always your own who disappointed you.

The Caribbean Petroleum men, *the most uncivil white people*, withheld promised maps, information, supplies. Territorial disputes between companies used to treating the land as if they owned it were heating up under the pressure of political change. Standard, too, was rushing to pull out as much oil as possible before the Colombian government yanked the concessions.

Even as he moved into the wilderness, he worried about Miriam, who tried not to think of him. Who would prepare her for the bridal chamber? To Mandy, he wrote, *There will be many things now that Muckie will want to know, and that you have experienced.*

On September 5th, Walter got the package: the adjustable ring he had sent to get her size and a surprise, her engagement photograph. *It took my breath away.* She looks straight into the camera, not quite smiling, her chin lowered as if in challenge. *A beautiful picture of a beautiful girl that is changing to a beautiful pure woman.* Not really beautiful, I think. Smoldering, incendiary, mulishly angry at her mother. He wouldn't be the only man to keep that photo near.

He had left her, a girl of eighteen, *full of hope, dreams, and longing.* Vanished, those letters, maybe half-imagined. What had he projected into them? What had she written? I myself have written I love you and in writing felt love move me. I've invented love and found someone to fit; I have been reinvented; I have surrendered the heavy box, the hammer, the drill, little pieces of myself.

His urgency. Light and shadow projected on a piece of paper. He wanted only to touch her. What could he write to her now? What to Mandy? *I don't want her to be married without any knowledge of my physical self. So many brides are terrified to death, purely because they have an unreasonable man that has no idea of the delicate soul of a pure virgin woman.*

And her physical self? *There must be a little dread that virgin girls have of certain things that come with married life.* Soon, she must move from one state of being into another, like an excited electron or a truffle melting on the tongue. How would he, knowing no more than she, turn one kind of trembling into another? *I will always try to control myself to have Muckie come to me.* Suppose she tried to imagine desire, in a world that worked to prevent her doing so. *She used to think it wrong for a woman to have passions and desires.* Again, she and I part ways. I have sought pleasure through flush, boredom, fury, rekindling—I decided coolly when to get rid of my virginity, more burden than treasure, and with whom.

Might she have written passion and made it so?

So he wrote to his future mother-in-law, my great-grandmother. Mandy encouraged him—oh, desire—reading *Green Mansions* now, in bed all day. A girl is mistaken for a bird and then for a saint before she dies, a virgin. A certain kind of man, a certain kind of mother, at a certain time, might believe in worse fates. At eighty, my father, already slipping into dementia, confessed to me he wished my mother had liked sex more. I wonder what she'd been taught to imagine, beyond the technical details she passed on, dutifully, when I asked. Am I progress? Or did I just marry better? Wingbeat in hand, capture and release. Walter, who counted every bird he saw but named only the mockingbird. Who was he? *Mother, I am banking on you to tell Muckie all about herself about men especially.* Who was less qualified to teach Miriam—Mandy, who had taken no pleasure in her marriage; Walter, who would give none? *I loved her for a long long time before I was ever conscious of her body at all.* Don't think about her body. *I have to come to her clean.* They knew less than nothing.

I wish you would give Muckie a little love as I would give it. Consider his temptations. Whether he had faltered. *It can't be done I know exactly, but she will now understand.* Mandy's own marriage bed, fruitful but I think hardly rich. Things would be different for Miriam and Walter. *Things.* She could have warned him.

If he could hear me now, what would I say? Who are you? I am looking, suddenly, not for her but for him.

A little love as I would give it. What we all have to learn, he should have made ready to teach her.

Three weeks later, Miriam moved her hand so her diamond caught the light, and people applauded her, as if she'd accomplished something.

The tripod, the alidade, the pick, the fossil. The pick raised and falling, its arc her body's able motion. Metal against rock. Force up her arms. The rock giving, fragment by fragment. Her body's motion, the rock giving.

I want to cut loose and run—to do things with just my own brains and nerve.

The ring took his whole savings.

I'm not good enough for him. When she wrote it, did she believe it? He lived for the wedding night; she dreaded it. *I can only be free, and a <u>virgin</u>, once!*

February. *There are no maps. We will make our own.* Reading, I am half exultant, half in cold terror, *much like an infant.* He and the senior geologist, Argabrite, Argie, would be mapping the remote Andes and, below, the llanos, the high grassy savannahs. *I am in the very best of health and in good spirits.* Walter packed light: paper, pens, pencils; seven photos of Miriam, including the engagement shot in its cardboard cover; her letters, lost to imagination; log books; gadgets. No Victrola. *The music I will miss, but not as much as Muckie's letters.* Would Miriam stick? *Please encourage my little girl. All she needs is to keep faith.*

The note from Murphy came to her at home between semesters. *Kid, may I write to you?* A little thrill. *I had a date to-nite. Oh my yes!* Nothing like Walter's letters, full of improving and informative anecdotes. *I went with my sister. Is that o.k.?* Nobody.

A boy from school. *I'd write a lot more if I knew it was all right.* She'd told him she was engaged. She could hardly help it if he wrote her.

I wish I had a lot of money so that I could go wherever I wanted to. But after all, I couldn't get away from myself. She knew this, at least.

Brutus is through his change already, Mandy wrote. *He won't be different in character.* Violence, extremity—how did Mandy imagine they wouldn't change him?

She said if I didn't want to get married, it was the last thing she would let me do.

But if she decided to break it off, she must do so to his face, after his return.

I'm trying so hard to live up to her expectations.

The road to San Cristóbal followed the face of the mountain, carved from solid rock. On mule back, Walter and two peons followed Argabrite through clouds, able to see only the cliff face next to them, though the view must have been something. Almost on the Colombian border, San Cristóbal's streets rose in dizzy switchbacks, houses clinging to the mountainside. There was no living to be made out of beauty and air—only out of what the white man would buy. Coffee, manpower, mules. I could have told him: Rima was a figment. *Girls are dependent.* They climbed into the paramo with its one tree, the red-trunked coloradito, a place so high and chill hummingbirds hibernate through every cold night. They tried to move south toward Bogotá, blocked by sheer drops into jungle, trees and shrubs and vines woven dense as a ball of yarn, like the landscape I sail over by tram in Medellín, above it all. *I can't say I am even tired as yet.*

Birds he couldn't name he left out of the log: cock-of-the-rock, crested quetzal, flowerpiercer, more species in Colombia than in any country on earth. I can't resist details, whether birds he ignored, whose names I will record as a gift for my bird-loving husband, or numbers he hankered after, recording miles traveled, direction, altitude, the barometer his idea of *traveling light.* Fourteen kilometers, eight thousand feet. Twenty kilometers, three thousand feet down and six thousand up. *I will have a lot of information concerning the country that is unknown now.* He measured, therefore he was.

March. The rainy season would start in April. Political tensions, high since the U.S. had taken possession of Panama, ratcheted higher. The Colombian congress declared the subsoil property of the state. The team descended into the llanos toward the Casanare, following on the heels of a group of Texas prospectors, mapping feverishly. If they were lucky, the early rains would be sporadic; they might have twenty days before the soil was soaked and rivers grew impassable.

Four saddle mules, two pack mules, *a beautiful bunch* traversing screes and cliff faces where a slip on slick trails meant falling a thousand feet. *The mules slid down this mountain on all fours.*

April. *The rivers are high.* The Texan had set out with *an elaborate string of mules loaded with camp chairs, cots, etc.* They slipped discreetly in his wake, buying food and shelter at settlements along the way. *We are sleeping in a rice hulling mill. There are pinching bugs and I woke in the night to find two bats in my hammock, a scorpion in my blanket, and a huge wood eating borer crawling over me.*

Sure he was right, he had no idea what he was making. Would he have changed a thing? I envy him, though Miriam hadn't written since January, though it would be months before Walter knew. Other things held her attention—Harry still; now Paul. *He's got a wonderful figure.* Murphy loping beside her, asking if he could carry her books. *Sweet Kid,* he wrote her, in letters she kept but didn't share. *Rosebud.*

What Walter wanted, what I want: pure exploration. *The Guaicaramo seeps are huge hot water springs. A beautiful rain bow of oil shows for a long ways.* On a rare clear evening, he looked out to see the llano light up at his feet, with *millions of fire flies and biscucuias, a huge fire bug with two continuous luminous eyes and a tail light, circling over the plains like fords in a traffic jam.*

The flatlands flooded. *When we reach the Casanare we will have crossed every river in the entire State.* Twenty-foot crocs, carnivorous fish. Just behind them, a pack team loaded with salt foundered in a current of electrons and went under. *I have read articles where these eels have killed horses & cows, but never believed it.* If they didn't get out soon, they could be trapped for months. They were low on everything, even tobacco. *A man can go without meals for a long time but a smoke must be had.*

One of the Texan's men died of pneumonia, and the rest pulled out. In Tauramena, the roof leaked, filling their hammocks with water. At midnight, Walter was wakened by a thump, *a sick horse that had strolled over and fallen down against the door. The horse thinking this was the Padres house came around to see the Priest.*

What to tell you and what to leave out? In a forest of words, every word draws me. Like Mandy, dying to follow, I am no better than he is, no more enlightened in my different moment, burning the oil he found. He travels a world of men, larger and freer than mine, his life built on the sweat and property of others, to which he feels entitled—a life I benefit from, one Miriam and I want. Except the red bugs that eat him, except for leeches and constant rain.

The day after they forded the Cauca, it rose behind them, impassable. In front of them, the Río Cusiana tore trees from its banks. *We can't move in any direction.* Three crops in a row lost to flooding. Malaria, yellow fever. No food, no turkeys to shoot, not even yucca or plantános, though pack trains waited on the other side for the waters to recede. *Abandoned houses, villages, and no growing boys or girls around with all the filled graveyards.*

May 15th dawned clear and dry. The savannah lay covered with water. Walter had broken a tooth and feared an abscess. Argie had dysentery. Both suffered parasites and infected insect bites. *They told us if it didn't rain for two days we <u>might</u> be able to cross the Cusiana on a bull.* They moved to a house on the riverbank. He and Argie reread all their magazines, including the ads. *We have*

discussed the latest styles of men and women of which we know
nothing and have solved all political problems of Colombia and
the United States.

He was writing no letters, only the journal I hold. He thought of lamplight, a head bent over his words, not my head. *Yesterday a man was swept away.* He hardly knew what to tell Miriam. *The body has been quite likely eaten by the various kinds of man-eating fishes that infest these rivers.* Her letters were so worn they fell apart in his hands.

And her? All this, and she never wrote a word in her journal suggesting she might be worried or moved. *Must I be reconciled to be the wife of a stranger?*

She enrolled in an advanced course in topographic mapping, one of the first two women to take it, putting on knickerbockers and carrying her surveying rod into the northern woods. To guarantee their failure, the professor sent the women on a steep traverse, an area he wouldn't have expected any student to finish. All day, she and Catherine hefted their equipment over boulders and up to the high ridges. By the time they returned to camp, well after nightfall, the professor was frantic. They had completed their map.

Back in Madison, Harry got on her nerves. *He's not worth it.* Murphy set her nerves singing. *He can be horrid.* Paul. *He wanted me to take his car. He says it's "our" car, but I couldn't.*

Twenty. Afraid to be alone, not to be alone. I know.
All she needs is to keep faith.
Shhh, Mandy says. Come here.

One last dry night. Finally, they could ford the river and begin their climb, scaling rock stairways *running a torrent of water,* navigating *huge boulders in the trail, everything you can think of that is bad.* The men walked, letting the mules go ahead to find the best route. *They are so tired now that they absolutely won't touch corn.*

Late May. The clouds dissolved. At ten thousand feet and counting, he ignored the cliff shearing fifteen hundred feet down and looked out at the vista, a green wave falling, and thought no longer about an ethereal bird girl but about flesh and blood he wanted. When they reached Bogotá, he would mail the letter he was writing in his head. *I am darned glad I come from the U.S.A. and that I will have a girl that comes from there.*

Mandy's fingers curled in Miriam's hair; Miriam's brow on her mother's shoulder. A mother's love, a lover's desire. *I only wish now that you will always reassure my little girl for me.* Shhh, Mandy says. Come here. She folds his Muckie into her arms, her grip too tight for Miriam to loosen, and keeps her there. *I want to bum.* She never will. She can't go anywhere but deeper into the interior, where she sees what she thinks is his face.

In Bogotá, he went straight to the office and cabled Miriam. From the company, he wanted two things: a raise and permission to go home and marry her.

Her letters are just about worn out. He had his tooth repaired; he'd lost twenty pounds. A nurse sliced two gusanos from Argabrite's arm. *The larvae were as large as large beans.*

People. Hotels, with *almost all a poor sucker of a rock hound could want in the line of comfort.* Gambling, women, bars. In field clothes and boots, he sat down for a drink with Mr. Shaw, their chief, come by boat up the hard rapids of the Magdalena just to see him. He ordered scotch and took a piece of ice in his mouth, letting it sit on his tongue.

The world of scotch and ice was the world of company politics; then as now, company politics were international politics. Walter had entered the mountains of Venezuela an employee of Standard Oil of Venezuela; he emerged from the Colombian jungles working for the South American Exploration Company, a camouflage division for Standard Oil of New Jersey. Mr. Shaw offered him a promotion. But Walter pulled out Miriam's photograph.

Another round, then. The beauty of the bride.

Having refused the job, he set out to prove he had loyalty and guile as well as strength, endurance, and accuracy. He took advantage of being a stranger to get *the jump on these birds*, asking questions in bars, visiting the Texan, reading his maps upside-down. *I have also the boundaries of the Jones, Celig concessions near Guaicarana.*

He waited for instructions from New York to make their way upriver. He cabled, *I wish we were already married.* He tried to remember how New York had looked from the bus—all those people—but no doubt it had changed. He kept seeing Miriam's face on the window, adrift between him and the grand avenues.

How could she be sure, after all that time, that he loved *her*, and not some idea of her?

At the end of June, Walter at last got his release. He journeyed down the mad Magdalena and overland by rail and burro and car, sailed north on seas calm as the lakes back home. *His environment won't have any particular effect on him. The mental stimulus and reaction comes almost wholly from you.* The morning they were to dock in New York, he took from his trunk the town clothes he'd set aside two years before. They sat strangely against his skin; his soft city shoes felt as if they might dissolve. Over the harbor, the statue lifted her torch before a skyline I wouldn't recognize. He stepped off the ship into early fall sunshine, scarcely knowing how to be, in this clean-and-pressed crowd, a man any longer. Then he saw her, shading her eyes with gloved hands. Almost two years between them reduced to a narrowing strip of water: he was lean and brown and quieter than ever; she, also thinner, looked at once like the girl he knew and like a woman with a secret life of her own.

He had dreamed of climbing into the taxi with Miriam and driving up Broadway, pointing out the sites, but with her newly bobbed hair and scarlet lips, slightly open as the taxi labored toward Times Square in a cloud of burning oil, she was both more and less than the girl he'd dreamed up while cicadas beat their wings with desire in the jungle. Her small hand with his diamond on it sat placidly in his large one, but he had spent so much time refining her image to his need that he hardly knew her. He had used all his patience to get here. She looked at everything but him.

They went to their separate rooms to dress for dinner. In his wardrobe hung starched shirts and neckties and suits sent from La Porte, his mother and sisters meeting her on the platform in Chicago to pass the cases when she changed trains. Those clothes still held the old shape of his body, but his field trunk contained his real life, the one he had carried out of the jungle, without small talk or evening kits, its smell when he opened it damp and dark and mineral. Under his boots, green with mold, was a wood box holding the army revolver he had bought in New York two years before and carried into the bush. He had put it away cleaned and oiled in Barranquilla; now, he pushed bullets into the chamber with the flat of his thumb. As dusk fell, he washed, shaved, and put on a boiled shirt and his dinner jacket. He tucked the gun in the back of his waistband and rode the elevator up to knock on Miriam's door.

Under his gaze, she moved aside, not meeting his eyes. When he showed her the gun, she backed herself up against the window, darkness over her head and city lights spread out below her like a train of sparks. To set her mind at ease, he raised the gun and pointed it at his own head. He imagined being the fellow down below, looking up at her silhouette against the light: bare swimmer's shoulders, the glimmer of pale blue silk and pearl. The glass must have been cold. She should have had a wrap. He needed her to understand.

If I invent details—pearls, silk, the man under the window—it is because I want to linger. I, too, have been spellbound, overtaken by a man's love not for me but for some idea. *How do I know all my beaux would miss me if I suddenly disappeared?* Would he pull the trigger? *Brutus might.* She'd meant to marry him. If she had

61

to throw herself over some cliff, why not this one? Then she'd seen how, after all, he was still only Walter, harder and more sure but somehow the same. *His environment won't have any particular effect on him.* Then he raised the pistol, calm, and he wasn't the same at all. He was larger, lit with violence. He had lived only for her. He wanted her to come with him into the bush.

Cockroaches, scorpions, vampire bats. *Hundreds of singing frogs, night birds, monkeys, and parrots.* There is no sign she had imagined it, but now there was the pistol. Who was she, who couldn't say she'd really loved anyone, to deny this? Hadn't she always been waiting for such a *One*? Always her question, and for too long my own—not, do I love, but rather, *Does he love me? How much?* His finger on the trigger, he, too, became an idea. *You never have loved me*—but that she would write later. *Waving the revolver around your head.* Most of her letters to him are gone; this one survives because she never sent it. Now, what could she do? She stepped away from the window. Arrows tipped with poison. Electric eels; the man-eating caribe. A man different than the pacifist I would eventually choose for myself, holding a pistol as if he knew exactly how to use it, in a room that no longer exists, in a vanished world.

She walked into his arms. The relief that flooded her when he lowered the gun and set it on the table felt like nothing so much as love.

Murphy: *Sweet Rosebud, I'm still weak.* She had written she was at the lake. *Sweet kid, why didn't you tell me Brutus was there? It was such a blow when he walked in.* Had she expected him to drive all that way to see her? *Please, please excuse me for acting so insane.*

Once you'd been shot at by Indians, a boy like Murphy held no terror. Once you'd held the gun to your own head and come out alive with what you wanted. Walter shook Murphy's hand, sat down on the sofa, and went to work on his pipe as if tamping tobacco was the only thing on his mind.

The man with three initials, who wanted to give them to her: *Mrs. P.E.M. Purcell. I just finished playing Pretty Lips. Please! I'm begging.* She didn't answer.

<u>Harry</u>: His letter waited in Milwaukee. *I've been in hell.* Handsome Harry, who had tried not to love her. *It's easier to jump up into an airship from the ground. I'll always wait now.* These are the love letters she kept—the ones from men she didn't marry.

Mandy smoothed Miriam's veil. Off-white lace and satin, seed pearls, white roses. Now, instead of looking straight at the camera, Miriam softened her face and dropped her lashes, gazing modest and maidenly at a place beyond the frame, as if she saw something there that was only for her, or as if to hide from us the look in her eyes.

CHAPTER 4

COLOMBIAN HONEYMOON: FIRST THINGS

To speak is also to be.

LOUISE GLÜCK

Oct 5th 1927, New York
*Just after sailing we received several Bon Voyage
Telegrams, Flowers from the Davidsons, and a box
of candy from Mrs. Wollaeger—our mother.*

WALTER'S JOURNAL

AS THE *METAPAN* PULLED AWAY from the dock, Mrs. Walter K. Link stood at the rail, ready to become a *woman geologist*, sailing off the map. She leaned against her husband, feeling the thread holding her to her old self dissolve. The city blurred on the horizon.

She'd undertaken a series of first events, leaving herself behind again and again. After the ceremony in Mandy's parlor, she stood in her bedroom *for the last time as a virgin* while Mandy straightened her collar and repaired her face. She stood for photographs on the porch then drove through fading light toward Chicago, leaving the hope chest with its cookbook behind. She was glad Walter couldn't drive. She'd given herself to a stranger sleeping off bootlegged champagne in the passenger seat, but it was her foot pressing the accelerator.

To me the Palmer House Hotel with its frescoed lobby means old-fashioned elegance; to her it represented modern luxury.

Mandy had warned her about the blood but not much else. As her husband labored over her body, Miriam sensed he was driven by a force beyond her. *He's awfully sweet to me in every way he knows how.* It took Walter urgently, but it did not take her. She wrote Mandy, *I weeped two nights in La Porte, and I could have a lot more times, but I thought I hadn't better.* During those long prenuptial evenings when they'd kissed into bruises, she'd felt— what? It was over quickly, and he was grateful. But she couldn't wish to repeat it.

Imagine beginning with disappointment at the heart. *I never thought I'd be such a baby.* But the boat's thrumming engines, New York a gleaming inspiration under the fall sun, came through him. *He gets my goat quite often, but he doesn't mean to.* His long fingers circled her throat. She made herself stand still. *I expect I'll get over my touchiness. As you say, men are so dumb!*

Hum of nerves. Soon, Walter would make their pitch to Argie, the grand idea, what she signed on for—as Chris and I made the pitch to our university, but with other offers in hand: they could have both of us or neither, at a time when such negotiations were still rare but beginning to succeed. Like Walter, Chris was the known and valuable quantity, I the one who needed to prove myself.

She believed Standard Oil couldn't refuse a trained geologist willing to work for food and a mule. Could it? She was eager, fit as any boy, braver, anxious to test herself. But they had to wait, Walter said, until Argie could see she was a girl of another order.

To Mandy: *P.S. She still obeys. I guess I must keep her a little longer.*

Her first cocktail: a Manhattan, with its brilliant cherry. Her first ocean voyage. In Jamaica, her first tropical landing; a black policeman in his bright uniform. *Yesterday, out of a clear sky, my "husband"(?) said, "Who said you weren't good looking?" I haven't quite recovered from the shock.* Coming: her first view of the Panama Canal; cobbled streets; another continent.

Bon voyage, 1927

At the Canal Zone, Mrs. Argabrite would embark on a Caribbean cruise, while Mrs. Link would continue with the men up the wild Magdalena. The couples played shuffleboard and walked the deck until cocktails. After dinner, they danced, Mrs. Link swinging with delight, Argie leaning into her. *He said I should take Brutus in hand—women had lots more sense, and it was better in every way when the lady takes charge.*

Her satin dress glowed phosphorescent green in the lantern light. Her first cigarette. Argie leaned over the flame as she exhaled, managing not to cough. What better time to ask? *He said I had enough sense—well, quien sabe?* Maybe he thought she was joking. Maybe her eyes were lit by her dress. Maybe he really imagined letting her come. *I'm going along on the mule part of the trip, down to the llanos—that will take about a month.* She was a different animal than Mrs. Argabrite. She had the same geology training he did. Maybe, under an ocean moon, he thought it could happen.

But even then, cocooned in smoke and moonlight, he hedged. *Then Brutus will bring me back most of the way.* A waste. *When I leave the party, Brutus and Argie go up and down rivers, being poled painfully up, mapping as they go.*

She believed she could do anything. Do I?

Filth, donkey trains, rotting plants and animals. No letters. *I'm beginning to understand how much it means to hear from home down here.* After four days in Cartagena, they boarded the *F. Peres Rosa*, a newly repurposed Mississippi paddle boat, for the trip up the Magdalena to Honda. *There's a barge on each side, and there's cargo and cattle on them.* Barefoot crew served dinner in the jackets they'd worn to load freight and clean the latrines. *For days I saw a man standing around on the upper deck in a bath robe and pajamas. This man happened to be the captain.* They passed machinery dumped in the river when the water was too low for heavy boats to clear the sandbars. But the trees pulsed with the calls of birds and frogs. One afternoon, a manatee, over ten feet long, smooth and breasted as a maiden, surfaced and swam alongside the boat, as curious about them as they were about her.

By the time I stand on the Magdalena's banks, its manatees have been hunted to extinction, its fish poisoned by chemicals from agribusiness. The water flows with sewage and trash; the birds that once clattered in huge flocks above its surface have lost their homes to deforestation. Ambush and insurrection brought an end to large passenger boat service in the sixties; now, barges with bullet holes in their hulls deliver equipment to the oil refineries, and flimsy public chalupas transport a dozen people at a time. Yet the river surges and flows with unrelenting power.

I've been driven to the airport yet again, my husband this time made marginally less reluctant by a festival program with my name in it and a promise that I will be attended at all times. Flying in relative comfort into the Andes, I imagine how Miriam bathed with a sponge and dressed for dinner. For her the men became charming. *You ought to see our parade—I carry the Flit gun 'cause the mosquitoes are bad, specially under the table, and Brutus carries a bottle of Worcestershire—we use that as disinfectant.* Chicken, rice, soup seasoned by a grimy thumb. For *dulce, a single prune. We all stared and then laughed till we cried.* Even what she might have recognized became unfamiliar. *They have a grande passion for playing a particularly tinny electric player piano, with rolls that have many more holes than they had originally—much of the beauty of such compositions as Collegiate is lost in silence.* The berths were so tiny she and Walter had to bunk separately, a torment to him and a relief to her. The Company had sent *a brand new mosquito bar.*

Voyager: from voir, to see, through my eyes and theirs. *Colombia is a rich in material resources of all kinds—Still they are extremely hostile toward the United States, whose capital wants to come in and exploit the country on a fair and square basis.* To Walter, exploit is a technical term, without negative connotation.

After dinner, all but the few first-class passengers hung their hammocks on the open lower decks. While the river slipped through flat country, Argie ruminated his Havana. It was time for Walter to face reality. Less than a year before, he and Argie had entered the jungle fit and tough and emerged with infections, malaria, dysentery, having escaped smallpox, cholera, yellow fever. *Absolutely no way to get out of here for help.* The gusanos in Argie's arm against the body of the beloved, smooth and clean and white. And what about her feminine malaise? If she ended up in a river (a bucking mule, a capsized raft), where caribe swarmed to a drop of blood? Indians, labor unrest, attacks. Pregnancy. Having no real idea, the men imagined the pack she couldn't lift, the brush she couldn't hack, the snake she'd be too frightened to behead. Staring at the murky water, I think what I can and can't do, though I might want to. I am less at home in my body than either of them were, but I inherited their stamina; I can read a map, run a rapid, rope myself in to rappel a cliff.

Never mind that she can climb anything and swims better than both of them. What changed between those two men when she walked into the room? Fidelity. Priorities. Survival. They are crossing a river, these two men and that woman, and everything goes to hell: capsize, and the flesh eaters gather. They imagine having to save her and don't question whom Walter would save if he had to choose. And if Argie had to decide between the woman whose right to be rescued was an invisible truth or the man on whom his safety relied? Reality, Argie reminded Walter, was where men died. Not a girl; not, if he could help it, on his watch. Better, he would argue, keep her out of the water.

Mommy, we've been married for six weeks and a day.

The two men sat smoking, looking toward a darkness behind which anything might be breathing, any weapon raised. *Sometimes for 15 and 20 minutes at a time the boat will fight the current without budging an inch.*

How could he not have known it would be this way?

Usually, people figure that when you get married it's all over.

He wanted to live suspended in that bright bubble with Miriam. But no matter how hard the current fought them, they kept moving upriver.

Assume Mandy handed her daughter over, perhaps in the nick of time, a virgin. Walter made the same claim for himself. What he understood at twenty-five about his body, I will never know: what it could lift and climb and clear and sleep through, what parasites it attracted, in what convulsive purges it rid itself of poisons. Virgin or not, he knew every thing about it but one. If I could send my voice into the past, what would I say? I know this: during their wedding trip to La Porte, for the first six weeks Miriam didn't write her mother, not once. *Not that anything was wrong.* And I think whatever Walter had taught himself, his focus now, when he entered a room with a bed and his new wife in it, should have been not on his own release, nor on learning one more thing about his own body, but on learning anything at all about a body like hers. Not even, after all, for Miriam—though imagine her sweet surprise. For himself alone, on the subject of female pleasure he should have been studious, as hardworking as he was on surveying, mapmaking, learning to wield his machete like a native and speak a Spanish his peons could understand. *He's most awfully sweet to me in every way he knows how.* If he was going to leave her behind while he went into the bush, he should have known what she was missing, should have left her something to miss.

What makes a man?

He leaves me absolutely cold, physically.

Quien sabe?

The real vision only the men shared, exhilarating and bleak. Only they could enter it.

It's a great life if you don't weaken, Miriam wrote Mandy. *But I won't be weakening.* No hay. Years later: *He leaves me cold. He always has.*

What might she have done? I have no idea.

Argie keeps reassuring us that we're not going anywhere and when we get there we won't see nothin'. Evenings beginning with cocktails, ending with brandy and bets over whether the captain would be wearing a jacket over his pajamas in the morning. *We got to the next bend—it's just like the rest.* Her honeymoon. *Brutus was just around to ask if I'd told you I smoked a cigarette.*

When she began her journey, there was a point. She was headed into the bush.

But we keep right on traveling to nowhere—that's our story and we stick by it.

Certainty, uncertainty. *I got a big kick the first time I saw clouds below us.* The prospect vanishing. If she had ridden with them down into the llanos, would she have become another woman altogether? Would my mother, would I?

I am in Colombia at last, for the International Poetry Festival in Medellín, founded in the nineties in response to the violence that had blown that city into legend. Before I go, Chris emails me links to websites about kidnappings, traffic, and cartels; I reply with articles about the museum, the botanical gardens, restaurants. In the twenties, Medellín was a village too small to mention, one valley west of the Magdalena; now, it rages with traffic, and its air thickens. In 1802, Alexander von Humboldt wrote, "the whole province of Antioquia is surrounded by mountains so difficult to pass that they who dislike entrusting themselves to the skill of a [human] bearer ... must relinquish all thoughts of leaving the country." Improbably, then, my grandfather traveled them by mule; now, when my host Jacqui and I visit the Parque Arví, a tram sails us up toward the Aburrá Valley over slums precariously perched where Walter must have dismounted to let the mule pick her own way down the mountain.

In the late twenties, some factions wanted to nationalize oil production. *It will drive out all the oil companies,* whose gated compounds lined the river. Talking late into the night with Colombian poets, I hesitantly tell them about my grandfather, and even now they set to re-arguing the politics. Some think the country should have struck a deal to take advantage of the U.S. expertise Walter vaunted, agreeing that the Colombian government didn't know how to manage the foreign-built refineries and Andean pipeline. Others sensibly question the good faith of the foreign companies. All of them believe that Pablo Escobar and the civil war, grinding at last to an end, were U.S. creations.

"The problem," Pamela, a young comedian and connoisseur assures me over the best rum I've ever drunk, "is North Americans are *stupid*." She pauses, a beat too long. "Not you." I demur and, after consulting with her, order another round, while talk turns to Medellín. My translator, the poet George Angel, bemoans the city's historical amnesia; they all lament its constant remaking, new buildings going up over old, though this, I have been finding, is the way of things.

If I thought I'd be able to slip free to wander the city, I was mistaken. Jacqui makes sure I don't walk outside the hotel alone, even during the day, even in the restaurant and museum districts. She takes me by the hand like a child when we need to cross the street—a solicitude that makes me smile, thinking how Chris would approve, until one of the European poets—male, not American, not led by the hand—steps into the path of a taxi and is carried off with a broken leg to the hospital. This, aside from a stolen backpack, is the only *incidente grave* during the ten-day festival.

Now that she wouldn't be riding along, Miriam half wanted the congress to nationalize oil and the expedition to fall through. I sympathize. I have reasons to be there, a job to perform. Another five months apart, and what would she do? Go home as a married woman? Sit in Bogotá, in the Hotel Europa's tiny Deco lobby? Look for work? *I've gathered that my spouse doesn't exactly like the idea of keeping me here at $125 a month.* For his own reasons, he'd brought her all this way. And.

Walter and Argie were as secretive and absorbed as lovers. While they were out making inquiries, she waited for invitations, for him to come home, for mail. *If you address it to Bogota, it takes*

72

at least a week, and almost two. Occasionally, she went to the office with Walter and practiced typing letters while he vanished for some mysterious meeting. *He left me to find my way home all alone. My sense of direction never fails me.* Mountains looming on one side, river and valley on the other. In Bogotá, we will all find our ways.

For what had Miriam's life equipped her? To be her husband's partner, a geologist? *I am going to set out on a job of typing for Argie, and earn me some money. Typing* meant composing the report herself from Argie's notes about oil laws. His name would appear at the top, put there by her fingers pounding the keys, an act of self-erasure to which I won't give in.

For what had her life equipped her? *Friday night was the big Armistice Day dance at the Anglo-American club; I had a wild time getting my husband into his boiled shirt.* She danced twenty-one dances straight. *Five were supposed to be with Brutus, but other fellows just took them away.* Not for the first or last time, he smoked and watched her spin in the arms of other men. An Englishman taught her to tango. Did he imagine she would change?

At night, starting late, the poets dance cumbia and Colombian salsa, which I pick up on the fly. Like Walter, my husband doesn't dance, but he is happy to know I get it out of my system without him. I learn to still my upper body and loosen my hips and legs, relaxing, when I have an able partner, into his hands. One young man dances so intensely I could almost fall in love—but he hands me on to a gallant and stately Macedonian poet, surprisingly masterful, and returns to his beautiful girlfriend, also thrilling to watch.

Days and evenings, I give readings at festival sites around town or further afield. One morning at the botanical garden, under a cacophony of birds, a woman gestures me over to sign her program, pointing at my photo, saying "Katarina?" and "Estados Unidos?"

Hospitably, her husband hands me an open bottle. The woman

Leaving Venezuela, Guasdualito, 1928

snatches it back, and for a moment I think I am off the hook, but after wiping the lip on her sleeve she returns it to me, smiling. My young escort, another Angel, watches to see what I'll do. I drink, and the husband shakes my hand. Angel smiles.

Dinners out, golf with borrowed clubs, horseback riding. He takes her by mule into the mountains and by train to see the Tequendama Falls twenty miles away—even today over two hours from Bogotá on landslide-prone mountain roads. They stay in the Hotel del Salto, then a recently converted mansion built into the cliff opposite the falls, which my taxi will approach through cloud forest on a road skirting a precipitous drop. The ornate building floats in rainbows; abandoned in the nineties, when the stench from the Bogotá River and the falls overwhelmed it, it has reopened as a museum. Dutiful, I tour the exhibit honoring botanist Aimé Bonpland, who explored the Andes with Humboldt. But, like them, I have come for the thrill of altitude, water tumbling four hundred feet. Then, the falls were pristine. Now, at their base, the river still foams lightly with raw sewage, though the smell has subsided.

First uncertainty wore on her, then certainty. *Congress adjourned today.* Walter still had his job.

What was there for her? She might become a governess. *And Daddy, I'm learning to tell the difference between a Martini, a Manhattan, and one or two other cocktails.*

Finally, he chose for her: the wild Magdalena, another tumult of water. Not allowed to travel with him, she would instead spend a week alone on the river, rescued from the danger she wanted and flung into the one she didn't. This time, there would be no cabin for the American Senora; she would sleep on deck in a hammock, effects in a bundle beside her, diamond ring pinned inside her brassiere.

Walter and Argie accompanied her on the train from Bogotá to Girardot. At the dock, both kissed her. As the boat drifted out into the stream, the two men stood together and waved. She was rounding the first bend when they dropped their hands as one and turned away as if released.

Then she was gone, coursing through a gash in the jungle. From the boat, no letters. I know only what she told me at her dining-room table. Rapids pounding against the hull. Rusted arms and cogs of abandoned machinery rippling below the surface, more perilous than snags. An automobile, submerged. None of Argabrite's jokes, no cocktails after dinner. Only the sternwheel turning. Her hammock cradled her above the deck; mosquitoes hit a constant note. One night, she jolted awake to a dark figure looming beside her. She sat up and spoke, and it moved away, silent, its face a shadow. Her hand moved to the strap of her brassiere.

Not long ago, when she was protecting the virginity that belonged to him, this would have been incomprehensible: Miriam, alone on the Magdalena, moving away at the speed of rushing water. She would remember it all her life, her first solo journey.

And Walter? *At midnight, I awoke cold. The stars sparkled, and the waning moon was on the horizon.* He was deep in love remembered and desired. She was still out of reach, but now, at last, a sure thing, safe the way he wanted her.

Last time, floods; this time, fire. *The canteens are empty.* Walter counted every swallow of water—every swallow without it. *The entire country is illuminated by the hundreds of fires all around, burning off the grasses and timbers. The savannahs had that hopeless weird aspect.* Along the trail, people asked for news, but Walter and Argie were subtle as thieves, pretending to be lost, looking for cattle, diamonds, anything but oil. Again, he wrote to bridge geography and time: a letter traversing both from his eye to Miriam's, now to mine. In grass-fringed marshes birds thrummed and turtles wallowed; crocodiles, otters, the capybara, a bulbous-faced rodent as big as I am. *This country is a country of extremes, and it takes hardy men to travel it.* He wanted Miriam to long to be with him, to understand why she was instead back where she started, tucked up in Mandy's house, which she had married him to escape. *The trails are strewn with the bleached bones of cattle.* The nights swarmed with mosquitos. *The darned things could bite as well as sing.* At bedtime, he burned off ticks with the ember from his cigarette.

The drive to Hispania, a mountain village with a tree-shaded square, takes three hours each way from Medellín, first through heavy city traffic, then over a treacherous summit, then down the other side in a barely controlled careen, a ride for which the new Apple Watch Chris has strapped to me credits me with 4,226 steps, though I sit the whole way. As usual, the van has no seat belts. Nokia cell phone, Treo, iPhone, watch—of all the devices he's given me, this one lets me tell him I am thinking of him in a moment, without using keys or distracting myself. When I lay my fingers on the watch's screen, it sends him my heartbeat, slightly elevated, by text; from his conference room, his comes back, a pink blob pulsing against my wrist.

A few miles from our destination, we meet a roadblock. Armed men pace each side of our van, peering through the windows at the motley group of poets and interpreters, all but me South American. I make the mistake of lifting my eyes at the wrong moment, my blue gaze meeting the eyes of a man who stops and barks in Spanish. Later, browsing Google images, I'm not sure if his uniform belongs to the army, the national police, or the FARC.

We're waved over. Pamela and Jacqui jump from the van. "Poetas," I hear them say, and "Hispania." The man with the gun leans against my window, inches away, watching me through the glass. Too late, I keep my eyes lowered. Against the guide book's instructions, I have my passport with me. If they find it, will they keep me there? Confiscate it? Let us go? I try to breathe.

Pamela makes a call. There is more talking, more waiting. Her cell rings, then, after long negotiations, Pamela and Jacqui return to the van. The mayor of Hispania has made a deal, or a bribe. We are free to go, but even now, nobody in the van looks my way;

nobody says a word about it. The event joins the list of things I won't mention to Chris until later, in company, as an amusing story.

During the panel in Hispania, I tell the children to read all they can—a mistake, I think, when a Colombian poet says no, they should live large and make love to many women. But afterwards, while the male poets find the bar, children crowd around me. I could have said anything and still become what I seek: exotic and strange. Jacqui interprets, smiling. The little girls comment on my eyes, reach to touch my cropped head, line up to have photos taken with me. One young boy tells me he has been to Miami, where he plans to move when he is grown. "I will be rich," he says, in English. "Shopping." Laughing, the children follow us out into the square—because we arrived so late, it is already twilight, and the spreading saman trees strung with fairy lights are folding up their leaves for the evening.

Halfway through, they come to Tame, strolling burros and cargo bulls laden with bananas. *At night the lights of the candles shine dully thru open doors onto the cool breeze swept streets.* In one direction, sloping plains. In another, snow-covered mountains. In a third, the silvas, a forest of palms and hardwoods, still belonging to its original inhabitants.

One morning he approached an Indian woman. *She had some kind of long contraption to pin her blanket.* He had no idea how to turn the trinkets he'd brought for trade into the spoils he desired. *We had a circus.* Imagine him on Main Street back home in La Porte, removing the brooch from a woman's blouse. *Finally we took it, and gave her a couple of pins.* He slid a cheap ring onto her finger as if making a vow, took a mother-of-pearl necklace from her neck. From then on, if an Indian had something he wanted, he shoved a few notes or a trinket into her hands and took it. By day's end, he had jewelry, bows, and arrows. Coca leaves to chew; lime to neutralize the acid. Chewing passed the time, leaving his mouth dry but deliciously numb. Flocks of leggy birds rising in pink and white clouds from the riverbanks. A moon gone bloody behind smoke. *The plains are mottled with silver and the night bird's calling. The world has a lonely beauty that sometimes makes a person mad.*

An invisible line in the middle of a river marked the border with Venezuela. On the other side, savannahs shimmered under the heat, yielding the occasional comic relief of a car driving straight at them over the roadless plain, shimmering like a ghost in dust and smoke.

Colombians, Venezuelans: to him, their flaws and virtues lay not in their characters—*They are not fit to govern themselves*—but in their stars. *It takes a good dictator to bring prosperity, because these Latin and Indian people can not agree among themselves what is good for them.* Good dictator, bad—all a matter of perspective and our national interest, we are told even now, as long as we're talking about some other country.

The end of his first long partnership, the beginning of his second. *Argabrite is and was the best and squarest man I ever hit and ever hoped to work with.* Two weeks in New York with Miriam, one in La Porte, two more in green Wisconsin. Then a promotion, from junior geologist to geologist with an assistant, and two more boats for both of them: the *President Pierce* from San Francisco to Singapore, first class passage—*He'll have to dress for dinner every night, I guess. Wonder if my collection of dresses will do?*—then a smaller craft to Batavia, Dutch East Indies. Flights for me, in the same stages. I wait for the right moment to break the news to Chris.

There would be no turning back for Miriam, not this time, from a three-year pull. A house, two servants. Everything on Standard Oil, even Miriam's travel and living expenses, plus his salary. *Getting paid for seeing the world—that, as the Bozo says, is the way to see it.*

Walter Link: Standard Oil explorer. The charming Mrs. Link: Standard Oil wife.

MODEL XI. (WEGVERKEERSBESLUIT B. B.)

Afgegeven aan *Wollaeger Marian hink.-*

geboren te *America*

den *16d December 190*

van beroep *Geen*

wonende *Bat ce*

tijdelijk verblijf houdende *Bat ce*

Dit rijbewijs is uitgereikt te

op den *11 December* 19*

en is mitsdien geldig tot den *1/2* 19*

De ~~Gouverneur~~ / Resident van *Batavia*

Voor dezen:

De *Hoofd-Commissari*

namens dezen

De Chef Voerwezen

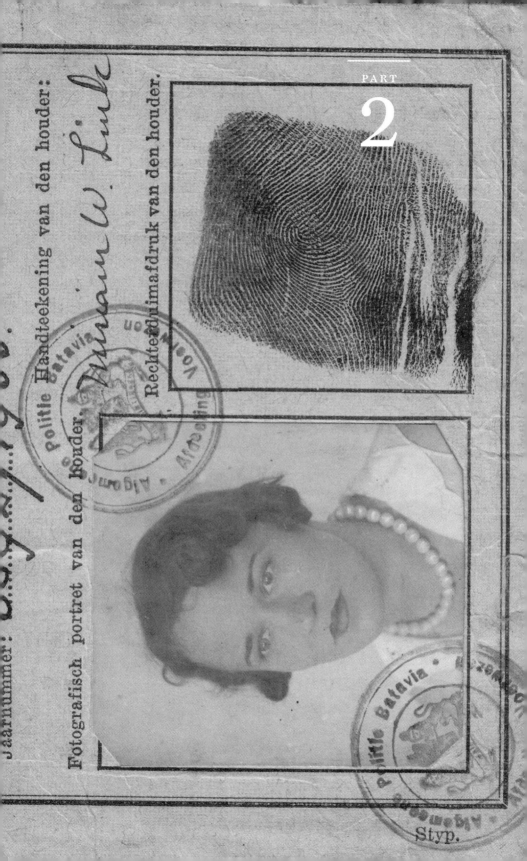

PART

2

Styp.

CHAPTER 5

INTERLUDE:
COMPASS POINTS

Train 1: Nebraska into Wyoming.

Sky lifts. Miriam rummages for pen and paper. *It gives you a feeling of space and serenity, with all sorts of time hanging around.* Walter aims his camera out the window and cranks. The land unfolds in black and white.

Train 2: Wyoming into Utah.

Engine straining. Clouds drag squalls into country I know like my own heart, where I have hefted packs two-thirds my weight and drunk straight from creeks, hung from cliff faces by ropes, slept under the stars, awakened to a rattlesnake stretched alongside my sleeping bag for warmth. *I'm going to start believing pretty soon that if you want something hard enough and long enough you'll get it.* Her husband considers contradictory forces: uplift, on which we ride; water and wind wearing stone down.

gan to find out what a hot train ride really means.

This is the sort of country we traveled thru all day — occasionally the mountains closed in, and we h[ad?] several tunnels, but usually we were in the middle of desert. Once in a while there'd b[e]

(thet's a sagebrush — so's all them funny-looking things)

Marginalia: letter from Miriam to Mandy, Utah, 1928

Train 3: The Salt Flats. Not a snapshot or a motion picture, but a drawing.

Desert, where I emerge squalling into another heat wave, 1959, and into Miriam's arms; where, having lain with my lover in our shared bed that morning, I marry him in her dress as she looks on. As she wasn't, as perhaps my mother wasn't, I am giddy with love, free to choose not a life determined for me but a man who will say more than once, "I married a poet, not a housekeeper," and smile. He won't know at first that he married restlessness, but we all cross a future we can't imagine. July 1928—the causeway over the lake, in my time needing repair, melts under the sun, the flats stretching *in blinding white heat, with mirages shimmering*. An ancient lakebed. *Time hanging around*. Sketched in her margin: mountains, scrubby sagebrush. Her eye, her mind, her hand under my eye, mind, hand. *An auto crossing, leaving a long white rising plume of dust* as she moves through me, standing now in her place, mortal, fugitive.

Mommy, he's sweeter than ever. She loves the idea—herself on a journey. *Here's yo-ho and we're off for the boundering main*.

This voyage of 2100 miles took the early explorers several months, and men suffered Scurvy, thirst and hunger. Now some ships make it in 4 days, and the Pioneers of Aeroplane flew to the island in 1927 in about one day.

WALTER'S JOURNAL, *On Board* Pres Monroe *bound for Singapore, July 27th–August 4th, 1928*

So far east, they sail west to get there, losing a day at the international date line—as will I, chasing them and the sun decades later, sailing the air and arriving in a few hours. A scientist, my husband Chris travels frequently if reluctantly, from conference to conference, cajoling me to join him when I can. It would never occur to me to try to stop him. Over a decade after our wedding,

Miriam, Kobe, 1928

I am perplexed to realize it hurts him that I would undertake these different trips, solo and with relish, traveling not toward conference rooms and academic credentials that can be counted, but into a sustained dream of memory and speculation that may count for nothing. I don't always hurry back.

Over the Pacific, I set my watch behind ten hours, forward a day. Our lost days will be restored when we come home, but those we get back will not be the ones we missed. For me, jet lag, sudden dislocation; for them, time suspended. She gossips with the chief engineer, reads the recreation board, swims in the tiny pool. Chess. Lectures. Dancing. *The days slip by so fast that it's hard to keep track of them.* She is too young to equate days with mortality. After dinner, he practices anthropology, a family habit, in the smoking room. *Many of the women do not conceal their desires and readily make fools of themselves.* Before them, the Orient casts a shadow into which they might vanish. *They think that the foreign world must be more wonderful than their own— how mistaken they are.*

When they cross the dateline—a day x-ed off—there are balloons and crackers at every seat. After dinner, prizes for the deck tournaments, a satiric wreath for Miriam, who won most of them. *Pallas Athena.*

At the bottom of the menu, a reminder: *Clocks will be retarded 8 minutes tonight.*

With their limited resources, Japan can never become a world power without conquest, and I don't suppose it is very likely that they can do that.
WALTER'S JOURNAL, *August 17th, 1928, Kobe, Japan*

The S.S. *Monroe* noses the pier as the sun sets, *the fishing boats looking like bubbles in the mist.* Miriam at the rail until bedtime. *The winches and derricks clattered and crashed all night, but one can get used to anything.* When the sun rises behind them, she is up, ready to disembark. *I'll have to start waking up, I guess.*

As natural as any dream. In Kobe, they travel by rickshaw, each driver wired hard with muscle. Walter buys his young wife kimonos, obi, and *clattering wooden sandals.* Another gift to himself, their sexy exoticism, their *life and originality.*

A ship must have eyes so that it may see. When the ship lies at anchor the eyes are covered with a bag, because the ship must sleep.
WALTER'S JOURNAL

Not there, but there. He watched the ship unload. *Several thousand tons of cargo, and that much more put on. All work is done amid chanting and song, and it is done well.*

He observes and records; I take note. In the tiny shops surrounding Shanghai's exquisite Yuyuan Garden, like me she bypasses cheap baubles and fingers rose and quartz crystal carved into beads, elephants, small, luminous monsters.

He doesn't notice what she wants.

She sails up Hong Kong's steep streets in a sedan chair, borne on the shoulders of men she hardly considers. *It would be peculiar to be in a city where everything was white people—we didn't see one all morning, and hardly any this afternoon.* Observing, observed, difference making her visible. Back to the ship they send nesting blackwood tables, two camphor chests—the small one sitting now on my own shelf—and a set of the hand-painted china Walter craves.

Under a narrow light I fly toward Hong Kong, hurtling through the night, alone with my thoughts, though beside me sleeps a saffron-robed monk, adrift on sandalwood. In the Hong Kong airport I trudge from shop to shop, buying nothing, trying to outwalk the air conditioning. I am exhausted, dirty, goose pimpled, but not lonely.

I can't wake up, it seems—and all these places are only places after all, with mere people in them.

Batavia at last. A fever heat. He supervises the unloading of trunks and cases, deciding what to declare and pay duty on, what to sneak through. *They are very strict here about fire arms, for fear they get into the hands of rebellious natives.*

She thinks of home, of her mother. *The water we're on reaches and touches the land you're on, and from here to you is merely a matter of traversing some material miles, after all.* All we've ever wanted: to be transported. *It feels as though it were only a dream.*

The Des Indes Hotel will be gone by the time I get there, but she's sketched the floor plan of their suite in the letter's margin. *The bed looks like those they always show belonging to Empress Thingummy—it is over six feet wide and seven feet long.* Life in the tropics will mean managing inconvenience and luxury, making a flounced drape of mosquito netting. Walter was out with his new friend Eastman, taking photographs—*chiefly of the cute little native women, I guess.*

All this magnificence, including excellent meals, costs 27 guilders per day.

Walter, already out. My mind following.

CHAPTER 6

A NICE NIGHT FOR BEAUTY

Oct 3rd, 1928, on board S.S. Van de Wiek
en route to Palembang
Muckie came down to the dock to see me off and I stood
and watched till she was no longer in sight. I never thought
that one person could grow to a man as she has to me.
WALTER'S JOURNAL

HIS FIRST EXPEDITION as lead geologist. His Dutch assistant, Agerbeck, waited on the dock to lead him through Palembang, half of it built on stilts or rafts over the Moesi River, rising and falling with the tide. *Coolies selling things to eat and drink, ringing a little bell,* chiming Chinese, Dutch, Malay—a cloud of tongues I trail through refinery-smudged air and words on the page, on crumbling sidewalks that suddenly give way to the sewers rumbling beneath, to the floating market, a street that flows with water when the river is full and now stinks of garbage. Women step gracefully along elevated blocks foundering in the mud, bend over rolls of batik or peer into bamboo cages stuffed with chickens, bead-eyes rolling and throats throbbing with panic. Now, also, Nike knockoffs, plastic Disney figures.

In my sun hat, I turn every head. One of the oldest cities in Indonesia, still this is not a tourist town. At last, a woman grabs my arm, says, in perfect American English, "Excuse me. What are you doing here?"

Chris's very question. The U.S. State Department has issued a travel warning for Indonesia, and I am traveling for reasons that make no sense to him in the age of Google. Still, he drove me to the airport, kissed me as if for the last time, said, "Be careful."

"Don't worry," I said this time as always, hefting my bags to the curb without his help. "I'll look both ways."

The woman repeats, "What are you doing?"

Jet-lagged, disoriented, I begin to answer. "My grandparents," I say.

"*Here*," she says, pointing to the mud beneath our feet. "You will be robbed." I am slow, my head fogged. Exasperated, she points at the bridge. "Get on a bus," she says, then mutters under her breath, "little fool."

My grandfather might have called me an adventuress, if not impossible. In this, he is like many people I will meet here, who will ask what I am doing, where my husband is. In my grandparents' time, a woman might follow a man to the resource-rich colonies, or come to find one in an economy of female scarcity, white and preferably in a class above her own.

The men came for oil, as many do today. Though most people here still live in dire poverty, now as then the ground is filthy with the substance that fueled the twentieth century through cycles of boom and bust and drove the imperialism—European, American—in which my grandparents unquestioningly participated. Oil drew them. Indirectly, then, oil draws me. It also carries me: in cars adding to the region's perpetual post-imperial haze; in the airplanes that fly me across oceans and continents.

The stench of refuse and raw sewage reaches the gates of the sultan's palace, the call to prayer wafting over all of it. I don't get on a bus, don't feel endangered, though I am already editing in my head what I will tell Chris. I walk decayed sidewalks through the old town, their last neighborhood in the Indies, where I can't know for certain which house was theirs or whether it still stands, then a mile back to the Sandjaja, good enough but not luxurious at $21 a night.

Behind me, my grandfather and Agerbeck haggle for goods and men: Chinese pit diggers and surveyors, Sumatran coolies to carry housing, tools, food for a hundred on their backs. They deal with Dutch officials for bodies, many conscripted or working off debts or sentences. My grandfather doesn't ask.

In Batavia, Miriam managed everything. Dutch came quickly on top of the German she'd learned at home as a child. She used her household allowance to pay bills as they came, not only cleaning but painting, plumbing, screwing shelves into walls—all things I, too, take for granted being able to do, but she would become exceptional at managing.

My mother married a man who, for the most part, took care of things. After sixty years, while my father tumbles into his mind's thickening fog, she has to figure out where to find the tax files and sprinkler valves, how to hire a handyman to fix a balky garage door and a service to shovel snow. She asks her children for advice she won't take. When the furnace fails, she still waits for my father to call someone, but he can no longer use the phone much less find the number. The garden falls into disarray. Having cooked and arranged housekeeping for decades, she now says, "I never realized how much your father did." Then she observes that he never learned to fold hospital corners.

Work accrues value or not, depending on who does it. The woman behind the man, Miriam sewed batik into curtains and scoured shops on the Pasar Baroe for used furniture good enough to refinish, swimming through the heat. I picture her riding as I will in bicycle rickshaws painted with wild patterns, a maelstrom of yellows, greens, blues, and reds. Borne before the spinning wheels, we are figureheads, windblown, nothing between us and what is coming. This is what I imagine, though in her case it is wrong, an anachronism.

Slowly we shall break into the habits of the jungle that will swallow us.

He left Agerbeck to supervise the building—thatched huts on wood floors for the white geologists, on bare earth for the workers—and chose five coolies to paddle him upriver. *The water being so very low, I saw outcrops that perhaps have never been seen by geologists before.* He drew furiously. It was raining in high country. By morning, up five feet, the river would be lapping at the coolies' beds.

I don't even know the rules. When I arrive in Jakarta, Amir, my driver, stands with a sign bearing my name, and I forget myself and reach to shake his hand. He backs away, smiling determinedly. When I realize he speaks no English, not even "hello," I consider phoning the travel agent. But surely she had good reason to send him for my eccentric itinerary. Maybe he knows the way, or he is her brother, or he needs the money.

The van crawls above a city sprawling through a fever-swamp on the north coast of Java. From the elevated highway, air-conditioned and sealed off, I scan modern Jakarta for any sign of the Batavia they knew. We drive through miles of houses constructed from what looks to me like trash. In my North American city, shanties made of odd boards, pieces of tin, shreds of fabric or cardboard cobbled into shapes that can, however provisionally, give shelter, are not homes; we call the people who occupy them "homeless."

Yet, as my grandparents would have known, people make homes where they live, from what they have. Laundry hangs from lines strung rooftop to rooftop. Cook-smoke rises from chimneys constructed out of cans. Every repurposing and device is a matter of pragmatism and routine, settlement, active domestic life: a variation on the themes of resourcefulness and penury. The slums that precariously scale the mountainsides above Medellín have this same makeshift quality, repurposing every scrap that has any

Walter was already out taking
photographs

life left, showing what at first appears as desperation, then reveals itself as determination and ingenuity.

A cluster of towers rises from the city of scrap, gleaming through air thick with humidity, wood smoke, and exhaust. As we draw close, Amir begins for the first time since we embarked to speak. He is adamant, but he has no more English than I have Indonesian. What does he want me to see in all that glass and steel? He jabs his finger toward the tallest, most polished tower. Finally, he slowly names it: "Mandarin Oriental," my hotel, at $79 a night apparently the fanciest real estate in the city. A middle-class academic at home, here, as they were, I am impossibly rich. I am put in my place, a place of disjunction: intense poverty in the literal shadow of wealth and luxury in which I participate, the present layered over a history I am coming to imagine. The air, an unregulated spew of carbon gases, is the visible sign of Indonesia's drive to enter a way of life, a standard of living, my grandparents helped create and most North Americans embrace, based on consumption and waste, in which entire countries are disposable—while, in these countries, almost nothing is disposed of. The day's news becomes toilet paper; even dung is dried and burned. Need, ingenuity. In the ultimate example of trickle-down, the slums are assembled from what is discarded by people in the soaring buildings they seem to support. That is a truth. The apparent mirage of hotels rising from decay and haze as if from their foundations—this, too, is a truth. A strange, unsupportable ecology of use, of which I am a part, whether I am here or at home, an ecology in which I have roots as deep as anyone's.

But what ecology, in its desire to sustain itself, hasn't made fragile compromises and surrenders along with demands? Just now, alone in a back seat, I am thinking about my grandparents and about my mother, who was born here. Suddenly, I am missing my husband, who I know is worrying about me. What is he doing?

"Every minute," Chris says, whenever we talk. "Where are you? When are you coming home?" His desire fills me with wonder. Surely I am easier to love in my absence than when I am there in front of him but hardly more present, distracted by the past and the words in my head. Yet, he wants me there. "You have all this," he says, gesturing at the piles of paper and books around me. "You don't need to *go* anywhere."

What does any woman need? I check the time on the Palm Treo he gave me before I left, and I am shaken briefly out of my dream of language. The Treo has international calling and texting, a camera that lets me send him pictures, all new and fancy four years before the iPhone will make such convenience commonplace. It's a kind of tether.

Still, I am on the other side of the earth, the side that for now is bathed in sunlight. It will be hours before I can phone without waking him.

For the moment, I am free.

The bathhouse was out back, past the kitchen and the servants' quarters—a tank of rain water and a couple of buckets. *Two or three or four baths a day seem to turn the trick,* cool water pouring over her head, just like the natives. *You can get used to anything.*

She didn't yet know the house was too modest and on the wrong side of the tracks. I photograph it from the street, having trudged on foot through the afternoon heat to find it, marking myself as usual as foreign, lunatic. A block west is Menteng, with its shaded embassies and mansions; here, where nobody walks, litter in the streets and a sidewalk eroded into gutter. Then the city had 435,000 souls; its population today approaches ten million. Archival photos show the colonial center in the twenties as almost bucolic, capturing only the occasional person, usually white, and perhaps a carriage or a couple of cars; now the streets teem with people, and traffic roars and honks through the smoky air.

Another bath, a dose of powder, a white evening gown, and Chanel No. 5. Her first party followed the Batavian model, down to the whisky-and-soda splits Marto, her houseboy, passed, and her guest list, everyone older than she, including Walter's new friend Mr. Eastman, *a mystery man scouting around for some oil co.*, and Lura Rhoades, *another geological widow.* She hadn't yet learned she loved the textures and spice of Indonesian food. Her Javanese cook, Minna, made roast beef, mashed potatoes, creamed asparagus, ice cream. *They never went home until 1:15. The only flaw was that the Boy Friend was absent.*

They mapped by section. A Chinese digger could dig a pit nine meters deep and three wide in under a day, reinforce it, carve into its sides narrow, slick steps Walter descended, peering at the walls looking for signs of structure, hoping they wouldn't collapse and bury him alive. *He who thinks this work is a Sunday School Picnic can follow me for one day.*

I watch him measure his life. *I need a stake—it has not been cut yet; then a note book, it is still in the bag.* Twenty-six, time moving through him. Leeches waited in the trees for any uptick in temperature to tell them a mammal passed, warm-blooded and mortal, below. He found one on his chest, full of blood, as big around as his finger. Others *in places I blush to mention, and so they were all the more painful.*

She still dreamed she might go with him on a car trip, to *Bali or Modura or eastern java.* She no longer imagined traveling 150 miles on foot, through ticks, thorns, red ants swarming like a lick of fire, cutting her own trail, any more than I do. Later, friends say, Jakarta, Palembang, as if I've returned trailing those names like a spell. "Who even goes there?" one friend asks, and my husband shrugs. For years, since he couldn't imagine traveling to such places, I didn't go either. Coming home, I think as much of what I didn't see as of what I did. *An unsatisfied woman,* wanting to go back.

Invitations piled up on the hall table. Tea, afternoon bridge, luncheon, golf. When she remembered, she missed him, the way she was supposed to, counting imaginary miles.

They made their own canoes to order

There is a wonderful moon that lights this wild and weird jungle in such a delicate pale light that a man is bound to get homesick, especially when he is in love with his wife. He enumerated the animals she would never encounter herself. A bobtailed monkey, biggest he'd seen. A white turtle. The neighborhood elephant, *a rogue cast out from the main herd, now wandering around all by himself,* leaving droppings big as tuffets. Under logs he found nests lined with grass and leaves: *wild men, wary as a tiger.*

Hardship and wonder. *It is all a very beautiful life.* Through his words, I plunge. *When one emerges from the jungle cover and into the light, the brightness is blinding.*

In her sheltered enclave, she didn't need to pay attention.

After clearing metal detectors and bomb sniffers at the gates of my shining glass hotel, I am led to the club floor and seated on a couch for private check-in and champagne. My $79 a night also includes breakfast and an evening cocktail.

She played golf at the club with Mr. Eastman then danced with Jim Farley at the Box, like most of glamorous old Batavia now gone. *Due to the dearth of girls here, it's all au fait.*

I walk under the afternoon sun through a city sinking like Venice into the sea, though here the canals are choked with trash. I finger batiks in a mall that will soon be bombed to almost nothing. It's not that I don't miss Chris, that I am never lonely, but here, however closely watched, I feel free to follow my preoccupations to whatever I might find.

Chinese peddlers unrolled fine pongee and shantung heavy as linen onto her dining table for dresses copied from Paris and London and tailored to her body, more than one seam blown in the hilarious wee hours. *I went to a cocktail party which started at 11:30 and our part of it never broke up until 3:00, after which we took a drive down to Tandjong Priok and watched the sunset from the yacht club.* A little break after sunset to bathe again and change for evening.

Tired, heat-sapped, I dine in at the hotel's world-class Chinese restaurant, surrounded by businessmen speaking English to each other in accents from around Asia. I promise myself that I'll find street food at Menteng FTS tomorrow. While I deploy my chopsticks primly if awkwardly, at the next table a Texan gripping a fork in his fist jokes that Indonesia is just like home: "'old money' and 'oil money' are synonymous."

I was brought home at 2:30 A.M. by an Englishman who was firmly convinced that I came from among wild Indians and ought to be wearing chaps and a 6-shooter.

The jungle wore on him. *Every morning I can scrape a nice crust of mould from my hat band.* Monstrous growth. *At night the ground is covered with phosphorescences.* The jungle floor lit up like a starry sky.

The flesh, too, eroded. A coolie came to him with festering boils. *I lanced one and drained it, but the poor devil could stand no more.* Lives in his hands.

At dawn, he heard invisible birds, *the mournful cries of the tailless monkeys.* When rain poured through the jungle canopy, each drop sounded hundreds of times as it fell from leaf to leaf, the storm multiplying in the ear. *I want to see the sky, the sun.* His long legs stepped off days. The engineers couldn't keep up, so when it was time to return to camp he struck out alone cross-country with his compass. Even the surveyor spent a night alone in the jungle, but never Walter. *If the man that makes the map loses himself I wonder how I should ever find my way.* Day by day, he was headed home.

At night, he lay awake on his cot, fitting map to land, a subterranean dream. *The coolies are singing some weird sounding song. Buenos Noches mi Amorcita—if only it were so—*

Most expats stuck to their own groups, but she worked on her Dutch and studied Portuguese and even Malay, practicing on Marto and Minna. From the jumble of her papers—books, diaries, old shopping lists—flutter sheets of jotted words. *I know almost two hundred.* With language, she might domesticate this place. *They do things a little differently.*

Her photos of the Kali Besar show colonial architecture, wooden boats with awnings, native women kneeling to scrub laundry. Today, the Kali Besar is still lined with picturesque if dingy colonial Dutch buildings, the few around Fatahillah Square—once Batavia City Square—saved from the frenzy of urban development. Most of Jakarta's canals, an elaborate system built to ease flooding in the rainy season, are clogged with silt and garbage. Nobody with a choice would think of washing in them, much less drinking their water.

After visiting the square's museums, I stop for lunch at the Cafe Batavia in a colonial building fitted out with dark wood and Deco furniture. Because there are so few tourists and the restaurant is expensive by Jakartan standards, I get a seat by a tall window overlooking the square with its colorful umbrellas, jugglers, tattoo artists, soldiers and police with guns slung over their shoulders. The menu ranges from club sandwiches to shrimp dumplings with mayonnaise to pancakes with syrup. But the soto ayam—a spicy chicken soup—tastes wonderful with my Bintang beer.

As I finish, I hear faint music, and two figures come into view— Ondel-ondel, I know from descriptions in Miriam's journal and my visit to the puppet museum, brocade-gowned, nine feet tall on stilts, with grass hair and wooden faces, the male red and the female white. They trail a little band behind: cymbals, bells, drums, some sort of push organ. Two men flank them, shaking buckets for coins, but I sit behind glass, too far above to pay my share.

All dressed up

The storm season settled in. *Every night one hears the crashing of huge trees, and it is a most terrifying noise in the stillness.* Branches and tangled roots blocked the trails. When the map finally resolved itself—no oil—the river was up forty feet. It swirled them through treetops in a tumult of reflected light. *Just before dark millions of huge bats came out of the jungle and covered the sky. Last night was a nice night for beauty, but a poor night for sleep.*

Emerging from the jungle, he felt half wild, estranged—from others, from himself. *My mind is feasting on the solid pleasure of my little Muckie, with her sparkling blue eyes and red soft lips that are mine alone.* They would sit in their little house, just the two of them. *That is a million times better than having the President of the United States or the King of England around.* So close. *I wish the cursed boat could fly—*

They went to the mountains for Christmas, Miriam driving the rental car while Walter took photos out the windows. There were hardly any cars, but the road was full of people, seven hundred per square Java mile. *One sees them trotting with a bamboo rod on their shoulders on which is suspended several baskets or tins etc, a contented lot of coolies.* It couldn't last—fields cultivated the same way for centuries; wooden plows. The Great War was finished, World War II a mirage, but even their presence exerted a force. *I wonder how long before the country breaks into the turmoil of revolution against the Dutch Rule.* Unlike his fellows, he smelled the whiff of violence wafting while peasants bowed to him, the master, the Toean in his automobile. By the time I arrive, even mountain roads are choked with cars, buses, and scooters along with bicycle rickshaws and carthorses, their harnesses jingling with bells and silver ornaments. Everyone sees me, my difference marked by pale eyes and strange dress, my solitary, undirected female wandering, but nobody bows or stands aside.

The Hotel Tjisoeroepan overlooked steeply-terraced rice

paddies, surrounding Walter, who for so long had seen no blue, with reflected sky. He was getting ready for a car trip to mid-Java—almost a pleasure jaunt through lovely country, a little light espionage to keep him busy. He wanted to take Miriam along, but Gallaher said no, so Walter claimed.

People left; new people arrived. Billee Gallaher, Walter's new boss, whose family lived in California next-door to Douglas Fairbanks. His wife Ludmilla, *a beautiful Russian girl* who escaped the revolution through Constantinople. Jim, whose wife died of smallpox a few days after they arrived. *He nearly went crazy for about a year.* In January, Miriam saw him every day. The mysterious Eastman, now Ted: *Harvard man, much given to poetry and introspection and analysis of other people, and thinks he's a bit of a lion with the ladies.* Colin McCulloch, a Scot. *He rode bucking broncos in Madison Square Garden.* The Brit, Bill Davis, *star of many polo games and riding contests*, who often lent her a pony. Walter didn't approve, but Walter was almost never there to know.

He finished in the field a few days early but sent no telegram. Tossed on the bed when he arrived were two evening dresses she'd tried and rejected. Made for her, with a nip and tuck they would have fit me. Where did they go?

He sat in the dark. At 3:00 A.M., headlights swept her batik curtains. Tires on gravel, laughter, a man's voice. Humming, she walked past, heels clicking time. He watched her gown slide off her shoulders into a shimmering blue pool. Another dress he hadn't seen before. In stockings and a froth of lace, she leaned to the mirror. She was unfastening her necklace when she caught sight of his shadow in the glass and began to scream.

I was glad to see him, of course. Tomorrow's bridge, any number of parties, golf, all blown. *I'd told everybody he wasn't coming till next week.*

Mine alone, as only a woman can be, yet she eluded him. He needed a plan to shift her attention. The next afternoon, she stepped onto the front porch to see a little roadster pulling up, a half-caste behind the wheel and Walter in the passenger seat. She didn't even grab her purse. *And o Boy, how she do ramble!* They arrived at Priok in time to watch the sun set over the water.

In the morning, she gave him his first driving lesson. His big feet sat awkwardly on the pedals, and the car lurched when he let out the clutch. He reversed without looking behind and ignored the speedometer, the buffalo on the road, a cyclist. By the time they returned he was getting the hang of it, but she was done in. In this as in so many things she cared about, he was more diligent than graceful. *I doubt whether he'll ever be a good driver.*

So began the cycle of separations and reunions. For him, every trip began poorly. Mosquitoes rose from the riverbanks in gauzy curtains, and men came down with malaria. But there were small gifts. A headman *trotted out the Gadisses for us,* the village virgins. *The village seems to only have about six of them.* Rarely, village women let him film them. *If one can not get pictures the native method of doing things is lost.* And, on the trail in the middle of the jungle, a glint of light: *a 5 dollar gold piece in the form of a pin.* In the mud at his feet, a gift. *Today Muckie and I have been married 18 months. I wonder how she is.*

It has seemed funny with Brutus gone again, but I'm getting used to it once more. The Javanese New Year, all color and motion and stir.

Miriam's calendar lists an ever-shifting set of expats, most of them men. *They treat me just like a kid sister.* Teasing so like flirting, an art she'd mastered. In the car he gave her she could go anywhere. *I had the flv up to 93 kil. Per on the way! It goes quickly this way, and so I don't get achey about Brutus.*

His wife and nobody he knew driving down to Priok in his car, his Victrola on the seat.

And o Boy, how she do ramble!

Monday afternoon I had a lovely ride. Yesterday I tried to play polo and reached too far for a ball and fell off, disgracefully.

Mandy was too distracted to attend to signs from across the sea. While the stock market expanded, Louis watched others became rich. It's familiar: the beautiful bubble growing. Louis's family was respectable, but hardly prosperous, especially since Prohibition shut down the brewery he'd married. And Mandy just sat on her principal. If he could take a little of her money and make something of it, what it returned he could call—couldn't he?—his own. She could have her three percent; her husband could have all the rest, and she would never know the difference.

Her brothers had been against Louis, beautiful Louis, from the beginning. Now, they insinuated, hinted, but real talk was for men. Everything happened out of earshot, out of her control. If only someone would speak out loud. If she could see.

At a cousin's, she met Mrs. Marth. Tidy, a little dull, she looked like any woman at church. But in the late afternoon when the drapes were drawn, she saw things in the cards, in tea leaves strewn across a saucer. A shadow, a whisper. When she traced some line in the leaves with her thin finger, Mandy could almost see it too.

Walter was down with malaria and hookworm. Miriam was raring to go. *He always lets his ailments depress him, and he thinks they're worse than they are.* She'd never seen him in the field, where he steeled himself against wild animals, disease, natural disaster, his own black imagination. She'd never returned from travels as he had, as I have to Chris, with rashes, intermittent fevers, stomach ills, a cough that holds on for months. Like my own husband, when he was home he wanted her home with him. He wanted her to want him there, to be taken care of.

Brutus is one of the best eggs in the world, but he is depressing to live with. He ran and reran his movies, editing sequences and titles. She cajoled him out to the golf club, but he was weak from fever, and the ball wouldn't behave. She no longer needed to let him win, but he couldn't bear losing to his own wife. He stomped off at the tenth hole, threatening to cancel the club membership. *He seems to think you have to scratch and be tight and uncongenial so that when you're 55 or 60 you can do anything you please, on a measly 5000 or so a year, because all the gorgeous high tide of your youth was directed along the ditch of sober plugging.* The fight wasn't over money but how they would live, who would decide— the question, perhaps, at the heart of every marriage. How much was enough. Back then, the answer should have been clear.

Is it that we didn't marry the right sort of people? She understood his virtues, could even tolerate them when she was used to them, she told herself, but he kept going away. *I get used to being independent and not <u>subject</u> to anyone, and he comes back. It's subjecting myself to him, just like getting married all over again each time.*

<u>Subject</u>. Even the word gives me a chill. It's not that they weren't alike, but that they were. Except. New York, her back against the glass, the gun raised. All the beds since, a corner of the pillow in her mouth. *It's so hard to overcome my rebellion because he leaves me absolutely cold, physically. And I can't let him know.* There it was, *brutal*: her chill at his touch. She turned to him anyway, most of the time. <u>Male and female, he made them.</u> *She still obeys*, a promise she should never have made, that she had to make. They couldn't change the structure that contained them. She didn't know how; he wouldn't have thought to. How could he not have known? How could she have been so invisible to him?

If he couldn't understand her, he should have admired her. And vice-versa.

To Mandy, a torrent of words. At home, silence. Miriam came back from tennis to find him sitting over his films, blinds drawn and the lights off, wondering when she'd be back. She was light as a feather, young, childless.

She had been invited to play in the Box cabaret show. Rehearsals would put her smooth cheek by any number of jowls. *A couple of duets with ukuleles, and a playlet—comic, with songs.* Miriam, of course, as ingénue, her small roundness packed into *white organdy, long tight bodice, little white buttons, round collar and long, dark blue ribbon.* For Mandy, in the letter's margin, and for me, a line drawing of her dress. He imagined himself watching another man croon love songs to his wife. I've got a man crazy for me.

The dark hid his face. Impatient, she clattered her racket down on the table, startling him, startling a shadow from a corner of the bookshelf—a hand-sized bat, hazarding ribbed wings around her backlit halo of hair. She screamed. Walter leapt from his chair, grabbed her tennis racket, and beat at the fluttering darkness. When the bat lay on the floor at her feet, he took her into his arms, kissing her hair where it was damp at her hairline.

Is it that we didn't marry the right sort of people? Chris and I, too, are different, our division of labor unpredictable. I kill black widows and set out poison for the river rats; he kills only the aggressive yellow jackets I am deadly allergic to, which he won't let me near. When a bird flies in, I catch it between my hands, and carry it outside; still, not squeamish, I dispose of the bodies of birds who have broken their necks against the plate glass windows and spray his rhododendrons with rendered blood to keep deer away.

I used to wonder that Chris didn't worry how heavy a load I chose to carry, that I was always the one to climb the roof—though, in truth, like Miriam, I like being strong for my size; I like to climb the roof and survey the neighborhood. I no longer wonder about his lack of jealousy, his disinclination to challenge men who flirt, hover, even suggest. All of this is unusual even now.

If we could only live together permanently, I could submerge all my interests and abilities and live entirely his way and so I shall sometime.

Why not imagine a different fate for them? Why can't I write a love story, two people bound even by difference, bound across time and space by words that might be burning, here, on my page, if they hadn't burnt out already? Another granddaughter might have invented this for them.

Submit. Subject. Words that chill me. It would be so easy to give in. Still, with all my liberties, I won't change their story, their bodies both mine and not mine; I can only imagine. Over the ocean, in my lengthening night, against my husband's wishes I head their way, toward the man packing for wild water, snakes, and poison arrows; toward the girl left alone with her flirtations, in just as much danger, nearing the brink, learning already to look at every man as a possible doorway out.

CHAPTER 7

GRAVITY

YESTERDAY MORNING Muckie went out Horseback Riding and when I saw her again she was lying unconscious on a table with a swollen face, covered with mud. She'd been riding a two-year-old known for spirit on the polo fields. All he had feared. Walter couldn't believe Dave had mounted Miriam on such a beast—but Miriam thought she could ride anything.

He held her hand while the doctor pressed at her skull. *To me there is a combination of which my wife is the Key. Why should such a thing happen to one that represents by far the cream of any white women in the City of Batavia?* If he needed her so much, why did he keep leaving her behind? An idea. In the X-ray, the bone looked like its ghost. Still looks, pasted in her album. The doctor's finger traced the fracture from the left eye socket all the way over the top of her head.

It seems so useless without her. The razor, hair falling away. Needle and thread. Her gaze skittered across his face. What if she never recognized him again? All that wooing. He wasn't sure he could persuade her a second time. *One reads of the downfall of people seeking power, land, gold—conquest—it is quite necessary to check the reign of a Napoleon—but why should something happen to two people who only care to have a simple happy life.*

Past midnight, the nurse sent him home to a dark house. He drew the curtains her hands had sewn. *I wonder now what the price of coming to the Indes must be.*

For a week, she swam in and out of herself. He waited for her to surface while his men waited in Palembang: Agerbeck, engineers, cook, coolies drawing pay, hours ticking by in guilders. He couldn't go until she knew him.

M: *Brutus left last Saturday. As a result he seems very vague.* She would tell me later how he left her alone in a hospital bed, still not in herself.

W: *One must do what earns the living. I think now there is no danger—*

(M: *I'm having the queerest sensation.* She dreamed a room too far away for her mother to reach, with slatted windows and palm fronds waving against a blue sky, a shadow crossing the doorway. *Or else I'm suffering from a hallucination.*)

W: *To hurt one almost kill one and then bring back again—If there is a God—*

And Mandy at her window looking at trees full of summer and light, the sheaf of cables in her hand—the dire first, the second. Miriam could have died, and for over a day while the news pulsed toward her through undersea wires, Mandy would have known nothing, though like Chris she had ways of keeping in touch. Had Mrs. Marth said something ominous? She imagined a shiver of knowledge had lifted her, at the moment of catastrophe, from sleep. *Darling Petty.* She must go to her. But when? Her brothers were constantly at her, and she couldn't get Louis to explain where the money had gone, didn't even know if she could raise her passage. Time equals space equals money.

M: O mommy, forgive me for breaking down, but I'll be so glad when you come and I can just crawl into your arms and weep and wail all I want to.

Blue hills with fantastic shapes formed by volcanic rocks, and a twisted mass of jungle so big the natives had never seen white men. Even with their new canvas tenting—lightweight and waterproof, *a thousand times better than thatching*—they had too much gear to carry over hard trails. They set out on foot anyway, counting on the river to rise so the boats could get through with food, housing, tools.

My youth and exceptional fitness saved the day—my bones are mending with extraordinary speed. For over a month, the doctor wouldn't talk of release, but even here she was at the center of things. Her room was crowded with young men fluffing pillows and blowing smoke rings out the window. Dave carried nightclothes home to Minna in the morning, bringing fresh ones back. He sold the horse at a loss. *You're my mommy and you know it's not my conceit—I'm one of the most popular girls here.*

Mandy was snubbed on the street. Acquaintances rang at the front door and asked for their money back. Summonses. Waiting for news from Batavia, she reread old letters and watched for the postman or, heaven forbid, the Western Union boy. She read every word I read. She had to wait weeks for each installment. When she grew impatient, she called Mrs. Marth. Turned her hand in Mrs. Marth's gloved hands, upended the teacup onto the saucer, leaves tracing odd scripts across the china.

Up the mountain

A man went down on the trail, gut-hobbled. *Arenta*: the first coolie he names in the journals. After the burial, the Javanese moved the tent where Arenta had died and even then refused to sleep on the side where his sleeping ghost now lay, invisible but no less present.

The scientist in him recorded it all precisely—not how he felt, but tools used and burial costs in guilders.

Even in hospital, she made tongues wag. *That's the trouble here— housekeeping is so simple most of these women can't keep busy.* But Miriam was getting tired of her hospital bed, her veranda, even her beaux. She wanted—what? Great love, preferably without difficulty. Freedom without regard for consequence. What everyone wants but not even a man gets. Her amnesia made her feel how strange this place was, how far from home. The stitches came out; her hair began to grow back. One eye wouldn't quite track—for the rest of her life she had to lift her chin and look down her nose at people.

Pale, uncertain, unlike herself, at the end of August she went home in Dave's charge, promising her doctor to be quiet. It had been six weeks. The house she'd furnished felt empty and lonely. *I'm sick of everything just now & only want my mummy, & to be a kid again and have a job, too.* Her desires, as always, confused; Walter in his jungle, distant as a dream.

He counted the dwindling rations again in his head, numbers refusing to add up. Despite his hunger he cut trail through a wild thicket where trees had been felled by wind, men, ravening elephants. *I used my compass and blazed the way.* One day's work: three kilometers. The rhythm of blade on vine, heartbeat in his ears. The diggers opened twenty pits. *All dusters.* He understood enough of the workers' mutterings to know their discontent, their fear, were directed at him.

Was she still in the hospital? October 1929—he'd been gone

three months. Banks were failing, the world economy grinding to a halt. He dreamed of leaves flaming. *I wonder how the football games came out today.* In the jungle's glaze of heat, time moved slowly, news more slowly still.

Only when the crash forced her brothers and banker to sit her down did Mandy learn what Louis had done. *Embezzlement—* though under the "Head and Master" laws, a husband had leeway. He'd withdrawn her entire principal and put it God knows where, patrimony reduced to pure speculation. Worse, he'd invested for others, borrowed money from friends—all lost. Her brothers planted themselves in her parlor and talked. *Worthless.* At last, with Miriam's letters in mind, deceptively meek, she drove her bargain. They would restore her principal, all of it. She would have a second chance. Their bargain, also hard: she must cut Louis and his debts loose before they would give her a penny. She must never marry again.

The next day, she filed for divorce. The day after that, free at last to go where she wished, she bought passage and embarked on a frenzy of shopping that emptied Louis's account. Five thousand miles. To Miriam, she wrote only that she was coming.

Miriam's letters to Mandy are unknowing, full of lists. *Patent leather pumps with high heels. Good-looking kid afternoon shoes of beige or whatever is* smart. *A white felt hat, a late model.* Records. Books. Mandy, an emissary from the world of department stores. *For yourself, bring house dresses for morning, sport or street dresses for bridge parties and calls and shopping.* Mandy would look at her daughter not through words on the page, a lens into the past; not through vagaries of scattered leaves or lines on a palm, whatever divination's claims on the future; but in the vulnerable flesh.

I have a very sane, levelheaded view of life, but otherwise I'm the same silly infant I always was.

They were wrapping up and heading back to the Moesi when the cook, Talib, told him they were low on food again. Walter unpacked the kitchen boxes, counting cans and sacks of rice— even less food than Talib had said. He found the cook's personal trunk padlocked and got his machete. *I cut the tin box and opened it.* Clothing, a Koran. A cigar box heavy with coins. Also butter, syrup, lard, canned pineapple and potatoes Talib hadn't already sold along the way. Even small-time pilfering, can by can, could add up to wealth, to disaster.

Walter sent the box upriver open for all his hungry men to see. *We are in their country and depend on them.* The ruler at the mercy of his slaves. *A white man is one to be cheated as much as possible.* But from now on, he would pack the food himself.

Our second wedding anniversary—

In the mountains, where the doctor had sent her, she sat on the veranda of the Grand Hotel Lembang. Still weak, she felt as woolly as the clouds obscuring her view, but under the grey stirred a desire to get on with things. Before leaving Batavia, she'd written Walter, suggesting he join her in Lembang when he finished—not telling him he'd have to, since she'd rented the house out; not mentioning money or that the company would not pay for her hospital stay. She wrote Mandy not to buy the clothes she'd asked for.

Kobe. Shanghai. Hong Kong. Miriam, Mandy, me in flight. *One good way of keeping fit is standing at the front of the main deck looking straight ahead with the glorious fresh air blowing right into your lungs.* To embark again for the first time, to be in motion.

Another digger was carried in with beriberi. *I tried the mirror on his breath.* Coolies and diggers sickened in twos and threes, all but the Javanese. One night, he visited their camp, the men falling silent as he stepped into the firelight. *Today I made my first speech in Malay.* Then he listened. In the morning, he set out alone for a nearby abandoned ledang, *overrun by moths, lizards, roaches, everything that creeps and crawls,* old gardens gone wild. Pods, roots, cucumbers, squash. That night, everyone ate fresh vegetables; the next day, sick coolies and diggers rose from their beds and went to work. Men fall sick: heal them. The cook thieves: catch and keep him. Talib would work for Walter for years.

On the trail, he spoke to a band of lumberjacks in broken Malay. They huddled, drew maps in the dirt with sticks, spoke man to man, the way he was comfortable doing, about a world measured in hours walked. Their expertise would save weeks of cutting. *I can never get any of the Englishmen to realize that.* He finished ahead of schedule and boarded his first airplane, *a trip that would have taken at least two days by ordinary travel.* They floated *above banks and banks of pure white clouds and rugged blue mountains.* Over straits strewn with tiny islands and reefs, the sky cleared. He would be in Miriam's arms at two.

Not bad for a tropical island, supposedly savage, eh?

Almost nobody had seen the earth from this height. A few pilots, madmen all; a few fortunate passengers like himself. A kind of genius. As if he'd flown open at the seams.

CHAPTER 8

INTERLUDE:
PURE SPECULATION

MOTHER DARLING darling darling! I'm the happiest woman in the world from here on. November, 1929, Lembang. Almost five months after Miriam's fall, *we're just a couple of happy kids getting a big kick out of everything chiefly out of just being alive & together.* A luxury I will follow them into, sinking myself into the Grand Hotel Lembang's cool swimming pool.

They have no real idea yet of the market's disarray, what it might have to do with them or theirs. He wants more than ever from the body he almost lost. He holds her hand, as much to keep as comfort her. All he has to do is change completely.

And her? *All this going out business doesn't intrigue me any more.* Part of the pattern, how she keeps persuading herself, pretending to be a willing captive to a romantic ideal. Chill air, fog burning off into long afternoons, sudden nightfalls. The man sees everything in her, more beauty and virtue than she has, and

Mandy on the ocean

more mystery—a habit of men, in my experience, and we women are easily persuaded. So much pressure, but she is in the mood to yield. She comes halfway across the vast Dutch bed to meet him and tries to respond to his movements. Feeling his moan, she almost believes she feels an answering chord. After, while he slips into sleep, something takes hold. Something she wants, yes? She thinks again, for the first time in over a year, that she might go out with him—into mid-Java with its beautiful hills, its bridal-path road lined with trees. *I'm positively dippy!*

In January, Walter leaves without her. *It'd be too expensive.* She'll make the best of things. *We're flat broke and owe the company a couple hundred guilders.* She might carry it off, if only. *He's going to a beautiful part of Java, too.*

I watch her waver between childhood and adulthood, submission and assertion, a line I know as I parse my course schedules and airplane timetables, wondering how long a trip I can reasonably manage this time around money, teaching, my skeptical husband. I make my reservations first, then tell Chris, and as always he tries to barter days, wondering why I need be gone so long, when he really wants to know why I am going at all.

I'll be so glad when you come. Her mother is on the ocean, so she reaches for her husband. What, for a woman like her, in her place and time, does it mean to grow up? What might it mean for me?

Suddenly Mandy is there, idea made flesh, straight-backed at the rail while the boat's horn blares. The past, the future converge on foreign ground, Miriam's body a confluence x-ed out. What now? Miriam longed for her mother. Five months of Mandy from breakfast to nightcap. Joy. Her daughter can hardly breathe. I know how this feels.

Walter makes sure the trunks Mandy has stuffed with tobacco, clothes, everything Miriam asked for and more, are on the bottom of the cart, those packed for inspection by Customs on top. Then they drink splits on the veranda and make plans: golf, swimming, bridge, luncheons, sunset drives to Priok with a carload of young men and the Victrola—Mandy's brought records—and dancing, which Mandy loves as much as Miriam does, as I do, in spite of her arthritic hips. As a married woman, she did all too little of it. The Box, Des Indes, Harmonie—demolished in 1985—had ballrooms with smooth and shining floors.

Miriam is all smiles, all despair. She can dance, but under her mother's eye her body will take another shape, and what new beau will think of holding her? No more abandon. No staying out until 4 a.m. She is haunted—by her mother, by the child Mandy reduces her to, by the child she carries, though she doesn't say a word yet. Her announcement will subject her more completely than anything else. X-ed out. For a little longer, she'll pretend she has breathing room.

Nearly sunset. Except for the native caddy, they are alone. While Miriam lines up her shot, Mandy looks west down the long slope toward the next hole and the jungle standing in dark relief against a red sky: the vista Miriam drew in the margin of one of her letters as a hieroglyph of shadows still suggested at the edge of the long lawn. While they watch the horizon change color, Mandy draws Miriam in under her arm and tells her what has happened, what she has put into motion.

Another life. Even when the market crashed, Miriam hardly worried, though her father borrowed money from Walter, too, enough to cover the hospital bill several times over. She will never get it back, nor her old home, her family, a world vanished. But Miriam says nothing about her own losses. She pets and comforts while Mandy weeps for herself, for once-beautiful Louis. Fury, heartbreak—she has always confided too much in her daughter. *Those worthless Wollaegers.* Miriam is one, as am I.

Another hole in the record. They are together, not writing but talking, words I can only imagine. It grows too dark to play. They will dine then dance at the Des Indes with Ted and Dave and that nice Bert Butler, the new Canadian Assistant Commissioner for Trade, who reminds Miriam of William Powell. Like her husband, he is better-looking than she is. Mandy approves how he renders his teasing of Miriam harmless by flirting as relentlessly with her mother. He has an unofficial fiancée in Scotland, distant enough to cause no distress.

They nap, then dress and meet for a split on the veranda, Miriam walking around barefoot, brightly painted, sitting on the chaise longue to light a cigarette. Mandy imagines being that young again, not thirty years ago but right now, when girls can wear lips the color of June cherries.

A plunging neckline. Crimson toenails. *It's really all comme il faut.*

Daughter and mother leave the bridge table early. The jealous thrill of watching a bright, winged cylinder of metal descend, open, and disgorge Walter, clean but carrying a bag of clothes reeking of jungle rot and sweat. He gets to do anything. She gets to feel his eyes linger on her face, move down her neck—Mandy, too, feels the gaze, as if it were caressing her own body.

Another shift: her mother and her husband allied again. Is she happy to give them what they want, to be already giving it, or is she beginning her new revolt? I, willfully child-free, don't know how this might go, what her logic might be. I have spared myself.

Mandy in the next room. Soon and for a long time, Miriam will be able to deny him, but not now. She neither helps nor hinders, only shushes him, her mother on the other side of the wall. For her own sake, to end things more quickly, she moves once he is inside her.

She's had false alarms—on the boat to Colombia and again on the one to Singapore, one period missed, two, three: travel stress, a new diet. Another fragility she and I shared. In each case, when the blood finally came, like me she was relieved, though unlike me she always knew children were part of a larger plan already made for her, one she wouldn't think to question. This, anyway, is different. She can't stop thinking about her parents, about the marriage that produced her flying apart.

His finish comes in a panic of breath. Nuzzling her breast, he drifts off to sleep. *The sweetest thing ever.*

The house slumbers around her. Miriam lies with eyes wide open, the future moving through her. In the morning she is sick. When she goes in to breakfast, she doesn't have to say a word. Mandy has already told him.

CHAPTER 9

AN ABSENCE AT HEART

JUST AFTER MANDY'S SHIP embarked for Europe, Miriam's smaller boat slid into the narrow strip of Indian Ocean separating Java from Sumatra. The two Dutch captains, sentimental, turned their vessels broadside so mother and daughter could wave at each other through spyglasses, then Miriam's ship steamed into the traffic jam at the Moesi's wide mouth—*lousy with praus and canoes* in the shadows of enormous oil tankers.

By now, Charles Bertram Butler was Walter's official best friend, approved companion to Miriam in his absence. He had supervised the loading of the ladies' luggage, instructed stewards, dispensed tips and bribes. Bert had handed her up the gangplank in Batavia; in Palembang, Walter handed her down.

The field at last—though not beautiful mid-Java. The baby did back flips on top of her bladder all the way to Talang Akar, four jolting hours. No car was comfortable now, much less *Brutus's dreadfully bumpy, rattly geological car.*

On the trail with the men, the baby kicked at her lungs. The jungle was even hotter than Batavia. As they walked, Walter lectured her about his new coring device: an oversized hand drill that could extract a cylinder of earth nine meters long and a few inches in diameter, in which Walter could read all the information he'd had to climb deep into a pit to learn a month before. When she paused to catch her breath, he imagined what the men would get up to while they waited for him to arrive.

At the drill site, Miriam lowered herself onto a fallen tree and massaged her ankles. The coolies assembled the device then spent a hard hour turning it, metal grinding on soil and stone. A few meters down, it failed with a labored crunch. They worked it out of the ground, repaired it, started again. At last they brought up a complete core, a snapshot of geologic time. Inch by inch, Walter pointed out where it was continuous and where a break indicated a rubble zone or anomaly. As if she couldn't see for herself. *At any rate, 's a great life as a geologist's wife.* No longer *as a geologist.* Never again.

She stayed behind at camp writing letters. *I wonder where you are.* All that time she'd yearned to get out. Now, sweltering under the tent's canvas, she wanted to go home. *I have nothing and no one, not even sewing.*

Desire was her condition. No matter where she was or what she had, she saw what was missing. Back home, Bert would take her to the markets, interesting himself gallantly in layettes and tiny hats. She wanted Milwaukee or Batavia, Mandy or Bert, a past that had never existed, an impossible future. *I wrote Daddy a hot letter.* The immovable mother, the weak father trying to get out from under: she saw herself in both. Willful. Waffle. I see myself, stubborn and wavering, how I will only go so far. She hoped for a daughter. She would mother according to Holt, scientifically, foregoing a nurse. *I'd rather not have anyone else messing around.* Like Joan, like me, everything different from her mother, and better.

126

The new device was a fragile miracle. Each time the earth broke it, Walter had to drive back to Palembang for parts. The expedition fell behind a week, two, three—though he was still weeks ahead of where he would have been, working the old way. He'd plotted and pleaded to get permission for Miriam to come to him; to entertain her, he spread out drawings made by his new assistant, *a half-caste boy from Soekaboemi*, who kept a sketchbook. *They're a scream.* In a letter's margin she traced one for Mandy: herself from the rear, blouse tucked into fitted trousers, a slender buoyancy. Another shows the Toean in a canoe, cranking his camera while an enormous python uncoils himself from a branch above, mouth opening around his head.

She disappoints him, herself, me. Didn't my mother tell me? He didn't understand she'd wanted, always, not to watch him do something, but to do it herself. Too late. Between injury, fever, and pregnancy, she had become, as I haven't yet, fragile, a woman, to be pampered—what he wanted and reviled. She missed house and friends, one friend, more than she'd ever missed her husband. *I was afraid I'd never have a baby if I stayed.* Her body ruled them both. Worn down, Walter took a precious day to drive her to Palembang and see her onto the boat.

Bert picked her up and drove her straightaway in the moonlight out to Priok.

Batavia stifled even at night. The swamp's miasma rose to the high ground occupied by Europeans and North Americans. Every afternoon, Bert brought ice and teased her in a way that made her feel not matronly and unwieldy but tender as a swelling bud.

A walk, a ride in the moonlight, cards, some music. *Bert is such a nice boy, even though he becomes slightly boring with time.*

Bert to Mandy: *Under the circumstances and now that Brutus is away again I like to spend a lot of time with Miriam.* His best friend's wife, his best friend's baby. *She is doing more than she knows towards keeping these lonely batchelors from going the way of the East and the future Mrs. B. & all the little Bs are going to owe her a great deal.*

Brutus's ratty geological car
(Sketch by H.W.T. Mulle)

Not disturbing. What did she know? What would she have known if she could have read her own letters, cold? *We decided once we were too much alike to ever be in love or get married.* Protesting. *Don't worry about these statements, Mommy, as I'm so dizzy about Brutus I can't think straight, and he's wild about his G.F. and we're the very best of friends.*

By the time I arrive in Jakarta, street names have changed, Bisschopsplein to Taman Suropati, Menteng Boulevard to Diponegoro. Almost all the old town has been demolished to make way for the present. The map Miriam drew in her letter to locate the new house relative to the old is all I have to find either, the railroad marked beside Pegangsaan, a tiny, one-block street. I walk out into the smoke and heat, exactly as Chris fears, ghosting locals lane by lane when I want to cross the relentless traffic (don't get run over, don't get kidnapped), expecting nothing—but I find it, Pegangsaan still, and their first bungalow, which I recognize from the photos of the two of them on the porch, ramshackle and vine covered, still on the wrong side of the tracks.

From Pengangsaan, I follow her directions and Diponegoro to the new house, its walls now topped with shards of glass and guarded by a man with a rifle slung over his back, where my uncle and then my mother came home as newborns. Two more bedrooms, separate servants' quarters, plus, sheer luxury, an indoor bath. Bert directed the workmen and dragged desk and sofa as instructed from corner to corner. Oh, he would make a good husband. Over splits, she read Mandy's latest letter aloud. Tony, her baby sister, was struggling at college. *Poor kid.* Lying shoeless on the chaise, she told Bert about Murphy and Al, about New York, the pistol, how she'd come to marry Walter. *I hope Tony doesn't marry as young as I did. One should have a chance to try one's luck and ability, if any, first. I've got as far as I'll ever get.* Tony shouldn't marry a geologist, for one thing. *One deserted wife in the family is enough.*

As the sun drops on tropics time toward the horizon, I find a café full of locals and order nasi goreng for dinner—fried rice with hot chilies and eggs, which I will also happily eat for breakfast—and lay her 1932 *Baedeker's* on the patterned vinyl cloth. The book has frayed and tattered more during the two years I've had it than in the two-thirds of a century before then. Its pages will gather more grease before I pay my check.

At midnight, she sent him away. *There is an eclipse of the moon.* The shadow of one heavenly body moving over the bright face of another. Another sleepless night.

For the first time, she shared Walter's obsession with measurements—except his didn't extend to the boy he'd wanted, who was now her business. *He's gaining about 6 oz. per week. He's 22 inches long, and powerful.* A prodigy, Peter slept eleven hours a night from the start. She imagined getting him out of diapers by the time they reached Milwaukee on leave. By then, he would be a year old.

After work, Bert would come for a split and a cigar. The men would smoke and stare at Miriam's brown head bent over her son's: Bert worshipping, Walter waiting for her eyes to turn to him. He hadn't yet thought to be jealous of Bert, but he was jealous of his son. He had believed a mother should look after her own babies, but he began to consider a nurse. Then she might drive out with him once in a while.

She wanted Walter to go. She didn't. She needed him to protect her from herself as Mandy had, holding her tight so she couldn't move. *I still feel like your bad child.* Peter's weight in ounces occupied only so much brain. *His back is strong—he can sit on his pottie with very little support.*

The night after Walter left, Miriam and Bert left Peter with Kokki, his new amah, and drove out to Priok. The night air was soft and light. Miriam had restrung her old uke, and Bert lay in the sand at her feet while she sang—you have stolen my heart, so don't go away—*under more stars than I've seen here. O hell why wasn't it Brutus?* Bert's face drawn like water to a moon. *Bert is beginning to waver about the girl*—the Scottish fiancée, all but forgotten. *Well too long absence doesn't make the heart grow fonder!*

Love's old sweet song. Some small disturbance. *We had heaps of fun talking about the origin of the universe and the theory of relativity. Then Bert got annoyed.* She tried not to think about him as she checked on Peter, brushed out her hair, creamed her face, and climbed, late, into bed. She was still awake an hour later, when the bed jolted. *And thrills, there was a tiny bit of earthquake!* All alone, still, the mattress giving way beneath her. *I looked underneath, but there wasn't a soul!*

Miriam, Walter, Bert. Starlight, reflected moon. I imagine them as puppets, wayang, a word with roots in shadow, imagination, soul, the invisible world and its set dramas projected on the screen's heavenly field. *Bert apologized violently for being childish.* If he wasn't careful, she would have to send him away. When she came too close to seeing—when their gazes brushed— she would bend to her baby. *I'd be pretty well lost without him.*

What did Mandy read between the lines? *He's one of the decentest, nicest, cleanest bachelors in captivity.* In her engagement diary, breaking into the list of appointments and invitations: *Filthy insult! Why can't Bert & I be friends and people leave us alone?* Protesting too much. She went out with him every day. *Late as usual—the last time!*

To keep him, she put something between them. Her sister Tony's face, the heartbroken age—her photo on Miriam's bedside table. *He wants to know what you say to my suggestion that we keep him in the family.* A proposal, made by Miriam, not to Tony but to Bert and Mandy: Why shouldn't Bert marry Tony? *What if.* What did she hope to get out of it? *Life is a funny proposition—*

When Walter returned, they all set out for Lake Tjigoemboeng.

Peter & I rode with Bert because his car has glass side shields and it was much better for Peter. Walter on holiday, driving his son's nurse with his son, his wife and her admirer following behind. *We must do something about Bert & Tony, and then we'd fix it for him & Brutus to go to the same places, and would it ever be swell!*

Almost May. At summer's end, Miriam and Walter would board ship for Europe then home, a six-month leave. *The only catch is leaving Bert.* The balance she kept them in, Bert and Walter, was so delicate a sigh could tip it. When Walter was away—short trips, a few weeks into Sumatra—she and Bert went everywhere together.

When did the broken-off gazes become one long one? The diary returned. *Bert & I simply bubbling.* Eyes catching over the dinner table, feet and legs brushing beneath. Walter wanted her to grow up; with Bert she was young, alight. *O Brutus, darling, please—why must you be away?* She wanted him away. *It makes it so difficult.* Bert was wherever she turned; she turned to him. Soon, he would sublet their house, would sleep in her bed, without her. She felt their impending departure like a physical pressure.

I read and write for a living; I know the deviousness of words. But for months, I have read and seen only the family version, which I had been taught to believe, the version of the world I have carried with me. Once I suspected, I had to go back to find clues that were there all along in her appointments diary, little notes among bridge engagements and golf games, what she can't not tell. *Situation getting a bit difficult in spots.* She canceled lunch dates and went off with Bert. *I refuse to be bored now—not enough time left!*

Early July: *Bert & I ate soup at the Harmonie and discussed things scientifically, but it didn't last long after we left.* In the car under the jungle's shadow, he kissed her in the bruised darkness. She hardly dared have him in—the bed in the other room a palpable thing, the pistol in its box, her husband not absent enough. *Brutus got home unexpectedly about 9:30.* Lipstick smudged but dress intact. *Lord, I am so lucky in my life.*

Walter's trips to Sumatra grew brief, briefer—a week, two nights, one. Her diary: *Silences—o, I do.* I'll say what Mandy said so long ago: *Darling Petty, be careful.* The female body at risk. If she can't seek danger abroad like him, she can seek it at home.

And when she's with both of them, *derelict*, can she look either in the eye? *I'm lucky in my boyfriends, and especially in my son—o bless him.* Motherhood, her last refuge. *If only I am fit to take care of him.*

Late July. Things not yet said, not done. How did Walter know he must come home? Intuition. Her little book, left in her desk drawer, in her purse, on the table. Mid-August. Lying beside her husband, her body pulsing with longing but not for him, she imagined giving over. One chance left, Walter's final short trip into the field. At last, she decided. *O please—give us just tomorrow night.*

A dressing table cluttered with creams, lipsticks, earrings rejected, the perfume bottle unstopped. At dinner, she could hardly look at Bert. He made her ravenous. She scraped the sauce from her plate. She sat right up against him on the bench seat as they drove back to her house; he grazed at her hair with his mouth as he turned into the drive, wheels crunching. Had she left that light on?

—The Ford, backed in behind the jasmine, almost hidden.

Is it better like this? Not even a kiss, not with Walter peering through the blinds. She had given herself every chance to escape the inevitable. She had escaped. *But it's so crushing!*

So near to her, kept from her, Bert asked Walter's permission to buy Miriam a gift.

Apparently he doesn't mind. Should she feel grateful or insulted? *Do you understand?* At the Pasar Baroe, I watch her hold baubles to her ears, her throat—an excuse for him to look at what he couldn't touch. Gifts a man might buy a mistress, not for her, until she saw it: *my lovely jade ring*—the ring I wear now, an

Looking on
(Sketch by H.W.T. Mulle, 1930)

inch-square piece of stone set in dark gold, a perfect fit. *Bless his heart.* Not pale but a lesser stone, deep and mottled as summer. All these years I believed it was a gift from Walter. His diamonds gone, the Colombian emeralds. This small thing she kept, its giving recorded in her tiny book.

A few more moments alone, snatched in a heartbeat. *Bert & I—a bit painful—yes, we really do.* August 29th: *Last kiss to Bert.*

After long pursuit, I catch them in Singapore. *It is well run because it is under British Rule.* They are on their way back while I'm arriving, our ways crossing in this city, this hotel—the same, not the same. *There are rickshaws and one sees carts drawn by water buffalo and by sacred cows, but besides those there are only the Malays and Chinese and Hindoes to remind you you're not in a European city.* When they stayed at Raffles, 1 Beach Road, the sand came right to the courtyard fronting my suite, and guests stepped out onto the veranda where I take breakfast to listen to dance music drifting from ships docked a few yards away. During the late thirties, a half-mile of ocean will be reclaimed; on my morning run, I cross traffic-choked streets under glass-and-steel buildings—Sony, shopping malls, bright new hotels—to get to the waterfront.

By the time I arrive, Raffles doesn't need the waterfront. It has become a minor industry, memorializing itself. The Long Bar where Somerset Maugham and Charlie Chaplin drank accommodates crowds of tourists looking for the original Singapore Sling. My suite is what theirs was—sitting room, bedroom, enormous bath, wooden shutters. They had a houseboy; I am assigned a personal valet—serious, professional in her suit—who can't understand why I never ask for anything but keep setting out alone in my hat into the city.

We walk into the room together, Walter, Miriam carrying Peter, and I. I wear the jade ring, severe and modern on my hand; she has not taken it off since Bert slipped it on her finger. She refuses to notice how her husband cannot keep his eyes from it. He is quieter than usual, sullen even, making us wait. Fruit and roses scent the humid air. Miriam bounces the baby. Walter remembers breaking a lock, uncovering Talib's secrets. *I knew damned well what it was about.* For once, his silence, though it disturbs her, is what she wants to conjure a different life. She'll have all winter to dream while the snow falls.

We are all exhausted. They've been two days on the sea, he wondering, half knowing, she keeping secrets and managing an infant in their cramped ship's cabin. I have left Chris bereft and willfully uncomprehending in Utah and traveled through time to stand where they stood at a window overlooking frangipane trees and birds-of-paradise at once, like Miriam, rooted and winged.

They left Peter with the hotel amah and *went to the tea dance, had dinner, and then danced to the strains of this ship's orchestra* on the veranda outside my door, turning in each other's arms, each nursing a different thought. In bed, she waited for him to touch her; he let her wait until morning, when he took her more roughly than usual.

In Singapore, tucked among clusters of skyscrapers and neon, neighborhood pockets stand as monuments to the city they knew: Chinatown, Little India, the Civic District, Kampong Glam, Alexandra Park. Like me, pacing the modern malls, then browsing antique stores at the Tanglin Shopping Centre—a pale jade and silver bracelet, a century-old embroidered wedding jacket, which I am small enough to wear—they shopped then dined on Japanese food. *We had a victrola and danced, and as the room was built over the water and the moon came up, it was decidedly romantic.* She wasn't thinking of him.

He said nothing in Singapore, where she could have boarded a ship back to Batavia, but waited until they'd sailed for Penang. A day out of port, he finally asked her, What is it? Or maybe he told her, It is.

He took it just as I knew he would—hard. What did she tell him? Only that she and Bert loved each other. And this: *I was never unfaithful.* Perhaps not with her body, though she had wanted—had planned too late—to be. *Shall we carry on or not?* Pleas, recriminations. *Finally letters to Bert, A.M. I can't leave him & Peter, so that's that.*

What did she imagine might happen? *In spite of his offers of freedom, he says now he couldn't let me go.* No job. Not a penny of her own for passage.

The next afternoon when she woke from her nap, he wasn't in their stateroom. She tried their chairs, the smoking room, the saloon. Passing the dining room, she heard a waltz and a woman's voice. Inside, while stewards checked place settings for the first seating, a couple moved across the wood, Walter uncertainly, the woman—one of the ship's professional dancers—providing rhythm and direction, leading him to lead her, counting their steps out loud through the whirl of strings and horns rising from the Victrola. *No dancing lessons—be yourself!* She had to admit it: the young woman managed Walter's big feet and uncertain tempo very well. But that was her job. Miriam didn't want to think about his feet. She wanted him to be another man, a prodigy, a master with the lightest of touches.

Be yourself. (Let that self be someone else.)

We marry and, if the marriage sticks, spend a lifetime negotiating the consequences. If Chris has wanted me to become the wife who is happy to stay home, I have wanted him to become happy for me to go. Then, what would we be? In what kind of marriage, bound as in all marriages for good and ill? I have staked out my freedom and thought of limits, when I did think of them, in terms of gender, having all my life worked to slip out from under the protection of men who assumed I wanted them coming between me and heavy boxes, flat tires, puddles, other men.

Chris never offered protection. He imagined I would take care of myself, which I do, but not the way he would have. At the outset he agreed that we would hire housecleaning, my only condition. We discovered later we meant different things by "taking care."

There was nothing Walter could do to please her. *I was never*

137

unfaithful. She eased the door closed. *Life is funny—not always pleasant, but interesting, as Bert & I decided long ago.*

The next day was their fourth anniversary. *At breakfast I found a <u>lovely</u> bunch of orchids and a Makassar silver medallion at my place—bless Brutus.*

It seemed like no time.

That evening we all had champagne in the smoking room.

Four years. Already, it seemed they'd been this way forever.

CHAPTER 10

INTERLUDE:
TRANSIT

SHE CHAFES UNDER his attentions, moodiness, unrelenting intimacy—a shared ship's cabin, trains' tiny sleeping compartments, also shared, the endless production of dirty diapers and only her to change them.

The joke Chris and I made, when the subject of children arose: "Who would take care of them?" Once a mother, is a woman ever really alone again? In my life, privacy and autonomy intersect. I have my own study, with a door that closes, at the other end of the house and on a different floor from Chris's. The increasingly rare intervals when he travels without me. And now, also, the intense and crowded solitude of my own travel.

At night, under what passed as love, one body worked out its ultimatum on the other. *It was either me or Butler, and she had to give her verdict.* She'd given it by the time they found Bert's letter to Walter waiting at the hotel in New York. *Some letter it was, explaining in detail how I neglected my wife.* He wanted to marry Miriam. Too late. While Walter reads Bert's words aloud, his voice sarcastic, Miriam hugs herself and shivers. *The right thing.* Another surrender. Another link in the chain—a girl, my mother, sets down roots within her, binding daughter to daughter, middle child to middle child, Miriam to Mandy, to my mother, to me. And to Walter: why expiate her sin this way, giving over at this delicate moment? Breaking the chain of generations, knowing history will continue regardless, I try to imagine how, like so many women, she may have thought in ceding her power she could regain it. Or, simply, how she longed for a girl, a new version of herself with the future folded inside, all potential.

July 1999. My mother and I walk on a wild Oregon beach, celebrating her birthday with a weekend on the coast. We talk, fall silent. The wind whips off the ocean; waves crash over the rocks. My mother wonders if I have not had children because of her.

Yes, but not exactly for the reasons she fears. I tell her I recently spoke with an old high-school sweetheart. You always did exactly what you wanted. When he knew me, I was, I remember, waiting more than doing. He had no idea. But against the times, their training, the odds, though I am female my parents raised me to believe I could someday do anything. And I did believe it: as a teen, climbing, whitewater rafting, skiing; in middle age, when I left my husband in the airport drop-off and flew off alone; at fifty, when I sailed the wild Drake Passage for Antarctica, while Chris sat home and, unlike my grandmother, worried about eventualities I refused to imagine.

Is it usual, at ten, to ask your mother why she had children? Simple: it was what a woman did, daughter becoming wife then mother, submission to an unspoken order implicit in every transition, one leading to another. My parents planned their first two babies, controlling what variables they could to increase chances the second, me, would be a girl. But it didn't occur to them not to have children. Like Miriam, like Mandy, Joan might have imagined something else, and did. A career in exploration. The job she turned down at NASA rather than ask her husband to move the children to Texas. Or maybe she did ask.

I can bring home the bacon; I would even fry it, except Chris is vegetarian. As a child, I said I would marry after thirty and have no children. I would become not a mommy or a nurse, but *lawyer, doctor, marine biologist, diplomat, fireman*, and always, from the age of seven, *poet*. I was thought adorable, but nobody believed me. In truth, I worshipped my mother. Still, if I am careful, if I am clever, with attention, I can escape.

The year I turned twenty-five, a *Newsweek* article claimed a woman over twenty-six had a better chance of being killed by terrorists than marrying. Just looking around, I could see there was a problem with the statistics. When my mother sent it to me, the first I knew she was thinking about my single state, I called her and listed the boyfriends I'd had. "Which should I have married?" I asked. Until Chris, not a one cared as much about my work as his own. If a man was going to idealize some part of me, that was the right part, though neither of us knew yet where it would take me. When we were first in love, either of us would have promised the other anything, even a child. But we have never regretted our choice.

As we turn at the top of the bluffs to look at the sun low on the waves, she says she wouldn't trade the experience of being a mother. I don't doubt her. It's hard to give up what we've bargained for.

The upper Midwest is iced solid. Miriam finds her long underwear and takes her furs out of storage, but she can't get warm. What she has remembered—blue and grey dusk of winter afternoons, her skis sliding over the tracks—has not included this worming chill.

Short days, long nights. Mandy is outside the bathroom in the morning when Miriam vomits; in the pantry when she has cravings; hovering on the other side of every wall. Miriam avoids any tête-à-tête, whispering instead on the sofa with Tony over a picture of Bertram Butler, as Miriam once, so far away, whispered with him over a picture of Tony. But when Miriam lies under Walter's laboring breath at night, she feels her mother's will working, with her husband's seed, in her body.

Walter gazes moodily out the window at snow piling silently under the eaves. He stopped writing Mandy when his wooing was over, but now he needs her again, and she him, along with tea leaves, to help her see. Of course, he tells her everything, even draws from his breast pocket Bert's proposal between men, that one should take the other's wife off his hands. *To me the whole thing was a terrible blow. When one is completely in love a thing like that hurts, and one wonders what is the matter with ones self.* Not I but *one.* Even on the threshold of introspection, he objectifies, steps outside himself to see his pain.

Tony and Miriam sit upstairs, mooning over Bert's photograph. *I don't believe that people should be married to each other and live with each other when there is no love. So I put it up to Muckie that way and she had to disregard the baby entirely.* Oh, my mother. Like you, Miriam disregarded nothing. Bert is her offering. She feels virtuous, generous, trapped.

In her cold childhood bed on his birthday, the day after Christmas, she whispers her news. Almost four months since she last saw Bert, and she isn't showing: the child must be his, though still he accuses her. But the news makes him neither tender nor kind. *I'm all sorts of things—why does he want to keep me?*

His wooing days are over. *Now I'm lazy if I get a babu—wonder if he'd work unnecessarily if he were a woman?* Not the work she wanted to do.

He could never have imagined.

Once they sail, Miriam stays in the cabin while her husband plays cards, joins deck games, drinks with the captain. *Men are funny creatures.* She washes diapers, mends socks, feeds the baby, vomits into the tiny sink. *I can't talk to people any more—don't like 'em around.* He drags her out to complete a table for bridge. He pulls her from her chair at dinner when the orchestra starts up. If nothing else, his dancing lessons have given him confidence. *Brutus is still the gay young thing. If he wants to dance,* o.k.

1932. The year of my mother's birth. This time, Shanghai is under siege, *shut down and locked up, the river cluttered with War craft of all nations.* On deck, Walter identifies flags and uniforms through binoculars. Planes fly low over the harbor, engines whining. *The Japs were having rough going of it.*

Miriam keeps Peter in the cabin. There is nothing she has to see. She is not giving in even to her own inclination, whatever it is. Suspended between places, between events, she has no idea where she will find herself, where she might set herself down.

Hardly a week after they land in Batavia, Walter will pack for the Celebes, for who knows how long. Pressed beneath that tropical sky, he might worry, leaving her alone again, pregnant again, in that same old place, with Bert. But Butler arrives late to meet their ship, walking in that *natural strutting way which Muckie hadn't fully realized. Nothing but a bantam rooster—*he can tell Miriam has seen it too, her eyes open at last.

What else can he do? Out in the jungle, he can't afford to worry. Trust—*a quality which was probably the most necessary thing for our married life.* He has a choice: believe or not believe. He thinks he has a choice. *At any rate the cure has been quite complete.* Both of them write so to Mandy. *The cure. Complete.* An official version, agreed upon.

As Brutus says.

CHAPTER 11

THE DEVIL AND THE
DEEP BLUE SEA

LOEWOEK LAY on a narrow shelf along the coast, its mountains soaring almost straight from the sea. *The S.S. Jacob pulled out at 10 AM and with it went the last communication of what we call a civilized world.* A packet of letters to Miriam, one to Mandy, letters he wrote to be shared, perhaps, but not to be read the way I read them. He stood on the dock, Maugham's tales tucked under his arm, tales I also read to draw near—the S.S. *Jacob* is straight out of the stories, *a junky ship, still used to fly around the islands,* as are the thatched huts on stilts, the small European fort. *With this isolation begins a new adventure.*

He walked to the Dutch controlleur's house with its deep veranda. Even here, the depression had hit: a world away, Americans skimped on coconut oil, kept their worn rattan chairs another year. The controlleur promised forty coolies. *This he is glad to do because in these times many of the natives cannot pay their taxes.* Not quite indentured labor. In a few weeks, Agerbeck would join him, but for now he was on his own. *I always feel like a little boy in a big strange mysterious place.* He tended to details, moving toward the moment he would overcome his resistance, *making the first start,* and the real work, its violent physicality, began. It was the part of every expedition he liked least. Here, though I will never enter this particular wilderness, I am with him—at the start of every adventure, of every book or project, the inertia, and the question, How do I begin?

The only thing to do is get it over with.

The first start. A vertical wilderness. I've followed him only in words. Now, I want to see what he saw. I remember ghostly images flickering in the darkness of his study in La Porte. Joan and her brothers complained wryly about the times he subjected them to his films and lectures, but my brothers and I were riveted. The films—where are they?

Walter set out with the minimum of equipment and food and only twenty coolies to their first camp on the wild Kienton River. In the morning, he took the two most agile men to scout the gorge. Above sheer cliffs rising hundreds of feet, a strip of sky glowed hot blue, but below, deep in rock shade and mist, he shivered. Late in the afternoon, something changed in the air, underfoot—vibration, more intuition than sound—and he paused, gazing upriver. Under the tumble of whitecaps, a shadow crept toward them, the line between clean water and silted so distinct he could have drawn it with a pen. Somewhere above, it was raining hard. The line swept past; the water, now the color of chocolate, began to rise with a surge of panic he contained, reduced to the size of a bean behind his ribs, as he turned the men around.

My heart is pounding. I, too, have been trapped in a narrow canyon with the river rising, cliff faces loosened by water shearing and plummeting around me—though not in a place where my body would never have been found. In twenty minutes, water had inundated the trail. Hugging cliffs, they stepped from boulder to slick boulder. Water swirled around their knees, waists, necks, sweeping with it branches and debris. Walter stumbled through the brown tumult pulling at his clothes, his feet in their heavy boots like blocks of cement. His two men, all but naked, were quick and sure. *They went places I could never even attempt to go, and when we crossed the river to the north side they stood on both sides of me in heavy swirling water and handed me across.* Ten more minutes. Ten more, driven by adrenaline, trying not to let it overtake them.

Almost an hour to travel a mile. Soon, the water would rise over their heads, and they would have no choice but to try to ride it. Desperate, he scanned the rock walls until he found a narrow opening. They stumbled, the water dragging at his trousers, the river's roar urging them upward, a hundred feet, two. Finally, they heaved over the lip of the gorge and lay panting, looking down into a wild chute through which entire trees now tumbled. A wash of relief, pure wonder. The current surged, rolling a boulder the size of Miriam's Ford as if it were nothing. The noise was terrific.

You can get used to anything. They started back along the edge of the gorge, over rocks and mud treacherously slick. Walter's feet, cold in their heavy boots, couldn't feel the ground. He didn't know he had misstepped until his gravity shifted, one boot sliding from under him. Beside him, the cliff curved into air, three hundred feet down into a raging flood. He tried to dig his other boot in, but the ground beneath it also dissolved—into mud slick as ice, into nothing.

Just as he gave over, a grip bruised his arm, holding him over the chasm. He didn't dare move, even to see which man had him. Again, his body, present, all in all.

What was there not to understand? *I should have been killed or at least fairly well busted up if those fellows had not rescued me.* A little Malay between them, flesh and blood, gravity. The

146

men could have let go, brushed off their hands, gone back to their villages. Instead, they hauled him away from that sheer edge, and he lived. If he had fallen, a different life for Miriam, for my mother still tucked in her body.

I have abandoned them both. I want to be with him, as will my mother, though into the wilderness he'll take only his sons, leaving her to find her own way, which he would never approve. Back at camp, still vibrating, he almost didn't know what to do with himself. Alive. He pulled out paper and pen. He wrote Mandy about coming in from the field full of need, wanting Miriam and music. *I don't think I ever willingly forced myself on her—I hope not.* He drew a map of the Celebes, an X to indicate where he was—an interior place, unnamed, as yet uncharted. Here, we are different. As always, I phone home daily—part of my bargain—but I don't want to be located, x-ed in or out, don't want Chris to know exactly where I am any more than he really wants to know. Walter couldn't help himself. *I never asked a question though I sometimes wanted to. To suspect a friend is worse than to be betrayed.*

The films are in my uncle Andy's garage, falling to dust, far too fragile to play. I arrange for them to be shipped to Western Cinema in Colorado, where the restorer says my grandfather had an eye, a sense of narrative, wit. It was rare for an amateur to edit film or cut in titles, especially so cleverly. The restorer suggests I sell or rent footage to "the industry," but I feel protective. What would my grandfather want? *If one cannot get pictures of them the native method of doing things is lost.* I Google the Smithsonian, call the number listed under <u>Donations</u>. I know, I explain to the man on the other end, that <u>Donations</u> means money. But we have films, little moving fragments of history. Does anyone want them?

So Walter moved through that extravagant gash up toward the river's source, which he felt under his feet before he heard it, a

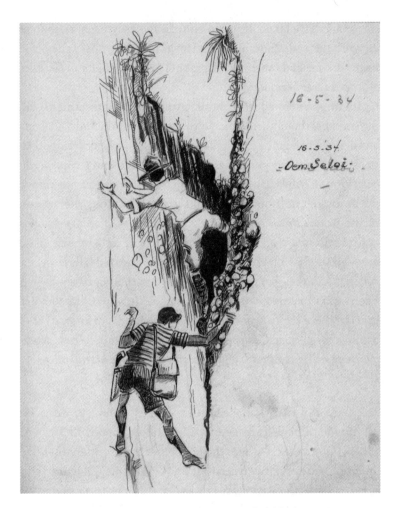

A vertical wilderness

trembling he first attributed to *quinine drunkenness, a nasty feeling that makes one's ears ring.* Waterfalls gushed straight from the mountain's face, their scale unreproducible in the sixteen-millimeter frame I watch, where the falls become lovely billows framed by foliage, his awe measured by the time the camera lingers.

They climbed freehand under heavy packs, huddling to rest on bare ledges trembling with ferns and slick with moss. *It is a quiet, weird country, and has a cold, hostile atmosphere.* After two days, they emerged into a valley ringed by still higher mountains, where streams and rivulets came together in a massive confluence before plunging underground. The spectacular fall they'd scaled wasn't the source, just the release of that subterranean aquifer. *The sudden rise of the main rivers is not such a mystery.* The water created as many problems of geology as of travel, falling over the exposures he needed to see, depositing silt. The rock was illegible.

As was his other life, in which Miriam played cards, dined, drank splits. Where was she now? He'd never been able to imagine her—what she might want or do—and she didn't know how to teach him even if he wanted to learn, didn't know the source of her malaise or how to ask for, even to know, what she wanted. Better to think about floods, snakes, dangers he could measure and was equipped to face.

In the evenings, he turned to music, to books. His tent, a circle of light. First Maugham, whose tropical betrayals only depressed him. Then Maupassant, *A Woman's Life.* Jeanne, innocent on the night of her marriage; Julien, unfaithful even in courtship. I read along, my head bent to the page. "Was *he* really the husband promised by a thousand whispering voices, thrown her way by a divinely beneficent providence? Was *he* really the man made for her, to whom her life would be devoted?" At first, I think, he imagined Julien as Bert. "He had one of those smiling faces that women dream of but all men dislike." But then, who was Miriam? Who was he? Exhausted, we read into the night. Late, he picked up his pencil. "And now! And now! Her whole life was shattered, all joy was dead, all her expectations blasted; the ghastly future with all its tortures, his betrayal, her despair, rose up before her eyes." He drew a firm underline: his heart to Jeanne's words. "It would be better to die; then everything would be over and done with."

Characters he could believe in. At night, he entered Maupassant's world entirely. I see it now: he was the innocent, female, the poor virgin offered, taken, betrayed.

I follow the films to the Smithsonian, a trip Chris almost approves, with its well-defined project, destination, and schedule. Every morning, I take the Metro into the suburban decline of Suitland, Maryland, which I walk as warily as I did Jakarta to an anonymous building with echoing concrete corridors and visible ductwork. Archivists Pam Wintle and Mark Matienzo have warned me to bring lunch with me, since I will find nothing nearby. They seat me at a light table, where I crank with white-gloved hand through the reels, peering at frames through a loupe, trying not to break anything. Mark is rightly nervous to have an amateur handling films that now belong to the future, and I try to repay his kindness and patience by making notes for them based on the journals— this, shot in Sumatra in 1929, this in the Celebes, 1932. A vanished world—and it's unusual, Pam tells me: his articulated awareness that he is shooting what can't survive, and that he is what will kill it. Of course, his awareness didn't stop him, any more than mine stops me. The film breaks, breaks again.

Walter had promised to meet Agerbeck in Pangimanan and bring him back to high country. The world was flooded, every trail impassable, but he left the coolies and hiked the river out of the mountains to the coast. At Loewoek, he dropped his shambled boots with the army captain and caught a ride over the pass in the rattletrap mail truck. From his shifting vantage above the high plateau, he sketched drainages arranging themselves in fissures east and west and maps to guide him when he was back down in them.

In Poh, the postman transferred him with a few sacks of letters, including his own, to a thatch-roofed boat with four paddlers. He lay on its wood bottom and drifted in and out of sleep while the men paddled a fast tempo. When they slid into harbor at 1:30 a.m., Agerbeck was smoking on the pier as if he'd expected the boss to arrive as horizontal cargo in the bottom of an overgrown canoe. They started back just after midday, beds of coral beneath them bright little worlds through which fish flickered, electric blue and yellow. In Loewoek, the army captain had not only gotten Walter's boots fixed but found two pairs of light canvas sneakers for wading to fit his size forty-four feet. *I almost kissed him.*

Men poling a boat.

The portable Victrola with its lid propped to show a record on the turntable, the heavy needle with its little horn. A title cut in: *The Victrola is a rank luxury.*

Cows and pigs being hoisted onto a ship. *The pigs make charming fellow passengers.*

My back and shoulders cramp. I crank through the frames, caught by his eye, tiny ghosts, a stilled world with his voice running through it, a voice I lean into. I can almost hear.

The ferocious Batoei stopped them cold. The natives feared the river as they would a ghost or monster: its rage, the pythons sheltering under its banks. Walter sent thirteen out sick. Out of a dozen fresh men, four deserted before they pulled out. The coolies muttered when he walked by, their fingers flashing against the evil eye.

They kept to the riverbank, hacking at foliage until they could crawl through. In mid-morning, Walter pushed through an opening

A mess of snake surveying the country. *I got a movie of it all.*

headfirst into a confusion of loops and coils, shimmering—*a mess of snake surveying the country.* A head bigger than his own, jaw built to unhinge. Eye to eye, ground level. He eased back through the gap in the brush, called for Agerbeck, who was carrying a rifle. The huge head turned again. The python licked the air, heavy with man-scent. Agerbeck took aim; the body writhed, still shining where sun penetrated the leaves. The head was gone.

None of the coolies would get close enough to touch it. The two white men looped a piece of rattan over what remained of its head and, sweating and heaving, pulled the beast out to full length—over twenty feet, a good foot across. The snake's belly was empty. *One step farther would have put me in the coils of the brute.* Nearby was a nest littered with hatched eggs. Walter looked at his feet—the tangled roots seemed, for a moment, to twist beneath his boots—and saw a hand-hammered gold medallion, lost who knows when, by what kind of man, to have come this way? Uncovered by rain, its glint catching his eye.

In the middle of any jungle, he kept finding gold. The skin of a python, a fossil. Moving pictures. Before supper, he wrote Miriam about how he wanted to wrap himself around her. *Business is picking up—I am having adventures this time.* They had to make nine kilometers a day to finish before the food ran out.

Midnight. By now, the Maupassant was dog-eared and worn. "Everything was deception and lying." He lay in bed tossing and scratching—where did those bites come from? Python, elephant, wild boar with its razor tusks—all worthy foes. But something too small to see was eating him alive.

—too small to film, though here's a leech on a white thigh, here a foot (his?) sprouting mold or mushrooms like a bad hunk of bread: *Fungal infections from stream water—*

—a plague of ticks—red, winged, tiny enough to pass through the mosquito netting. The rains kept coming; the river rose, *wide and terrible*. If they could build a raft and get it once to the far shore, they might run a line and ferry men and goods in shifts.

Walter, Agerbeck, the mandoer, the natives felled and stripped bamboo trees, lashed them together, lowered the raft to the riverbank, rappelled the cliff and passed down their gear. Walter christened the raft with a bottle of beer and secured it with rope. He lined the men up on the riverbank, all of them tiny now in black and white. *Crossing the Delaware was a snap compared to this. Note the coolie taking off with a line.*

The first coolie stood in the bow holding the line's free end while the others pushed the raft out into the current, hanging on as long as they could before giving it a mighty heave toward the other side. The current carried it back into midstream before the man could leap for the far shore. Man after man took his turn on the raft. They labored through afternoon, wet and exhausted from battling the river. Walter might have to think of something else.

The mandoer was short and scrawny, used to command more than labor, and Walter had left him almost for last. Again, the men pushed the raft out. Again, the current began to take it. If Walter hadn't been filming he would already have turned away in disgust when the mandoer *plunged off the* bow into the furious water, momentarily swallowed; his head surfaced, disappeared, after a breathless second reappeared, then his shoulders, and he pushed the last few feet up the steep bank. *I got a movie of it all.* His triumph, proof that <u>here</u>, against the forces of nature, he knew what to do.

(I, at last not only reading but watching, almost there, make my note—On the Batoei River, 1932, crossing in a flood.) Once the raft was secured on both banks, they needed six men on a rope and three poling to move it back and forth. (A title, cut in: *Bend your knees and bow your head, and pull that rope until you're dead.*) By noon, gear and men were sodden. But all were on the other bank.

My husband, my high school sweetheart, my friends—they think I am wild, that I fling myself into danger, that I want to make myself spectacular. Watching this, safe in Suitland, I know: my failure is not that I'm female, which is no excuse these days, but that I am smaller than I look, mere, modern, above all, bookish. I will never be larger than life. Even from her, I am a tragic falling off.

Continuous outcrops, H2S seepages and an oil seep, on a monocline. Oil, finally. And he was flooded out, water *swishing merrily under the tents.* They were out of food, but he wouldn't give up now. In the morning, he left the surveyor and a few men behind with the gear and continued with the rest downriver, where he'd heard there was toko, a small native store. He found an abandoned hut settling back into jungle. He shot two fresh doves on the way, a morsel for everyone to whet their appetites. At last, they straggled into Loewoek, where he paid off the men who had finished their contracts. The new men also wanted to be released, but he needed to get food to the surveyor, and now that he'd found oil he was determined to finish. Any coolie who ran away would get hard labor and forfeit his pay. *They put on a demonstration of weeping, pain, hysteria like I never saw before—it did them no good.*

Walter ordered twenty-five more coolies like so many cans of potatoes at the controlleur's office in Loewoek, but by now the locals knew their pay would go to taxes before they ever saw it, and news swirled about curses, invisible biting demons, famine and flood, snakes as big and monstrous as legend. Finally, Walter left with twenty new men and promises of more to follow. *Somehow this gang gives me the creeps.* That night, an earthquake rolled through the jungle and under the flimsy town. For five full minutes, the houses danced on their stilts.

Nature couldn't frighten him, if humans would cooperate. But the next day, seven men set off after breakfast without a word or coin in hand. The day after that, he awakened to find only ten men. He needed thirty to carry gear and food. *They stole away like thieves. I am sitting in the soup. I hope they all die.* He was content to be tired and wet, to do backbreaking labor *just like an ordinary coolie,* as long as he was moving forward, his life in his own hands. He never thought about their lives any more than Muckie's, about their hands, which had saved him. *It seems such a waste of one's precious young life.* One day, two. If the mandoer came back with no coolies and he had to cut out, the Victrola would stay behind. His camera, his films, lost to the jungle. Another day passed.

Here, he is not much different than the man I remember reciting Robert Service forty years later, though he is unshaven, dark rather than hoary, and haggard. His narrow head is bowed, his long hands tented, eyes gazing into the jungle while dance music pours out of the Victrola's speaker. As the record turns, does he imagine another man or himself spinning her in his arms, silk pouring over her hips like fast water?

Four days. No mandoer, no men, no sugar, no potatoes. That night, there was a second earthquake. *You could see the tremendous trees move and sway. The whole earth felt in motion with a sort of billowy wave feeling.* The earth turning to nothing while he rides his cot. After it stopped, he lit his lantern and smoked his pipe, gazing into the dark. Eventually, he reached for pen and paper and wrote to Mandy—all this, and news from his last trip to town: one of his own wells had come in, the first to deliver oil for any company geologist since he'd arrived in the Indies.

On the fifth day, Agerbeck shot one dove, a mouthful of meat for him and Walter, each. On the eighth evening, just as Walter decided he was abandoned, the mandoer materialized out of the dense jungle. Only two men at his shoulders. The runaways had *plied the country with stories,* all true.

I'm all blown up. If they continued, they would starve. (A pan of the clearing, tent frames bereft of their canvas. *Deserted camps always carry the sadness of a past glory, even if occupied for only a day.*)

They built four rafts and floated to Loewoek, to the world,

where Walter found letters from Miriam and news that another well had come in. He and Agerbeck went to the club for their first iced drinks in two months, toasting failure, toasting success.

He was sitting a few days later in his rented house on a veranda overlooking the bay when the village chief arrived, asking for wages for the men who had slipped off into the jungle. *Now I ask you.* Until that moment, Walter had planned to let the runaways go. But as soon as the man left, Walter walked to the Government Office, filled out paperwork for filing charges, and handed it to the controlleur with the money he'd withheld for taxes. There would have been more, he pointed out, if the men had finished their work.

In a few days, the government had rounded up half the men. *These birds were rather surprised when we walked into the court room.*

They had left, the men said, because their loads were heavy. (Huge round baskets, as big as the men, shoulder straps of twine.)

They'd never complained about the loads.

The interpreter said, "Did you not realize that your running away would probably cause these gentlemen an undue amount of danger that in cases might be fatal?"

Yes, the men answered, they had known it. Their faces unreadable.

The controlleur insisted on punishment. They could have paid their taxes. Two months hard labor, no pay. Not so different from what they'd fled, only safer, without Walter in charge. *I am glad they got socked in the neck for the trick they pulled on us.*

Were the two who had saved him from going over the cliff among them?

In a high meadow, he remembered, he had one afternoon come upon the men unexpectedly. *They are always complaining about their loads, but there they were merrily playing soccer football at a terrific pace with a hand-made rattan ball.*

A dozen men, having laid down their loads, running and playing. (I would like to see a movie of that.) Proof, to him, of something he already knew.

Now I ask you.

CHAPTER 12

ABSENT FRIENDS

Love is a strong thing—it is real, it is beautiful, it is harsh, it is unreasonable—but it is still the greatest force in the world.

LETTER FROM WALTER TO MANDY

It was as if, when one has been thinking about absent friends and lost the habit of seeing them round one every day, one experienced on meeting them again a check to one's affection, until the bonds of a common life were re-established.

MAUPASSANT

WALTER SETTLED INTO the chair beside his wife, relieved to find it unoccupied. Later, he fetched his straw hat and strolled his betrayer to the club. The new pattern of their afternoons. *We are friends in a way. I could cheerfully murder him.* To keep her old beau in her life, Miriam had organized a Dutch fiancée, Tine, for him; she had brought them together at her table and exerted her own charm, until they believed what they felt for her they felt for each other. They were planning a London wedding after his leave in Canada. *That is, if no serious break occurs before then!*

And Miriam Joan was the girl Miriam had longed for, *almost too beautiful to be real.* Even Walter wrote, *She is the most beautiful girl baby I have ever seen, and behaves perfectly.* He and Miriam left the children with Kokki and went out for bridge, dancing, picnics. *Brutus and I are so happy that we just sort of shine all over.*

The new year, 1933. Miriam had just turned 25, Walter 30. *We are getting old.*

Around the fire, the Dajaks showed Walter tattoos protecting their flesh from disease and weapon, mirrors of the spirit world living in this one: tigers, sacred hornbills, tuba roots, garing trees, sun bears, *orang utans*—such close cousins the Dajak called them "orang," meaning "men"—flying snakes and pigs, moths the white men never believed in, sipping crocodile tears. They chewed over the lumber market, smoking, passing cane liquor. *Who said the depression didn't reach the wild man of Borneo?*

The Atan River was low, the work easy, the Dajaks performing *the best piece of canoe handling I have ever seen.* He couldn't believe he felt so good.

What can be seen: *here,* Tine and Bert in each other's arms in Miriam's sitting room, held together by her will; *there,* a photograph taken four months later on Mandy's front steps, Bert and Tony gazing into each other's eyes, a door closing behind them as the shutter opens.

On his way to the States on leave, Bert stopped in Singapore, where he bought an engagement ring and sent it back to Miriam, with instructions to give it to Tine at a surprise announcement party. The announcement appeared, and Tine quit her job and left for London to prepare for the wedding and ship her possessions back to Batavia.

A few weeks later, Miss Polly Prospect, gossip columnist for the *Wisconsin News*, interviewed Mandy. "I've just heard of the grandest and most breath-taking romance, so thrilling I can hardly wait to pass it on to you."

In a quarter-page photo, Tony trails her fingers over a globe's surface, eyes fixed on some unidentifiable place she never, unlike her mother and sister, wanted to go. Instructed by Miss Prospect,

Tony looking into the future

I have imagined her look as dreamy, but her daughter, my mother's cousin Stancia, identifies it: terror. In Miss Prospect's tale, Mandy, visiting her eldest daughter in Batavia, befriends a young bachelor and shows him a photograph of her second daughter, whose face draws him to Wauwatosa. Within a day of his arrival, he asks Mandy's permission to court Tony. Two weeks later, she leaves with him for Canada.

Swooning prose. Mandy as cupid. Family gospel for over seventy years, though it was Miriam who had written, *Shall we keep him in the family?* The family medium, playing short odds on Mandy's hints, predicted the event. Who was Mandy to apply the brakes? As with Miriam and Walter, she concerned herself with getting the pair from proposal to altar, through vows that would seal everything.

Imagine Miriam at her writing desk, two letters before her: one from Bert postmarked Milwaukee—*He would marry Tony if he could*—and one from Tine, written a week or so later, asking if she could stay with the Links when she returned to Batavia, alone. *Poor Tine.* She'd spent everything on the wedding that would not happen. Poor Miriam, who had brought both courtships about. *Under the circumstances, I would put her up for the next two years.* Had she never expected her daydreams to bear fruit? *It is better that Bert didn't marry her out of duty—they never would have been happy.* In the winter, Tine's sandy head on her shoulder, Miriam had dismissed *the usual black doubts.* She should have known.

No letter from Mandy, no cable. Miriam had wanted Bert back with her in the Far East, married to her grateful little sister. *He is the only man I know, bar one, that I'd be willing to have Tony marry.* The only getaway allowed. Miriam had forgotten that marriage is a closed system, and now she was out of the loop. She kept writing *if, if, if.* And happiness? *Marriage is a gamble.* She sealed the letter. What would she write to Walter now?

161

At Meloh, the chief showed Walter parangs from five generations, a sword that could stop the winds. Severed heads, spirits sentenced to live in the longhouse with their enemies. Walter tried to barter for a mandoer, a shield, a head to add to his collection, but the chief refused. *Poor as these people are, they cherish the old weapons they used in the days when they made war against each other. Blood flowed freely—and they had a lot of fun.* How old-fashioned he was, I am realizing, like me in love with talismans despite the obsession with instruments and efficiency that made him a techie in his time, always ready to use a machine if one was available. I think how Chris deploys the power drill, I the screwdriver. I shovel one side of our long, steep driveway by hand, while on the other he runs a snow blower so heavy I have to lift my feet from the ground to ride it down without digging up the bricks. Still, he hands over the chain saw, which, with its bite and power, makes me laugh out loud.

Over all loomed the coming war, when the Dajak, fighting first with the Dutch against the Japanese, then driving out the Dutch, would add fresh souls to their collections.

In the morning Walter and Muller would wade down the leech-infested river. But for tonight, white lightning and music from Walter's phonograph—the Radja had never seen a phonograph—in a village surrounded by carved images of the dead. *Just why the men are made with a tremendous penis either in the normal state or erect they don't seem to know.* In his collection. *Sexual intercourse is a practical art.*

Miss Prospect's columns came with a formal announcement from Mandy. A letter followed, with a three-quarter page newspaper photograph of bride and groom in traveling clothes. September 24th. Mandy laments there are no wedding photographs good enough to print—no shot of Tony to displace the portrait of Miriam with downcast eyes. Into that envelope, Miriam tucked a clipping from the Batavia paper, 1 June 1933, announcing the engagement of Bertram C. Butler to Miss Tine J. van Stralen. Not part of the family story turned to ink by Miss Prospect and taken up by my grandmother and great-grandmother. A clue for me to come across, wondering what I'd misheard.

BRIEFLY, THREE RAPIDS

I don't think a cloud crossed the sky all day. If it did I was too much absorbed in getting out with my skin than to look at it.
WALTER'S JOURNAL

First. *Just above the gorge we piled up on a nice big rock, and all men had to hit the water in order to keep the raft from going over.*

Ten minutes later, the interpreter shouting something Walter can't understand. *The raft was brought to shore over a rapid that would have beaten the brains out of anyone.*

Later still. *I guess our escape was more thrilling than I thought.* In panic, watching the raft carry the Toean into the rapid, the man *yelled to "jump and swim" but I can't understand Dajak, so that was that.*

AND, BRIEFLY, FORMS OF LUCK

Making Long Wai the day the food ran out. *We had payday, and the gals all came out in their best costumes.*

A day of rest while the swelling from fire-ant bites on his hands and feet went down. *After all, there is no use in killing off your men.* As he's learned the hard way.

The motors' arrival. *Mail from Muckie.*

A vein of coal. *A nice fire in our tent.*

A sambar deer—huge and maned. Steaks, dried venison for the trail. Then Walter spotted a wild pig on the opposite bank, seventy-five meters away. *I got it right between the eyes.*

With very good luck we might make Long Hoet tomorrow. They made camp by dark. *Tonight it can rain as hard as it wants to, cause we are on the way down.*

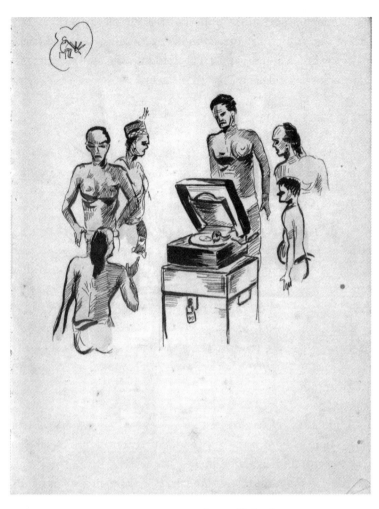

The Radja had never seen
a phonograph

At last, Walter sat in his tent in Borneo, Muckie's news in hand. *Dearest Mandy*. Too late. *He is still in love with Muckie.*

I remember Bert dimly as my mother's uncle, father to the impossibly glamorous Stancia. *You will probably see two sisters who are now the best of friends come at each other's throats*. A bitter taste. The glint of gold and jade. *I almost beat up a man who told me about it—I owe him an apology but he isn't here any more.*

I read on, divided, having been in my life betrayer and betrayed— the betrayals of my marriage having been not for another man's sake, but only for my own. Maybe, then, it had nothing to do with him. What she had was never enough, much less four walls, with or without him inside. He got the world they'd both wanted; she got a house to fill and keep. As much as he loved to go home, he would never have sat and waited for her, alone.

One of the family. His brother.

When Bert handed Tony off the boat there was almost nobody to meet his new bride, *quite a few of the Britishers having taken Tine up violently*. Just the Links (*of which*, Walter wrote, *one member was doubtful*) and three others. The thousand guilders Bert had paid to settle Tine's breach-of-promise suit couldn't settle her pride or her future. Whenever the Butlers crossed her gaze she fluttered, fainted, *had to be taken home. She is giving back none of the wedding presents.* Many of Miriam's old friends declined invitations to her cocktail party for the Butlers. *I have given quite a few friends the proverbial gate.*

Tony snubbed back when snubbed, failed to return notes, declined invitations, danced like Isadora Duncan in her parlor with the shades up, tossing the long hair she refused to cut. She slept until noon and was at least an hour late to everything. When she was alive, she drove the whole family crazy, but looking back I have to admire her for staking her ground, however passive her resistance. *Standing in the middle of a room and thinking for a long time of what to do next does not constitute the state of being*

Leaving again

'busy.' She knew, as my mother would also learn, how to annoy my grandmother. *She doesn't give a damn.*

And Tony had opinions. *She thinks it's awful for a married woman to go out with another man*—well, Bert should know. *The little egg. If only she weren't quite so proud of all her concoctions and her taste, she could be very attractive.* Whenever Miriam was pointing out one of Tony's shortcomings, Bert waltzed in, kissed his wife, and told her she was the most beautiful woman in Batavia. *Not that I'd want for him to think differently!* Having married the man who still loved her sister to escape her mother and college, she refused to subject herself. She declined to enter into Miriam's plan for the Butlers and Links to be inseparable. *They claim to like being alone all the time.*

Walter wanted to find relief in this but couldn't. Three years, a six-month separation, two pregnancies—Bert had loved Miriam through it all. *He was certainly doing what he said he couldn't help. He also wanted to stay away but wanting her was stronger by far.*

Walking with Walter, Bert rehearsed the version he took home to Tony every day. *He has met someone he loves the way I love Muckie.* Walter listened, a scientist lost in a problem, saying nothing. *Only it was sort of a kick to Muckie. I confess, I love the way he defends her. We all live in contradiction. In geology we must always put together the things we find. The final result must bear the scrutiny of others.* There to be read like layers of sediment, the past was what it was. Bert was no man of science.

When Bert was finally promoted and posted to Singapore, Miriam was relieved, and Walter spent four months in Batavia. *The last two especially were the sweetest things I have ever experienced before. Much better than a honeymoon could ever be.* Miriam had nobody else. If she let him make love to her, she could talk to him late into the night about Tony, about what was wrong with Bert, about herself. She turned to him alone.

Everything. *I finally told Brutus why I'd married him.* Having told him, she did not tell her journal, or Mandy, or the future.

Across all these years, I am testing answers. For adventure. To escape. Because he held a gun to his own head and not yours. Because he was *absolutely a man*. Because, like Tony, like Mandy, you had to marry somebody. What did she tell him? What led to her *final adjustment on an entirely new footing?* What footing? *I am quite uninterested in all the eligible bachelors, fortunately in a way, but unfortunately in another way, because my life with Brutus is so more complete now.*

Unfortunately? Again, against everything I know, against the evidence of her own wording, I believe her. Like Walter, like her, I can't stop being a sucker for her conversions, her perennial good intentions.

Why does her voice feel like the glove on my own hand?

CHAPTER 13

INTERLUDE: PRESENT TENSE, WITH BREAKFAST

WATCHING STANCIA'S HAIR flare in the light through the cafe windows, I can't believe how much she looks like old photos of Mandy, brought to color, to life, in her narrow face and long upper lip. Down from Vancouver for a convention, she is Tony's and Bert's late last child, named Constance after her mother. Even in her sixties, my first cousin once removed has a young man hovering at her elbow.

She knows all about Bert and Miriam, her "Auntie Cyclone." For the family habit of giving children more information than they strictly need, I am grateful.

Mandy's father, Adam Gettleman, was "wildly unfaithful" to all his wives, including his fourth and last, Mandy's mother; he was divorced as well as widowed well before the last century's turn, when only grave sin led to such opportunity. My own mother will doubt it all.

Mandy was still crazy in love with Louis when she divorced him, forced by her brothers, Mandy told Stancia, not bribed, though a second patrimony changed hands, though Miriam's journals, her fury of letters, and my mother's memories suggest Mandy came to the end of her own rope. The record versus an old woman's retrospect and lifelong anger; one granddaughter's word against another. The tendency, running in the family, to romanticize, and to blame anyone else, or genes, for one's unhappy choices. Can both be true?

Bert told Stancia he arrived in Milwaukee not knowing his engagement had been announced; that Miriam, jealous of Tony, placed the notice, though it came out when Bert was still steaming across the ocean. The ring, the party: the moment's record versus memory passed down, stories that solidify a family, or wobble it. Who takes the blame?

In Canada, Tony met Bert's bosses, who had to bless the young diplomat's marriage. The Foreign Service might have saved Stancia her childhood efforts to get Tony out of bed and into the ensembles Bert selected in the morning in time to make her afternoon engagements. But in Ottawa Tony was all charm and punctuality. Everyone approved.

On the night before their wedding, Tony crept to Miriam's childhood bedroom where Bert slept, took off her gown, laid herself beside him under Miriam's childhood quilt. There, he entered her for the first time, his feet braced against the hope chest at the foot of the bed.

I can't help ask: How do you know? Every time they visited Mandy, Tony drew Stancia through the door of Miriam's old room, sat her on the edge of the bed, told her again.

And love? Stancia confirms that Miriam was the love of Bert's life, and Tony knew it. Miriam would have made a perfect diplomat's wife, Bert's ideal match. Tony flung china, cultivated lateness with a vengeance. How much female fury can any one family produce? Bert never forgave Miriam either—for not loving him enough, for having loved him.

170

Auntie Cyclone. Like me, Stancia betrayed her own mother for Miriam.

What happened to the hope chest? Nobody knows. Another thing vanished.

Stancia is a professional spiritualist and alternative healer. She peppers her conversation with science, some of it right. As the conversation winds out I am lulled, even as I recognize elisions, sleights of mind that allow her to move from neurons to heart tissue to the physics of light and time to chakras to her own perhaps inevitable failures as a mother, then to her granddaughter's birth and memories from another, earlier life which prove, Stancia believes, that my cousin thrice removed, whom I've never met, is my reincarnated great-grandmother. Does she believe it too? Her first name is my middle name—Amanda.

"Mandy was fey, you know," Stancia says. I travel in one of a few circles in which the word is still used this way, usually in regard to literary texts. Stancia asks if I, too, have a long second toe, a physical sign of a link to that other world, another family trait. I'm thinking how different we are, how different our realities, when suddenly, watching her watch me with eyes the color of mine, the color of Miriam's, I have a sense of what people may mean when they comment on the intensity of my own gaze. "When you look away," a colleague of Chris's once said, "it's like I disappear." Another man, after watching me at a large dinner: "You have no capacity for partial attention."

My attention is usually in tatters. But like Stancia, I am looking for explanations. I live surrounded by poets but also by scientists: husband, mother, father, brothers, uncles, friends. To the extent the universe is knowable, like Walter I believe it's knowable through science. At the same time, I understand it to be bigger than I am. For me, poetry lives in the space dividing the known and the unknown, and sometimes, briefly, opens a little gap in the thin membrane between. As the physicist V.V. Raman says, "Poetry is to the human condition ... what the telescope and the microscope are to the scientist."

Mandy, fey. I think, she was searching. But I have now a clearer idea of how she could have been both the people I've come to consider her to be: brilliant and hard-headed, yes; also under unreasonable sway, needing to be exceptional and, like Miriam, living in a female body, having no outlet for the exception she was.

When my mother was small, Mandy told her how, at the moment Amelia Earhart's plane was lost, a cry yanked her from her nap. Later, Miriam told Joan the same story, as if it had happened to her. Tony told it too, about herself.

Fey. What do I know? I listen to my cousin spinning stories. I am a spinner, too.

CHAPTER 14

THE NIGHT MAIL

Beautiful flight again, but not salig *this time*—bet is niet
"heel iets anders"—*your definition isn't so good*—*you
have no idea what it's like on a girl's wedding night.*
MIRIAM'S JOURNAL, July 6, 1934

In every crowd ... are certain persons who seem just like
the rest, and yet they bear amazing messages.
ANTOINE DE SAINT-EXUPÉRY, *Night Flight*

MIRIAM LOADED SUITCASES, a box of books, the kids, and Kokki
into the car and headed over the mountains toward Selabintanah,
tooting slow through foot- and buffalo- and bicycle- traffic, moving
it aside. Even now, the drive takes four tooth-breaking hours, 120
kilometers over roads jammed with tiny green buses, motorbikes,
pedestrians, horse carts, bicycle rickshaws, all jostling for space
on narrow, rutted pavement.

Since passing Indonesian customs a week ago, I haven't
seen another Westerner. The State Department warning covers
not only North Americans but also Europeans and Australians.
Wherever I walk, people greet me—those with little English,
"Hello Mister"; with slightly more, "Hello Miss." Those with more
English, kindly: "be careful." In my ambling female solitude, my
lack of care is apparent. Those with more English ask where my
husband is. "Coming soon," I say, unused to being marked out,

following my guidebook's tips for women traveling alone in this place where Chris would never come. "Jalan jalan," I say, "just walking." Everywhere, walking alone, I'm warned not to.

In the colonial Dutch East Indies, she could drive into these mountains with two small children and a native nurse, honking equally at people, dogs, buffalo, no questions asked. Pale, crew-cut, with Miriam's blue eyes, from the back seat of a van moving through pedestrian, animal, and wheeled traffic at walking-pace, even without her jaunty hat, I turn heads.

Then as now, the Grand Hotel Selabintanah sat at the bottom of Goenoeng Gede, its stone gates, now abandoned, in 1934 tended by a keeper whose job was to keep the natives off their sacred mountain. As dusk fell, Miriam entered another world. The rising mist felt silky on her skin. She was glad she'd brought extra blankets for the children. The half-caste desk clerk checked her in, and the boy carried her bags down a rain-slicked path to her bungalow, while monkeys hooted from the trees, narrating her passage.

She arrived as I do just before dinner. Guests lined up at the desk to pick up letters and reserve horses or tennis courts; they chattered in Dutch in the bar. For me, a dark lobby, one bulb shining down a hall behind the unoccupied desk. No bell. When I was planning my travel, it took me days online to find the place still existed, but in spite of the darkness everything looks clean and operational. I clear my throat, call Hello? Again, a little louder.

A young woman appears. She seems surprised to see my name in her book and asks where my husband is, in English no better than my wholly inadequate Indonesian. As I watch the bellboy carry my duffel across the dark grounds, I realize nobody else is here. I've eaten nothing since breakfast, before I got on the plane in Sumatra, but the hotel restaurant remains dark, chairs upended on the tables. Why am I their only guest? I will never know, having no words to ask, as she has no words to tell me.

My driver asks her a question. The two speak rapidly in Indonesian. He gestures me back to the van and drives me down into the crowded town, its smoke and noise, and pulls over at a grocery store. Flocks of women in head scarves move along the aisles, picking over produce, some familiar, some alien. No, the fare is ordinary. I am alien. Exhausted, hungry, I wander under the lights. Heads turn. I find foods I can eat without cooking—oranges, mangoes, and bananas, safe because of their peels; an avocado. Trail mix with nuts. Bottled water. No wine, of course. At home, I eat the darkest bitter chocolate, but here I buy Toblerone because I know what it is. Dutch licorice, more to my taste, black and salty.

My grandmother has bathed, donned an evening dress, and walked to the restaurant, its lights blazing and glassware gleaming. Her shawl—peach silk, embroidered with scarlet roses—she will send me one Christmas when I am in college. I still wear it.

My driver was kind to see my need. He drops me off and drives away. Does he have a bed here, or will he sleep in the van? I don't know how to ask.

Now, online photos show updated rooms, but that night my bungalow is as it must have been for her, down to Art Deco furniture and the shock of a cold-water bath. The quiet, punctuated by the cries of monkeys and birds settling for the night, has a physical presence, as does the volcano looming in the dark. I eat under a bare bulb on the terrace, spot lit. After testing the locks on the doors and windows and checking my phone to find I have no coverage and can't call home, I shiver through my bath and go to bed.

My mind will not stop moving from floating market to volcano to supermarket, everything strange. *A jungled night. A poor night for sleep.* Music pulses, grows louder—I have been hearing it for some time, just beneath my awareness. People singing, calling. I put on my robe and step onto my terrace. Light flickers up the mountain. A ritual—the rhythm and tone of the music intensifies, haunting. Fire pulses through the dense trees.

I could dress and go up. Nancy Drew would, in any of the books Miriam sent every Christmas until I turned twelve. And her? Whatever this is, it wouldn't have happened in 1932 with the hotel full of Dutch. I am completely alone. In Salt Lake City, Chris has a copy of my itinerary, but I can't call him for my own peace of mind any more than for his. This is what I love about travel: the illusion of being adrift on the earth, untethered, unlocatable. No one who knows me knows where on earth I am. But here, I am not protected by a bubble of whiteness and a colonial legal code. I am suspect by nationality, vulnerable by gender in a way I usually decline to think about, alone, a little afraid, trying impossibly to go unnoticed. My grandfather stepped into the coolie's camp and unleashed his meager Malay; I will not venture alone at midnight onto the sacred mountain, with its god who would hardly welcome me hovering, even having come from so far away, looking for something I can't explain. Chris would call me sensible for once. I am a coward.

The music throbs for hours. Footsteps pass beneath my window, and every time I hold still, wondering if those people know I am here, a woman without my husband, and that I cannot even understand my driver. I lie awake, waiting for a step to pause, for a hand on my doorknob. I get up twice to check the locks. Only later will I wonder why I thought anyone might consider me at all, plunged as they were into dance, music, their lives.

Just before dawn, I doze. I get up groggy, dress, walk up through the grounds toward the mountain. The path, though well-traveled, is abandoned. I smell ashes. The jungle is so thick the site could be anywhere, just a few feet off the trail, and I might never find it. The air blows fresh and the birds, waking, have begun to sing, to stretch their wings on the breeze.

Finally, about two-thirds into her stack, she reached it—*A Woman's Life*, the copy Walter brought back from that arduous journey. The children down for their naps, she took it to the pool. Like him, she was reading, as always, to find herself, to put words to her yearnings. "Was *he* really the husband promised by a thousand whispering voices, thrown her way by a divinely beneficent providence? Was *he* really the man made for her, to whom her life would be devoted?" She was ready to be courted, with Jeanne, by the idea of providence.

A man stopped at her chair to tell her he had followed her poems printed in club circulars and newsletters. *I'll laugh at the idea I was swept off my feet—and good heavens, the man is 42!* I know how this works. *Isn't that the attraction—the experience and knowledge and insight—and technique—that go with his age?* She sent him away, advising him to write some poetry himself. *He seemed intrigued by the idea.* Oh, she was young.

Providence, wooing, tender wonders—events we pass to reach the novel's heart. Reading how, on the eve of Jeanne's wedding, her parents refuse to answer questions about the marriage bed, leaving her in her husband's hands, Miriam almost put down the book. "It is for him to lift the veil that has hidden the tender secret of life." Though Jeanne has seen animals mate all her childhood, sex surprises her. "She was thinking with despair in her heart, in the disillusion of an intoxication which she had dreamed so different, of anticipated pleasure now destroyed and a happiness now gone forever; she said to herself, 'So that's what he calls being his wife! That's all there is to it!'"

Being his wife. Not the initiatory moment, nor even the moment, if it ever comes, of delight, but entry into time, a continuous present. "Something was weighing on her mind, a presentiment of the long, drawn-out boredom of the new life in front of her." There is no escape. What she is, she will be. "It was the end of expectation." At first, Miriam hardly noticed the stray lines, penciled messages. But eventually his marks drew her eye— perhaps Walter had underlined these passages for her. A message. She'd brought her abandoned journal. After dinner, I carry it out onto the terrace where again she wrote, *Do you understand?*

Maybe now. But reading, he marked not Jeanne's delicate qualms, which so moved Miriam, but Julien's every deception. His voice, his questions. Betrayal, disappointment; she followed

177

Balinese dancers: *Everyone but me knows the story*

his pencilings as the novel led Walter and now her toward an idea waiting to be articulated. *Judging by the passages, he has lost all trustfulness and belief, and he doesn't have the same love for me that he had before.* Nothing spoken. Instead, the sharp point on her skin, inscribing, writing her over. <u>Faithless</u>. If not with her body, with her heart.

Hurt, dense, vindictive, cruel? —maybe he'd put the book on the shelf and forgotten it. But I see him, still carrying that dark jungle inside, laying it on her bedside table for whenever she got to it. *If it weren't for my children, I should either go away or unobtrusively do away with myself.* Bliss, despair. Illness, health. Two worlds: he carried both inside.

"She had nothing to do today or tomorrow or ever again."

Cold bath, early dinner, back to her terrace and the book. Walter slept or lay awake wondering where she was, or—who knows?—lost himself in the jungle etched on a woman's skin. "Why did this estrangement not cause her more pain? Was life like this?" She might have felt a freedom she didn't know what to do with. "These little scattered lights in the field suddenly gave her a keen sense of the isolation of all human beings, with everything to keep them apart and divide them." She tried to remember when she and Walter had really spoken.

It is late, and I am still trying to figure out how I am implicated. I fell in love so many times in my teens and twenties, usually spending a couple of years in a peaceful domesticity that gave me space to work before my lover's attempts to get my attention, often by enacting rules, grew tedious. I would take a new man before— as a way of—getting rid of the old, sidestepping conversation and moving straight into resentment, which I understood better than my heart but couldn't articulate. Miriam wanted a love that promised to change everything, as if the self, the female self, could be found <u>out there</u>, in the arms of a mysterious other. I once believed this, too. My parents—my mother wishing in this as in all else to be unlike Miriam—endured unhappiness and perhaps betrayal to stay married during the sixties, when people began to mistake sex for freedom and so many parents dismantled families for new love, not knowing they would wake up in six months or three years and find the world old again, themselves no wiser, no happier, no less who they had always been.

I can see what each might have lost. Chris and I pass a quarter century together. Like every couple, we suffer periods of boredom, of rage; we threaten to separate, pack boxes, make up in a fury of bedsheets. I chafe under meal planning, cooking, cleaning up—but we both prefer my cooking, and these are the only gender-traditional chores I do. I won't let him touch my laundry, but he does his own; he cares for our plants, feeds the birds, shares the shopping, cleans his own messes, which are no worse than mine. He buys a Roomba and an industrial carpet cleaner. I was thirty when I married, and beginning to grow up. If I'd married at nineteen, how would I have begun? How ended?

Even now, not wise yet, I know better than to trust myself. Even now, we are restless. Working to hold on. *It's a heavenly night with a strange, wild, dramatic full moon.* A poet, I have become what she wanted to be, as does my own mother late in life. Of Miriam's life, I have desired the freedoms, not the obligations. Why did she not see how remarkable it was and just enjoy it? *And a gorgeous wind rattling the palm.* I have pursued her as if she were myself. Now, rereading her words under the bare bulb, I find her not trying to record or delete or write over or justify or elide her life, but to invent. The beginning of art, though she portrays herself as she wishes to be, *immaculate, simply elemental,* not— the end of writing—as human, among others for whom she wants to make something. *I wanted to write, but didn't dare.* I have been lucky. The freedom she sought was my freedom, and she'd lost so much time. She felt her youth slipping off her, though she wasn't thirty, not even close.

Could she set herself aside? *It is hard to put down some thoughts if there is the possibility of their not staying private.* For whom did she write? For Walter, still clumsy, having learned nothing of the *practical art* on the body of his wife, on any body? *I*

180

can't let him know. Did she still believe he would never read this? Was she sending a message?

Months earlier, Walter wrote Mandy from his jungle, *A man with a past has better chances of being a successful husband than some innocent dumb guy.*

As if she'd conjured it: the Havik's body suspended beneath a great wooden wing, propellers shimmering the air. Havik, Hawk: I've conjured it, reading toward this, the arrival of the man my mother always suspected. Unlike Bert, he will not take me by surprise.

Since October 1931, when KLM began service between Amsterdam and Batavia, Miriam had watched planes landing and taking off at the airfield—puddle jumpers that carried Walter up to Palembang; Fokker F.XIIs fitted for long hauls to Europe— imagining herself leaving the earth in a roar, entering the clouds.

Evert van Dijk and his copilot, Adriaan Viruly, were famous in Batavia by June of 1934, when they landed in smoke and noise on the muddy field at Lembang to the cheers of colonists escaped to the mountains. The group at Selabintanah's remote resort had made the winding three-hour drive over the stunning pass in caravan to fetch them.

That evening at Selabintanah, his dress uniform gleaming with embroidery and metal, van Dijk whirled Miriam onto the dance floor to applause from the other tables—*Purely physical, in magnificent condition, bubbling with animal spirits—the most cocksure man extant.* They danced the last half of one number and the first half of the next before the second pilot cut in—Viruly, too thin, with bad teeth, a large nose, an underhung jaw. *Ugly as sin.* As he maneuvered her around the floor, deftly avoiding collisions, she could see him thinking through the shape his sentences might take. *Chiefly mental & philosophical, reserved at first,* renowned among the Dutch as an author and lecturer as well as a pilot. She sat next to van Dijk at dinner but listened to Viruly across the table. *Never saw such a contrast before.* When

181

she rose before dessert pleading a headache, Viruly leapt to his feet to walk her to her cottage.

The stone path passed under an arbor hung with jasmine. In fragrant air, he asked how she had arrived in the Indies. *Relativity again.* Told her to call him Jons. At midnight, he shook her hand and saw her through her door.

His constant attendance. While she dined with a Dutch landowner, he haunted her terrace, chain smoking. On a warm night, they walked through the jungle to a nearby tea plantation, Miriam in her evening gown, silver silk with a scarf trailing from one shoulder like a single diaphanous wing. Moonlight coated the leaves, it was so thick. *He makes me feel strong and intelligent, with infinite possibilities.*

He spread a blanket under the tea plants, the green fragrance falling. She asked him what it was like to soar above the clouds; to plot a night course, following village lights; to be overtaken by a fogbank trusting only the altimeter, an instrument that could tell you how far you were above the sea, not what mountain or building might loom in mist or darkness. Awash in fragrant shadow, she told him she wished to write, had been practicing in her journal but didn't know how to move beyond details both too intimate and not intimate enough. The heart of the problem. The moon, huge and yellow, pressed through the tracery of leaves. Lying on his side, his head propped on one hand, he looked dreamily down at the glow in her eyes, the silver fabric of the dress pooling around her, reflecting reflected light.

A few days later, he drove to Lembang with van Dijk. At the desk, he left two small volumes wrapped in brown paper. Strange, for her to be dining alone. She could feel people watching her. What was she reading? *A diary is really a strange sort of thing. One can't detail all one's vagaries of thought.* But his journal wasn't only about him. What she encountered there, so personal, was not only his self, but his self enlarged to include her, present from his first arrival: her intelligence, her energy and vigor. Perhaps this is what she fell for. *One is so <u>unsuspecting</u>, and all the early entries* *sound so innocent, in a way—in the light of the present, of course.* In absence, in front of everyone, he wooed her, simply by having seen her.

Why did she need a man to see herself? *Jons' diary makes me feel more immature than ever. I seem to be battling against a small shell which contains my mind. I wish J. could help me break through my little sphere into the infinite.*

The next time, she drove with him to Lembang. She had her own room at the Grand Hotel, but they stood at the sleek wood desk side by side. *Being stared at.* The other guests knew his well-photographed face. *We created a sensation trotting into the dining room.* After dinner, they danced. *Slightly bitten.* Her children were a mountain pass away, her husband in a jungle surrounded by sea. Jons's wife was in Amsterdam, across continents and oceans. Jons's hand, his mouth—everything unfolded. *Bitten by a wolf.* She marked a beginning here, July 1, the way he did: *A.M.,* after Miriam.

July 1. Walter wrote Mandy from Bare-Bare. *Our little Muckie has changed quite a lot, I think.* He was always behind, exactly as many weeks as he'd been away.

Sitting in the p.m., talking and dining and smoking. My mother would be two in less than a month. Among her earliest memories: Miriam bending to the mirror to touch up her lipstick then floating away on the arm of a ribboned uniform in a cloud of Chanel No. 5, which Joan has always refused to wear; the door closing behind her, shutting her off from the world. That day, Miriam and Jons rode horseback to the top of the Goenoeng Payang and bought *limonade* from the Italian marquesa—*gone native*—at the summit. There was nobody who mattered to watch them. *Sitting on top of the world, in the sun, perfectly happy.*

She left the children with Kokki and flew all over Java with Jons and van Dijk, not thinking of Miriam Joan's eyes, her reflection in them getting smaller. She never wanted to come down. On July

4th she flew with them from Lembang to Batavia, the first leg in their long journey back to Holland. Van Dijk, hung over, napped on one of the long chairs in the passenger cabin. *Actually me in the cockpit* behind a red steering wheel, engines rumbling overhead. Dials bobbled on the dash; between the seats, a bristle of levers, red and black.

The runway unfolded; the Havik's nose lifted and the trees fell away. They climbed over rice paddies and hilltops tangled with green. Where to look?—opening horizons; his hands, brisk and calm on the switches. He showed her which numbers and arrows to watch, laid his gloved hand on hers and pulled. She felt the plane's vibration beneath her palms, its resistance. Then, he lifted his hands and she was steering, banking the plane, returning it to level. They climbed toward a heart-shaped puff of cloud, pierced it, and for long seconds flew blind, in her hands, trusting the gauges.

Sailboat, horse, automobile: she loved anything that could move her. She'd taught her husband to drive; she'd taught this man, almost her lover, to ride. But this was something else—a flight of sparks above the clouds. A start. When Batavia came into view, she eased the Havik down until she could almost make out the features of women working the rice fields, the patterns on their batiks. When van Dijk poked his head through the cockpit door, Jons was back in control, setting the plane down. They might have been riding a feather.

The Europe-bound passengers waited with a festive crowd to see them off with noisemakers, confetti, crepe, even, this July 4th, a small American flag. She could only shake Jons's hand goodbye. Through drifts of weather: Batavia to Palembang to Singapore to Rangoon to Jodphur; a stop in Jask to refuel. Baghdad, Gaza, Alexandria, Athens—over the Mediterranean, the pilots changed from tropical khakis back into blue uniforms. Now, the whole trip takes under fifteen hours. To them, the ten-day marathon felt breathless with speed: eighteen countries; nine overnight stops. The pilots didn't fly in the dark but had to entertain over salad, take a spin on the dance floor. Athens to Amsterdam, and rest.

Ten days later, they would fly the same route back.

He would be gone a month. But this was different. *O Mommy, I do have fun living—and I'm riding high again now—pray for me a bit, no?* Thirty days. *Something is almost sure to spoil it.*

Have I had fun living? Reading on that mountainside, thinking about my own marriage, I remember being a graduate student in Houston with a boyfriend out of mind in Salt Lake City. Free enough. I had promised to drive editor and poet Howard Moss from his hotel to campus. On route to his hotel, my rattletrap Toyota began to hesitate, then buck. Nervous, barely on time, I nursed it into the parking lot, where it stalled for good.

Mr. Moss was polite as I dialed the English Department on the desk phone, apologizing profusely. A few feet away, one of the other hotel guests, a man in his forties whose name I don't remember, watched me as I spoke, then touched my arm and dangled a set of keys on a Mercedes fob. "I don't need my car today."

I was twenty-two.

"Will you be back in time to have lunch with me?"

He showed me how to lower the SEL's convertible's top. I pulled out of the parking lot, testing the acceleration with a thrill but too embarrassed to speak. Just as I was about to apologize again, Mr. Moss said, "And do you walk on water?"

Over lunch, the man asked about my studies, about poetry, catching and keeping my eyes whenever I let him. Brown curls, a bit of a paunch. He was flying his private plane to Austin the next day for meetings; did I want to come along?

Classes or adventure. A crossroads. What creates attraction, I wonder? The plane alone would have persuaded Miriam, though I didn't think of her then, knowing little about her young life. But though I watched hawks with envy, I knew even then I wanted— the life I have, lived mostly in books, quiet except for brief, occasionally wrenching interruptions. Not to be pulled at, not to be indebted. What would this man want next? He assured me, no strings, but I'd heard that before. I weighed possible trouble, possible pleasure.

Maybe I was wrong, or just a coward. I might have married a trucker at seventeen, a lawyer at twenty-three, a rock-and-roll drummer who would never make it and would retire to a plumbing job in New Jersey; I might have let a construction magnate stake me at the Las Vegas poker tables, thrown myself into any number of lives attached to existing, immutable trajectories set by men. If I'd known what I know now, would I have abandoned my studies, strapped myself into a rich man's airplane, and let him teach me to fly?

I am physically far from chipper. Autumn, 1934, her boat came into view of Bali, a blur of white emerging from the horizon's haze.

I am falling from the sky, again, to that same end.

Mentally and spiritually I'm quite awake. I'm at another turning point. She sat on deck, writing and drawing, working to realign herself with her almost forgotten life and the husband who defined it for her. *He is the complement to something in me. He has brought me into this sort of life and is a recessive (?) part— of it.* As the island loomed on the horizon, dark green adrift on a jade sea, she wrote as if writing could help her understand her capitulation. *If I have any brains or ability, I can rise above the minor hindrances of marriage.* If Jons had taught her anything. *Most important is the knowledge that I am free—that my beloved family and house can't keep me from expressing myself.*

One marriage, two people. Two last nights apart. She sweats in a Balinese inn; he lies awake on the boat in anticipatory bliss. Soon, he will bury himself in her, and she, seeing no choice, will let him.

Decades later, I am driven away from the tourist hotels along the strip where a few months before a bomb killed over two hundred people and blew the Balinese economy to bits. Something is

186

unraveling. My car heads inland to Ubud, the old artistic center. I will stay at a spa carved into a hillside, at its center the painter Walter Spies's house, an abandoned temple on the other side of the gorge. I'll visit every place named in her diary, beginning here, with a cocktail. I have bent over guidebooks and her journal, puzzling out her handwriting, the strange Dutch spellings, trying to match words with books and maps. I will go anywhere, looking for her.

And him? He has my sympathy, but oh, I do not want to be merely, grudgingly tolerated. I want from Chris what Walter wanted from Miriam: for him to love and miss me even as I cast myself away from him, onto the world. I want him to have his own occupations, lest his love become a burden. Walter would have my sympathy entirely, except—machete, python, elephant. When he was out, he was transformed. As was she. Drive, fly, sail to earth's end: none of us will get all the love we want, or all the freedom.

In late afternoon, I walk out into thick air, *to the so-called sacred forest.* On Monkey Forest Road, now lined with artists' studios and boutiques, I browse for a sarong to wear into the temples. I considered bringing one my grandmother sent me before she died, shocking pink splotched with orange and green, but though it looks like a sixties tie-dye it is old and fragile, at home in the box it arrived in, still addressed in her hand. In Singapore, I saw an almost identical cloth hanging on an antique-store wall. They were asking two thousand dollars.

The sacred forest is mostly eucalyptus, a temple at its heart. Monkeys swing from trees, clamber over statues—large monkeys, young monkeys, mothers carrying tiny babies, stringing behind me in a chattering parade. Small, with short, tufted hair and a mobile face, I smile to see myself as Chris does, as an adorable animal, and I wonder if I look familiar. Really, I look like someone carrying toys or food. They pull at my zippers and slip clever hands into my pockets; they sit on the bench beside me sucking their toes or tuck themselves into the temple's nooks and crannies, among carved stones.

I give her no privacy. I stalk her into the monkey temple, later to the bat temple on the coast, soft rock crumbling under weather until the ornate designs vanish. A pity, she says, until her guide explains how erosion keeps tradition alive. The carvings portray the invisible world pressing against this one, so perhaps it is right they should blur, reemerge identically under a new hand, stories I can't decode. What might have been remade since she stood in my place? Demons, gods, the cheery, bespectacled Dutchman bicycling the wall at Poera Madoewekarang? I move through the mountains, in and out of phone coverage. At Ubud's Poera Taman Sarisvahti, devoted to the goddess of poetry and music, words and numbers, my work and Chris's, I wander boardwalks over lotus ponds to make my offering, not because I believe but because it's what one does.

At Tejakoela, Miriam and Walter stopped to swim in the sea, risking cholera, as do I. At Kintamani, they stayed overnight (*dead silence and blackness—swell place for a murder*). At Bangli, I find still the *great banyan in the court*, a house nestling in its high branches. The priest climbs down to receive my offering. Over lunch at Goenoeng Batoer, I read her journal, raising my head from the page to glimpse blue lake emerging from the mist, receding again. No paradise. Everywhere the society of dogs— crook-legged, mangy, in flaming misery, snuffling under my table for crumbs—and the temples, people living in the courtyards, men sleeping, women cooking, carrying on under niches where the idols are set for ceremonies. The material and the spiritual, the past and present, travel hand in glove. Hand and glove are the same. There are so many worlds besides my own. I have known this, not known it.

At the temples of Goenoeng Abang, I negotiate for a guide. If I were male, I might venture onto the mountain alone against the guidebook's advice, but there may be restrictions peculiar to women, and the gods, or the people who protect them, are testy.

Already mist breaks over the summit, which means it's too late to begin the climb to the top, but I mount temple to temple, most closed to nonbelievers. At one that is open, I make my offering. A priest lights incense, sprinkles my hair with petals and rice while I bend my head. Not praying, exactly. Trying to feel what might be here.

At night, as they did, I watch dances staged and abbreviated for tourists, with our small attention spans, smaller tolerance for ambiguity. Cold drinks at the bar. I ask questions, and when questioned I answer. Wayan, my driver, wants to know if I'm a nun. With my cropped head, I'm often mistaken for Buddhist, but I could also belong to one of the local animist sects. I don't look like a typical American tourist, or go typical places. I describe my grandmother's sarong and the wayang figures dancing over my staircase and regret aloud that she carried the batiks away, but he shrugs. If she hadn't, they would have rotted in the tropical damp or been sold to an exporter—if they'd survived the war. For me, he says, they are what they should be: time machines, space machines, links to the past and to the invisible world in this one.

At once tender and businesslike, Wayan helps me fix my sarong and sash for the temples, so I don't look sloppy, slapdash, American. He tells me to which begging children, at which temples, I should give money. After seeing me climb off the back of a motorcycle in town, he gently warns me not to go with strangers—but the man offered to take me to a funeral celebration, a fire burial, and after hesitating, I allowed myself to be persuaded. It took all day. Puppets and gamelan music played while the celebrants picnicked and chatted, mostly ignoring me. The body, gilded and draped in bright silks, burned inside an enormous bull, the flames purifying and releasing its soul.

Wayan admits a Ngaben is worth seeing. But he also saw: when I climbed off the back of his bike in Ubud, the man grabbed my wrist. He was asking double the price we'd agreed. I handed him what I'd promised and pulled away, then turned to see Wayan watching from across the square.

On my last evening, Wayan drives me deep into the jungle. All business, he ties my sarong and sash himself, makes sure I've covered knees and armpits, considered unclean in both men and women, though I could show my breasts if I chose. His own small village, his home temple. *The real thing*, the performance will last most of the night. As the music begins, a man hands me a bottle of water, but most people ignore me.

A black, lion-like devil (2 men)—a marvelous sight. A row of brilliantly-clad girls on the temple wall, with flowers in their hair, the gamelan players under an awning, two umbrella bearers finishing the dance with the dragon. Everyone but me knows the story behind the story, set in the shadow world. The sun drops; Wayan whispers in my ear, narrating, but the gamelan music pulses, hypnotic, carrying me back to the night I spent alone on the mountain. *A witch doctor, change of men under the dragon, a man apparently in an epileptic fit.* Her Dutch friend declared the man hysterical. *They give themselves up wholly. Even his painted mask registered shock and dismay.* At last, the kris dance. All eyes on the knife, its ripple in the torchlight. *Rather terrifying to the uninitiated.* Then, darkness, quiet. Human laughter fading into the night. The dirt road dark and narrow until the moon rises huge over the fields.

That morning is my last in Ubud. Soon I will catch airplanes to Taipei then Los Angeles, another world, also in this one. I am already half gone. For the first time since I arrived, I indulge in a massage, a fruity drink by the pool. Back in my cottage, I lay a cheap sarong on the floor in front of the tiny mirror and stand on it in my bathing suit. The room is dimly lit, but sun from the east window, set high in the wall, falls on my hair and shoulders and feet. I snap the number-one guard—an eighth inch—onto my hair clippers.

The first cut makes a clean swath from nape to crown. Hair drifts, glinting gold, copper, the beginnings of silver. I take another pass, another, before a movement catches my eye. At the undraped windows under my porch stand five young, sarong-clad men, noses pressed to the glass. All week they have carried my luggage, lit my mosquito coils, turned down my bed. When I turn to them, they laugh and applaud. They don't move away. It's not they who have been caught, who are novel. I turn back to the mirror. With their eyes on me, I stand in my shaft of sunlight and finish the job.

During their week in Bali, Miriam wrote travelogue, description, analysis, judgment. *Native women, in spite of their beautiful skins and natural grace, don't average nearly the beauty of civilized women. Men surpass the average civilized man.* We don't have Walter's opinion. She never mentioned him beyond a comment about his boils.

To Mandy, Walter wrote only about the two of them. *We did see quite a bit, but after all that was not the point, and we did have a swell honeymoon.*

During their last night on Bali, she dreamt of Jons, the wife and children she had never met. *They kept crowding around me with troubled incoherent questions.* Walter awakened her with his hand on her shoulder, *unheedingly reassuring.*

After they sailed, she sat on deck, *small fishing boats dotted in groups, a Makassar sailing ship drifting rather proudly by.* An idle description, a drawing of the scene. Then the pen moves in her hand. *And I've discovered once again that there's no use trying to kid myself—it just isn't there, and I'm going to*—the sentence interrupted here by a second drawing: mountains and clouds in dotted lines—*have to make myself, too.*

Back in the cloud forest of Selabintanah, Jons's presence-in-absence engaged her more than Walter's persistent, oppressive presence. *The person who should interest me perennially would be the one whom I could never anticipate, one who was always dreaming new things.* Falling in love with another absence. To keep him close, she read Saint-Exupery's *Night Flight*, which he'd given her before he left. *Have I found that person?* A pilot vanishes into a South American night, leaving behind the woman who loves him. What if he were present? *I am trying to concentrate (on what?), to find myself (is it worth it?). Perhaps I would find out if I were uninterrupted for a bit.* Always, there were Walter and the children, constant noise forcing her to turn her attention from her thoughts to them. *I'm waiting for something to happen.* After a week in Selabintanah they would pack up and move to Palembang.

Here, tucked into her journal: a snapshot, a man profiled (large nose, underhung jaw) against the light coming through an airplane's side window. *I can't write anything, but you understand. Letters are the truest mirrors of all—some letters.* These, too, are lost or destroyed, except the lines he quoted from Longfellow, recorded in her journal: *"Tell me not, in mournful numbers, / Life is but an empty dream."* I finish the quatrain: "For the soul is dead that slumbers, / And things are not what they seem."

What a liar a diary is.
MIRIAM'S JOURNAL, September 14th 1934

On the day Jons was to land in Palembang, she spent the morning in a fret of waiting. How would she get away tonight? *What a lot of degrees of consciousness there are!* She padded around the new house in her kimono, for once not caring if the blonde across the street told all the Dutch housewives she hadn't dressed until noon. She took Miriam Joan onto the terrace with a coffee—got up for newspaper, then slippers, then pillow. *A new-blown rose, with a wormhole in a petal, the oriole-like bird warbling, the beauty of the baby's face.* With just enough time, she went to her bath.

At last, she stood on the airfield in her new hat and watched the plane fly low over the jungle, growling. In spite of the hours of travel Jons was clean and brisk in his pressed khakis. *We could say nothing but the most ordinary things.* His cheek to hers, she felt him breathing her in, as she did him, sweat and soap. She wanted to tear off her gloves. *The other people were like colored shadows. I was only subconsciously aware of MacKall's intent observation of my face, upturned to Jons, undoubtedly revealing.* She wanted to be seen, wanted, perhaps, to be caught. But Walter, still in love, couldn't afford to catch her.

Back home, she found her nerves tuned to their highest string. *He is real, physically, again.* She'd just settled in on the terrace with her journal when she heard it—the shriek, Kokki's raised voice. Peter. *He drives me almost beyond endurance.* The shrieks got louder; she heard him call <u>Mommy</u>, then the baby began to cry too. She sat with her head in her hands. Peter was four, Miriam Joan two. She couldn't go to them. She might grab them, shake and slap them, just for keeping her, for making her what she was. *God preserve me from using any such methods on my precious brats—it will take control, as I inherit traits of Mandy's that I <u>must not</u> develop.* Somehow, she held herself together until the wailing quieted: Kokki had gotten them to sleep.

Beloved trap. Children, position, a comfortable life. *I have everything I could possibly need to make me perfectly happy but the state of being in love with my husband.* She would have to decide: *Is the world really well-lost for love? I'll never find out, apparently, as I can't kick over the traces.* But she couldn't help thinking, *Perhaps I should have my way.*

That night, she felt Walter watching her in the mirror as she put on her makeup. *A woman must be afraid to think of her lover when she is with her husband. He might see the reflection of the lover in her eyes.* For a flickering moment, she thought what marriage might be. *Built on two separate and <u>inviolable</u> personalities bound by affection, sympathy, and tastes.* She almost turned away from the mirror, back to him. But whatever he sensed—deceit, vulnerability, shame—roused him. He was shouting before his hands were on her. *Reminds me of my childhood, when Mandy whipped, tongue-lashed, and insulted me into nerve-washed, blindly resentful obedience.*

Reminds me of my childhood. Safe in my chair, I still want to duck. *Why does he drive me from him?* She hunched, her hands over her head, as if she could keep his words from hitting her. *She could have made me do anything by gentleness—and so could Brutus, by leaving me as I am. Or does he know that I'm weak and foolish, & is he trying to cure me?*

Another man's name written on her skin.

The day of Jons's dinner and lecture in Pladjoe. The two men are still strangers. A stroke of luck, good or ill: *B. suddenly called away to nurse an oil well.* Jons landed in Palembang, and she spent the morning, then lunched with him before they caught the boat for the Dutch refinery at Pladjoe. *Serenely making an entrance at the social hall with hundreds of eyes round with conjecture—"wie is dat?"*

She understood the lecture, all in Dutch, *perfectly.* A midnight supper, Miriam seated beside Jons, in the thick of the conversation. *Wie is dat?* Jons called the old men elephants for their growing ears and noses, how they never forgot, their respectable, quiet wives. He was twenty-nine, almost as young as she. On their way out, he lifted a bottle of champagne from behind the bar and slipped it under his coat. She could hear voices rising behind them, his name, her own name at their backs.

The boat was almost empty. They stood in the bow. *One of life's delicious whimsies: here and there shore lights making silhouettes and patches of light haze.* He popped the cork. *Wie is dat*—a girl from Milwaukee. *And a young Dutch aviator, lion of the literary world, knows my ineffable thoughts, a reality among shadows.* Deep in romance, in contradiction, his coat around her shoulders. Champagne from the bottle, bubbles in her nose, two heads together over the rail.

The next afternoon, she went to the airfield to see him off then took to her bed. *I'm in a strange mood.* He was in Batavia now, only a short flight, but already he seemed oceans away. *Perhaps it's one of seeing plain truth instead of everything colored by my optimism.* What she had been waiting for? Had it happened? *I fled from myself to a movie.*

He'd left his coat. When he landed to refuel on his way back to Holland, she met him at the airfield to return it. In front of everyone—Elliots, Calmeyer, Westerman—he folded the jacket gently and pressed it back into her hands: his smell, the shape of his shoulders and torso. She wouldn't see him again until after Christmas. *After all, it was quite comme il faut.*

CHAPTER 15

SEVENTH HAPPINESS

*White thunderheads piled high with a blinding white and
silver gleam; add flying below the dull, grey clouds—coming
into Singapore and landing to find a cold wind blowing.*
MIRIAM'S JOURNAL

The second happiness, we suppose, is Talking, but it is very rare.
CHRISTOPHER MORLEY, *Inward Ho!*

TONY WAVED THE PLANE in, ginger hair tossing. Walter would
arrive on Christmas Eve and stay through his birthday. Jons was
making his way stage by stage, to land just before New Year. For
almost three months, they'd had only letters. He'd asked her to
send her journals, but she couldn't find the courage.

The Butlers lived in the wilds of Tanglin in one of the new
black-and-whites, freighted with history by the time I walk in its
sultry shade—Tony's sewing piled on the sofa, Bert's papers on
the dining table. The grounds, hemmed in by now-tamed jungle,
harbored mosquitoes, bats, toads, the occasional python. Miriam
wondered what the maid and houseboy did all day.

She left Kokki to settle the kids for their naps and joined Bert
on the terrace. Tony had vanished. Bert fussed at the drinks
cart, then, before she knew it, pulled his chair close and took her
hands in his. *"We both realize now it was a bit foolish." He is smug*

now in his happy marriage, & sure of things. Did he protest too much? She thought of the Scottish fiancée she'd never met, his first; herself, Tine. *Strange coincidence*: on the plane she'd been reading Rupert Brooke. "Gently he tombs the poor dim last time." Oh, they had wanted each other. He'd laid his flayed heart before her, begged her to marry him. "But THIS—ah, God!—is Love!" She'd regretted her refusal—so many evenings, lonely in her husband's presence—before she'd met Jons. Now, she thought about Bert's habit of correcting Tony in public.

Of course, Tony had engineered this scene. He went on: realizations, assurances, professions of gratitude and brotherly tenderness.

—Better oblivion hide dead true loves,
   Better the night enfold,
Than men, to eke the praise of new loves,
   Should lie about the old!

It helps him to make Tony happy—more power to him! She didn't think of the harm she'd done them both, of how he needed to protect himself from his own heart.

Under the lamp in her room, she opened his letter. *I wonder what you would say if I were as I am, if I did what I wanted to do. Well darling I am quite sure you would probably be a sought after attractive young grass widow by now, because you wouldn't put up with me.*

Under Tony's lamp, she copied sections into her journal. She didn't know yet what had provoked this, the *poison pen* letter he'd received in the field—some anonymous busybody listing Ted, Calmeyer, Dumoulin, all the lovesick men. She wrote, *Brutus— the Galahad?* He became almost attractive, a man she might like. *I know nothing about him. The husband whose happiness I tried to guard because he deserved everything, including a more passionate wife than me. Young & strong & made for love as we both are, loving each other but being separated for months we may be courting disaster.* The idea thrilled her.

197

Christmas night she turned to him of her own accord, for comfort, then lay nestled against him. She talked while he, drowsy and content, listened. *He said in effect that Bert and his criticisms were crazy.* About the anonymous letter, he held his tongue. When he boarded the plane to Sumatra on the 27th, Walter had regained his confidence. She had turned to him. She finally saw Bert for who he was. After the plane left the ground, he pulled out a sheet of paper and wrote his annual Christmas letter to Mandy. *Finally my wife loves me.*

There is a colossal cosmic grin tonight. On December 30th, Jons, just landed, called for her at the Butlers' under Toni's disapproving eye. They went out for Chinese food then strolled up Government Hill under the trees. *There is the sound of gongs & tom toms and barking dogs from the Chinese kampoeng.* I've taken the same walk in the heat of the day, the bay flat as a steel counter, and in their footsteps, at night. *Essence of living—time, life, now flowing past.* Leaves rustling darkly. The city in constellations: *Here a lighthouse; there a government building, a ship, a theatre, an avenue, a palace, an hotel, glowing sparks in rows and masses.* I've come half a world. I still don't know what I'm looking for. *And an American woman and a Dutch man, standing on the highest point of the town.*

He knew what he wanted. *"Take me out of this sea of trivialities back to our world."* He'd offered heart, journals, inner life, his body, *"our heads among the stars & the world lying in dawn's half-light at our feet."* He offered to take her heart, inner life, body in hand. What was she waiting for? *All the old spirit of the last days at Selabintanah.* As he pressed, she was already remembering the moment, bittersweet. *Given a golden dream, does one wish for a dreamless slumber?* She turned her profile to him, remote, already writing it down.

"I've never needed you so."

Did he ask her to leave Walter? To come back to the Sea View, where the pilots stayed? As famous as Raffles in its day, the beautiful beachfront building was replaced in the sixties with a high-rise, now, too, preserved only in photographs and words. From Palembang he would fly to Batavia. It would be days before they saw each other again.

And what did she want? *Unselfish love, love unaccompanied by passion.* I don't know how that would work.

She left him in the taxi at the end of the lane, crept into the house, grabbed her journals from her desk. Sent him away, that time, with them in hand. Then, she stood at her window looking out over the dark lawn until dawn, until she heard an airplane overhead.

I wanted the moon—and got its reflection. I had no serenity and wanted none. If she could turn restless spirit directly into words. If she had the courage of her desires; if she knew what they actually were. *Did I say too many silly things?* The impossible: *love unaccompanied by passion.* To see herself.

That afternoon, she drove out to the airfield to meet the flight from Palembang. The new pilot, van Sluis, left his seat as soon as he saw her. *I went cold.* The letter was four sheets, both sides. Jons must have stayed up as she had until dawn, reading, madly scribbling.

Back at the house, she stood in the center of the China carpet, light from her window pouring in over the page she held. *Life is lyric again! How to put it without sounding mad? My faith in my new life was justified!* At last, he'd discovered how to make love to her. He told her she could write. He read her and wrote back. *I want not the "inner stillness" of The Fountain, but a stillness approaching that, yet keeping in touch with the current of Life. I have that with Jons.* She parsed desire. She loved him, loved, at the moment, herself as he saw her. *I'm conscious of my physical existence, of being a woman.* Not *being with him*; imagining being with him, his gaze defining her. Not his touch, but his voice on the page. *I must lapse into silence—*

The year turning over. She hummed, getting ready for that night's party. *When twelve o'clock approached and people became excited and familiar, I became silent—I sent Brutus a cheerful thought and loving wishes for his health & happiness—and ceased thinking—only felt a presence that means Life—Love to me. My faith was justified.*

There is no happy life for woman—the advantage that the world offers her is her choice in self-sacrifice.

WILLIAM DEAN HOWELLS, from Miriam's journal

They were both back in Palembang, *everything gleaming and in perfect order,* unlike Tony's house, or mine. Walter went out to a stag party, a small reprieve. In the morning, he came into the dining room and put the anonymous letter detailing her conquests down on top of her buttered toast. At first, he said, he had decided not to credit it. Then last night, at the party—

Was she interested in every white man in the Dutch East Indies but him? *He said the gossip was 50% my fault.* He recited sections from memory. *Heartless. Coils.*

She tried to imagine *the blonde,* Gladys, a disappointed wife writing a list of heartsick men, addressing it. *I have been silly, & reckless— but at the time things always seem so simple & harmless.* Her toast was cold, her coffee tepid. *(It's about time you grew up, woman!)*

She left her dishes for the boy and went onto the terrace. Beside herself, she felt an end coming. *Any good fight might smash the whole thing to bits.* She wanted that smash. *And then what?* She wanted to destroy everything but risk nothing.

There have been happy women.

Anything was better, he thought, even the dust bowl. They would leave in April: six weeks in Europe, summer in Milwaukee and La Porte. By fall, they would be in Ada, Oklahoma. The end.

Desperate, she made her plans. *Why shouldn't Brutus see me off for once?* She would do some shopping in Singapore, say goodbye to Tony. She booked seats on Jons's plane for herself and the kids, a flight for Walter five days later, and berths for them all out of Singapore the day after that, and presented Walter with the tickets. At least the poison-pen had distracted him from Jons.

So quick, the end. Walter, filming them as they boarded the airplane, so I see them through the loupe from his point of view, his eye behind the lens flat and hard. Under throbbing engines, she had to tear Miriam Joan from Kokki's arms. Joan will miss Kokki all her life. *A gale of propeller wind.* Viruly brought the children into the cockpit, let them place their small hands on the levers. Then she took them back to the passenger compartment.

No invitation had come from the Butlers. *Free.* Jons bade the passengers, some continuing to Amsterdam in the morning, good night. She took the room adjoining his at the Sea View, settled the children into their cots, kissed them. Peter, for once, was quiet, but Miriam Joan fussed, clinging to the bodice of her mother's dress and refusing to let go. The hotel's amah was a silent shadow in the chair by the window.

We went to the Jap place for food, with the moon shining over the sea. Moon. The gramophone, the dance. *He is "the pilot Viruly" occasionally.* Already she could see him from a distance. Their last night. Months spent waiting, suspended, and now—.

Even now, having pored over everything, I don't know what was denied or granted. What did she want, really? *Unaccompanied by passion*—is that what *unselfish love* is?

She goes to his bed. Doesn't she? Doesn't she watch, sleepy under the sheets, while he shaves in the predawn and puts on his tropical uniform, freshly pressed by the valet? Do I want her to? My own head turning, though after Chris I haven't wanted anyone else enough to risk his loss.

And yet, and yet. Bed was never where she took her pleasure. What happened there hadn't been the point, not to her. She would have done it for him, not herself.

He left the next morning at 5:00—& then I did feel lost.

CHAPTER 16

INTERLUDE:
IN TRANSIT

EUROPE, 1935. In Rome, *Jews who fled, white and big, doing work that would degrade them in the Orient.* Their nanny. Their guide, whose eyes fill with tears as he watches her kiss Peter and Miriam Joan. The posters say *Viva il Re, Ditto il Duce, Viva il Fascismo.* In sunny Florence, she feels a chill. *There are spies everywhere.* She sits in the café at the corner, watching for *the mystery man* who telephones daily from the booth across the street.

Their train across the Alps stops at the Austrian border. The police read her letters. *Afraid of espionage or propaganda?* German name, blue eyes—when they finish, the soldiers tousle the children's blonde heads and let them leave the train to touch their first snow. In Germany, there are brownshirts and soldiers everywhere. *Nothing can be stopped.*

In Amsterdam, husband and lover meet at last at Jons's favorite restaurant. She can't even take Jons's arm. He has brought a copy of his new book, *Alles o.k.!*, and Walter flips through the photographs, lingering at the Havik's cockpit as if he sees her shadow. What does the inscription say? Her journal doesn't tell me. If Viruly's books were in her effects when she died, my mother didn't keep them. I have to scour the internet for a copy from a used bookseller, and then it's in Dutch. I buy it anyway.

Poor Miriam. Poor fugitive. Nothing to raise anyone's suspicion —only instinct, hair lifting on the back of a neck.

Walter watches, helpless but for small, tyrannical gestures. He still finds her impossible to know, though she fears herself to be as legible as type. Viruly offers a personal tour of Amsterdam; Walter declines and takes her on a taxi tour, *in solitary splendor*. Viruly offers to fly them to the coast to catch their boat; Walter prefers the bus, roaring in a cloud of diesel down a Dutch highway. That evening, they will cross the Channel to catch their ship. He will know within a few yards where she is, with whom.

He will know where her body is. The mind is its own swift vessel.

CHAPTER 17

DEPRESSION: DATELINE ADA, OKLAHOMA, 1935

... never wandering around the world again, until,
perhaps, we were quite elderly, & then as wistful voyagers;
revisiting places in which we left no trace ...
MIRIAM'S JOURNAL

DUST DEVILS in the yard, a patch of dirt. The Tulsa neighborhood where I play with Peter's children in the sixties will be green with lawns and shade trees; in 1935, Miriam finds peeling paint, no front porch or shutters. Inside, a draft flapped through torn shades and drew dust in skiffs across the floors. Someone had painted the toilet seat brown, the paint now cracked and peeling. Mothballs, small animal death. *We'll have to put the washmachine on a screened back porch.*

Close your eyes: It's all there. Ice in her glass. The boy at her elbow. Rain on the terrace roof. *He likes it better here in every way.*

Looking at the sky, he could tell the rain would stop before it settled the dust but resigned himself to office work. *In the tropics we would be working anyway in spite of rain and high water.* He'd worked through typhoons to get home sooner. Walked off fever to get to her. He longed to leave so he could do it again.

Mornings were frigid. A gas heater in the parlor, no heat in the bedrooms. *He never does anything around the house, except, & I suppose it's a lot—he gets his own breakfast.* Rummaging, clattering—she kept her eyes closed, hoping he'd remember to light the heater. *He forgets half the time, so it's no warmer when the kids & I get up.* Then she drifted back to sleep. *Never mind, Ma, don't worry about me—I'm going to stop seeing limitations.* He would never have to rub his hands raw on a pile of wet laundry, feeding clothes into the mangle while wind whipped through the screen. *What we'll do in winter I don't know.*

At noon he strolled downtown through air momentarily clear and fine, past meager shop windows, through the park where men congregated on benches, by the soup kitchen where they lined up for lunch. A few, new to misfortune, wore suits and felt hats; they turned their backs so passersby couldn't see their faces. Others had obviously been sleeping rough. Walter wanted to think these men hadn't worked hard enough, been smart enough, paid due attention, that they were utterly unlike him. The sight of them lined up, hands in their pockets, gave him the shudders.

The radio played hillbilly banjo music all morning, followed by a report about farm relief. She tried to submit, to submerge. *Don't worry about me.* When, at night, a voice arrived over the wires—Willem Hendrik van Loon's—accented in Dutch like the one she loved, she closed her eyes and fell in. His commentaries came when the air was quiet, static reminding her how far the familiar strains traveled to reach her.

No invitations, nothing to do. Once, Walter dragged a couple of geologists and one of their wives home for dinner. The men talked oil while the wife *chased peas. The people who knew me in Milwaukee and the Indies would hardly recognize in me now the vibrant Miriam (not Mrs. Link!) they knew—foolish, reckless, careless, perhaps, but abundantly alive!* She kept her friends in a world made of words. *Once, in Singapore, Tony derided me for 'spending my life writing letters.'* After the post, she swept again, napped, played with the children, swept yet again. *This is, after all, the answer to a woman's dream, I suppose.* Wind scoured the country, pulling its veil of dust.

The children's coughing troubled his dreams. Farms failed. Businesses faltered. Soup lines lengthened. Walter saw a couple, the woman holding a boy and girl by the hands and watching the man, who never lifted his eyes from the ground. In his stomach, Walter felt a weight like a stone.

He gave Miriam a budget but no allowance and made her account for every cent—his excuse not their finances but those of the nation. *I'll show him. I can live on a lot less.* Who had foreseen their shabby furniture? Her inadequate winter clothes? At night in bed, she imagined running away with the children. Miriam Joan would like that. *She doesn't like B., & always calls him "Peter's Daddy."* Milwaukee. Batavia. Holland.

Dust in their hair, clothes, bedding; rising on the horizon, its stinging dark—every time, she thought she would never see the sun and sky again. Deepening cold. Her fingers split from feeding clothes through the wringer under the winter wind.

I'm looking for no one. Like that, she was done with romance. In the cold wind and dust, she was going to do something. But what? Fidelity, I think, was for me a matter of finding the man who was happy seeing me at work, concentrated on the page; who, from the beginning and through hard times, saw not my surface but my self and still lets it surprise him.

She wrote Hendrik van Loon a letter, in Dutch. *He invited comment—it may have been silly. Time to try writing a bit,* time to herself at last. *It gripes the old man.*

From under the building shadow of war, Jons sent an article he'd published on pacifism. She decided to translate it. *No harm in trying!* Keeping close the lines and habits of his mind for an hour a day. She liked weighing one meaning next to another, feeling her way toward something beyond literal sense, a kind of consistency. And as I know, translating her letters and journals not from one language to another but from her time and space into mine, it beat facing an empty page. Jons's words, his voice in her ear, provided

Miriam Joan and Peter, Ada, c. 1935

the given; van Loon reminded her of the tune. She was inhabited. Housework, letters, children. Surely, a *normal woman* would be satisfied. What was a normal woman then? What is one now? Like her, I have my doubts. Unlike her, I have never cared to be normal. *M. Joan, especially, is a glowing cherub, and sings all day—"Happy is the donkey, Don't you hear him bray." She's rare.* I always thought my mother had dropped the "Miriam" later, to set herself apart. A name, bestowed then reclaimed. Mommy, Muckie, Miriam sat at the window watching dust rise—sometimes, you couldn't see the hand in front of your face—and remembered standing on a ship's deck breathing glorious air. *I am not going to sit quietly here for the rest of my life, seeing nothing and spending nothing, never busting loose.*

In January, a letter from Viruly, to waft her. *I have known what it is to be perfectly happy.* A tease in her ear. *He understands my wild mind.* In the photo, he poses among Notre Dame's gargoyles, gazing over ancient rooftops, a wild-faced creature carved in stone. *Did they tell you what I think of you?* To be with him in Paris. *They know, of course—they've seen it in blue moon-&-star-light, in 5 o'clock grey, silent mist, in lashing storms.*

She polished her translation of his article, translated his response to the inevitable attacks, sent both off to *Magazine Digest*, then churned out her own piece about his refusal to fight and sent it—why not?—to the *Saturday Evening Post*. The post office; a nap. *Tonight we are dissipating.* After supper, Walter would take her to see *A Tale of Two Cities. —Gosh, Mommy, I have certainly come down in the world when I regard a movie as news, no?*

She still had ideas. *A book of poems, small & delicate, named Wind-Bells. A good dedication: "To a sunny morning when Life was good on the Marquesa's mountain."* Her own radio program? Ukulele music—she visited the local station manager, played for him, met with him over lunch, tea, cocktails. They were planning the show's launch when someone warned his wife about her, and he withdrew.

Even the wind's howling grew ordinary. The wet sheets she put up in the windows at night to catch dust; the kids coughing in their beds. *If other people can stick it, I suppose I should be able to. I'm happier, now that I'm really working on my stories, and have finished one.* The days ground through their routine; nights, the house slept and she could think of herself, almost, as alone.

May: *The thin, acid hum of mosquitoes. I can't remain in abeyance much longer—*

Late June: Her translation—condensed—came out in the *Magazine Digest.* Two copies and a check for ten dollars. My mother knew nothing about this work, that Miriam had ever been so serious, taken so seriously. *They changed the title from "War?" to "Pacifists Must Fight", which is rather silly.* It made her a minor celebrity in Ada. A local reporter called, wanting to do an article.

And in the same mail with her *Magazine Digest*s, a reply at last from Hendrik Willem van Loon, who had seen the translation. *It's all in Dutch, & it's a beaut! Now aren't you popping?* She left both out on the hall table for Walter when he got home, but he just looked down his long nose at the parlor, cluttered with toys, then at the kitchen where the breakfast and lunch dishes sat in the sink.

July, Milwaukee: Six whole weeks with Mandy and the kids, no Walter. Green balm for the eyes, and finally her life was moving. With Mandy, she visited Mrs. Marth, who had nothing to tell— *except that I was nervous & worn down & must rest or I'd be ill for a long time.* Except that she was a sensitive herself, and should trust her intuitions. Except that she was prone to self-delusion.

Louise Ivey, a medium back in Ada, had told her she was *prophetic.* But if so, why couldn't she see her future, not the slightest detail? *Well—¿quien sabe? Why can't they ever produce any of these "wonderful proofs" for me?* As usual, she couldn't see herself. Van Loon had continued to write, had invited her to visit. *I think he, better than any other can tell me whether I'm ridiculously mad, with delusions of grandeur, or gloriously sane*

& on the right track. Still looking for a man to see her.

Late, with her head in Mandy's lap, she broached the idea. She could take the rest Mrs. Marth said she needed. A week on the coast of Massachusetts, a day in Connecticut with van Loon, alone, without the children.

Have I a right to go? The question I keep answering yes. She knew what Walter would say. *I'm a wife & mother & have duties (and no money!).* Walter, of course, had given her barely enough to pay Mandy expenses for the summer, a way of keeping her under wraps. But oh, to get on that train. *Wouldn't I be a fool if I didn't? Haven't I a duty to my growth & development?* A small question, two huge questions at its heart. *Would I be better off without my dreams?*

Who could say? Not Miriam. Not Mrs. Marth. Not Mandy, whose daughter was so unhappy with the husband Mandy had chosen. Was Miriam simply unable to adjust, to submit? If so, whose fault was it?

Yes.

When she pulled up beneath the porte cochere, the famous Dutchman was standing in the front door waving both arms. His wife was away. *He's very tall & fat, explosive, active mind leaping from one subject to another.* Not what she'd expected. *Profanity & no patience with human stupidity—not the ironic tolerance displayed in his books & radio talks. He was off the record, of course.* The record was not a reproduction. What was it? *My moods are so different.* She wanted to know how he did it—constructed a self for his radio program, for his books, not *representative* of his moods, but beyond them, entire. The leap she could never quite make, from her quotidian self into that other space.

I was entirely calm—I don't flutter any more. She'd missed men, had missed eyes on her. Hank took her to walk the beach, leaning his big body in and down to hear her under the wind. After supper, they sat on the terrace, listening to the sea. She declined his pressing invitation to spend the night, but left late enough to make me wonder, the moon blazing on the water. *He kissed my hand in farewell, & waved until lost to sight. Well!— it made me feel alive & temporarily vital & attractive again.* In the photos, she is clearly older, a little grey, a little plumper than before. Reflected in a man's eyes, she felt herself.

Fall. Waiting in Ada were letters from Viruly and van Loon, who wanted to see her again. She copied his letter for Mandy. *"Will you the next time be honest and let the dear family go to the devil when you come in search of wisdom."* That part, certainly. *"Alas for my poor wisdom. I got a letter from the editor of the satevepost refusing my last article because it was* TOO INTELLIGENT. *Will you kindly put that on your piano and play it in nine flats?"*

The society editor of the local paper asked for an article about the Indies, which she wrote under a pseudonym. *I would hate anyone to think that I am trying to be something or somebody.* Would hate, especially, for Walter to think so, or to publish, subsumed, under his name. Still, half-a-dozen people called before the day was out, and the local AAUW asked her to give a speech. *They sat actually spell-bound for over an hour—and now I'm to be asked to do it with enlargements to a bigger group.* Even to her, Java looked romantic. *I am asking the Okla. City paper if they want feature articles—might as well get $35 or so for them.*

Time was speeding up. The days were shrinking; she was filling them. She knew people. Women, anyway. People—women—knew her.

I've ordered the two chairs I bought from Jack re-upholstered, and a slip-cover for the couch. The bill: eighty-one dollars. *Brutus didn't faint—he raised his eye-brows slightly.* Perhaps she could change him, if she changed herself, or at least what she showed him. *The record.* That night, she turned to him. *Am I making progress in this marriage? Are both of us not?*

Time speeding up, the year hurtling toward its end. She voted for Alf Landon, a geologist and oil man, because Walter did, *as a protest* against the New Deal, *the social parasites.* A quarter of Oklahomans out of work. I think of my mother's hard turn to the Left, how some conversations don't change. I am the one in our house to read the news and decide whom and what we will vote for. Division of labor: I fill out the ballots, Chris signs his, I send them off.

Van Loon had never responded to the article she'd sent, but now, emboldened, she wrote again, asking his opinion. *For private consumption he is much more apoplectic than otherwise.*

(December. Walter sent his semi-annual letter to Mandy. *A lot of water has gone under the bridge since last summer but nothing much has happened.* His anxiety had shifted away from his wife, onto his bankbook and the soup lines. *We just about manage to hold our own.* The fifteenth: the day before Miriam's birthday. *I have pawned the Crown Jewels to get her a Beautyrest and a good spring. Then I hope the hard bed thing will end for a while at least. I guess it will be something else then.* Why she did she keep on wanting?)

The dark of winter, her birthday, Christmas, Walter's birthday party. She cooked dinner herself. *People say more and more that they like to come here to eat, as they did in the Indies.* She'd only had to adjust her expectations. At New Year's, Swedish meatballs on toothpicks, deviled eggs, cocktails, hilarity rising as midnight neared, came, passed. 1937, the year rolling over—at what moment does one reality turn into another? The moon's shadow, dust blowing across the earth. Dreamy in her new dress, she felt the old charm. *I enjoyed it all, even to washing the dishes!* A house full of people laughing, a little tight. For the first time in months, she enjoyed looking forward. What would the year bring? Walter talked of Louisiana, Montana, even the Indies. Far away. *Am I a child of yours or not?*

Van Loon wasn't the first to say it, but he said it without caresses. *You can be a writer who HAS GOT SOMETHING TO SAY SAYS IT AND STOPS TALKING. When people say .... dear Miriam is so clever and writes so well ... tell them to go fly a kite. Don't listen to anybody but the DAIMOON.... It is harder work than you ever dreamed of doing. If I have set you to work seriously I shall not have lived in vain."* Her article came back from the *Saturday Evening Post* with a personal note from the editor. *Stop talking.* She sat down again in silence, heard—

a terrific gale roaring through the trees. She went out on the porch. Already the world had shrunk to two or three blocks. *The sun looks pretty sick.* Before the storm was over, they would be shut in by swirling dust, Peter and Miriam Joan whimpering. She couldn't touch them for the shock, static electricity so powerful it could knock a man down.

Time swirling, speeding again. Where would they be, six months from now? She still longed to believe desire and event could fuse. She longed to do something, to become. She went to see Louise Ivey, wrote down the predictions she liked. *Next June is the turning point in my life.* New posting, new location. *No more vegetating in this backwoods!* How she floated it out there then dropped it—*a complete change in everything, including marriage.* Talk about what might be next, for the company, for them, over fences and bridge tables, between herself and Walter under the covers at night.

A box from Tony arrived. Toys, a little kimono for Miriam Joan, *six yards of the loveliest Japanese silk I've ever seen for me.* She stitched one of the batiks into a casual dress with a nipped waist and wide skirt. She took art lessons, played bridge, talked, like everyone, of Europe, of war, of the need for oil. *Brutus is slated to be one of the outstanding geologists of this country, and one of these days he'll step into a really big job.* Many of their friends were backing Fascism. *Only as a means of straightening out a lot of abuses and to pave the way for a real and individualistic democracy.* She thought of her letters from Viruly and van Loon, their own travels through Europe the year before—how frightened people had been in Germany, Austria, Italy. *I'm sure I don't know.*

She was still trying to find herself, to find what to do to be.

At seven, I knew. Poet—and, since there was no other word for it, fireman.

Women kept asking where she'd gotten the fabric for her dress. She wrote to Eddie Muh in Batavia for samples. *A capitalist like all the rest.* Half the cloth was sold to acquaintances before she opened the box. She contacted store drapery departments. *It could be worked into a nice business, without my actually becoming a business woman with a shop.* Walter could hardly object. This is what astonishes me: how far he moved, from wanting her in the field with him to wanting to keep her entirely at home, to exert that kind of power.

As Chris works to cut back on conference travel, my own career on its different rhythm picks up. I am almost finished following Miriam, but my new poetry publisher wants me to read in Los Angeles, New York, London. I receive invitations from across the U.S. and from Melbourne, Canberra, Saarbrücken, Montreal, eventually Medellín. Chris keeps imagining I, too, will subside, but I feel myself building steam. When I receive an invitation, I say yes, book tickets, then tell him in my own time.

(*She still obeys.* Except when she didn't.)

Then it came. *The turning point,* a few weeks ahead of prophecy, and once again she had to drop everything. *I'm still punch-drunk—our whole life is going to change now.* The job Walter had been waiting for: Chief Geologist and Assistant Manager for the Standard Oil Company of Louisiana. Shreveport. He was becoming what she'd wanted. *It makes me wonder whether I can keep up with him.*

Just when she was going to do something.

CHAPTER 18

SWING TIME, INCLUDING INTERLUDE (PARENTHETICAL)

Heaven is not built of country seats
But little queer suburban streets.
CHRISTOPHER MORLEY, "To the Little House"

A DREAM OF LAWN; rose canes leafing. Neighbor women in hats and gloves bearing cakes prepared in their kitchens as in the colonies by "little brown hands," a phrase she still used years later, setting me to work. *I'll be darned if the Methodist lady pillar didn't descend on me again. She is a very prunes and prisms sort of dame and is cross-eyed—altogether a specimen.*

Calls, bridge, afternoon teas. Walter was taking her Friday night to the Fountain Room, where Shreveport's elite dined and danced. *I have become the sort of wife he has always wanted—dull, without spirit or initiative, and completely domesticated. —And he has become what I never thought he would: quite a social light and attraction, but without shedding any of his light on me at all.*

Walter opened an account for her at M. Levy Company, *"Shreveport's Greatest Clothiers."* A parade of tulle and lace, lamé and sequins, gowns this year plunging front and back, draped and clinging—the model, not too pretty, turning smartly on the showroom's marble floor. For day: suits with matching shoes and gloves, afternoon dresses, cashmere sweaters with three-quarter-length sleeves she sent me when I was in college, which I still own. The depression deepened again, before, everyone hoped, its last turn up and out—but for the Links things had never looked better.

On Friday afternoon, she had her hair done, *in anticipation.* Her gown was cut to show off her back and shoulders. *I have a magnificent body, too powerful & developed around the shoulders and legs for real beauty, but virile, symmetrical, and good to look at in spite of childbearing and the strain and wear of my damned restless temperament.* Striding through the gilded lobby, she caught sight of her reflection: visible again, golden and plumed, skirts swirling. In the center of the dining room an enormous fountain played; the orchestra rode a brassy swing. Walter introduced her to a small group—a tall blonde surrounded by four men—already hilarious. *The most brazen gal I ever saw, super sexy, & blaringly blazoned nymphomaniac in every line and feature,* whispering something to Walter that made him glance quickly at Miriam then away. *The supremely funny part of it all is that I am in love with him now.* Clara's gown made Miriam's look modest. None of the men could keep his eyes off her. She had flash and elegance, qualities Walter had once admired in Miriam. Once, she'd loved him only when he was absent.

One of the men asked Clara to dance, and Walter swung Miriam onto the floor, the band covering "Oh, Lady Be Good!"—could she blossom yet? Did she need him to do it?—almost what it should have been, two bodies whirling in time, suspended between cocktails and dinner, between downtown's neon glow and the distant light of the moon.

About marriage, I've learned you don't want to turn your back on it. It's a wild animal, requiring attention and alertness. Or it becomes a solid thing, an iceberg in a climate that's always frozen.

Only the people inside it know what it is.

What each of them knows is different.

What Walter adored in Miriam he tried to change: liveliness, once an attraction, quickly turning to threat. Love of clothes, of dancing, her desire to plunge headlong into the world. What she tried to erase: Walter's firmness, his desire for control, *absolutely a man*. His desire to plunge; his freedom to do so.

And if both succeed in changing the other? Will there be anything left to love?

There is always a dance of negotiation, of what either partner expects or thinks she, he, has a right to expect.

You don't have to understand why I want something, I have learned over the years to remind my husband. Only that I do. A dress that makes me a work of art. Money I've earned. Music moving me. To be in transit, in transition, transported. To be at work, in myself and abroad. Never to be entirely safe. To be left alone.

All this, all these years. In trade, I'm still learning not just to go my own way, but to narrate my passage. Not to pretend what I do is none of his business.

It is August. They are in New York, so close to van Loon, to his *guest room that overlooks nothing but sky and water*, she can all but hear him shouting. He was proofing the *Arts*—750 pages, 182 plates she couldn't wait to see. *"I anticipate your visit with great impatience. Please come. Both of you."* She imagined Walter stepping into this corner of her life. She wanted, now, to impress him, to let him see her manage van Loon's bluster, his desire. *"I am a one-man opposition. We have got to talk about all of these things."*

Walter wore a bespoke suit to the office. He stopped in the hall to shake hands with the new assistant geologists, told them to pack plenty of socks and tobacco. Behind closed doors, he pleaded with the only geologist higher on the ladder for a couple of godforsaken areas in Arkansas everyone else was wrong about. Marshaled more numbers, pleaded again.

Please come. She postponed their visit. She shopped on Fifth Avenue—day dresses, a suit with a cutaway jacket—spending more the longer Walter delayed, a form of protest. Late afternoons, she met him in the hotel bar for cocktails.

At last, he returned to the hotel gloating. He had Arkansas. And they were leaving in the morning for Niagara Falls. A surprise for her, the second honeymoon he craved—or rather a third. Then they would drive to Milwaukee, pick up the kids, and head for La Porte.

Had he ever meant to stop in Connecticut? Had he heard a thing she'd said?

We must talk. When had she heard those words from Walter?

The falls, the long bridge, rainbows rising in scattered mist— Still imagining what he wanted would make her happy. The motel bed. The weight of expectation she would not meet. She was not free. She kept forgetting. She wrote her apology as best she could.

In September, she pointed the car toward Shreveport. Indiana had been nice after all—sitting under autumn's first cool spell, watching the kids with their cousins, Alfred's four. *I'd love having four kids like theirs.* Miriam Joan was five already. She thought she missed having an infant. She didn't know what she was missing, still didn't know herself.

Two were more than enough, Walter told her, rolling up his sweater for a pillow.

The children stayed awake with her, singing quietly. Outside Shreveport, they passed an airplane beacon, its beam sweeping the humid darkness. Miriam Joan said, *"I wish I weren't heavy. Then I could sit on it."* Oh, flight.

She thought it would be swell—and so it would.

While she was in Milwaukee, he'd made the house his own: shoes he'd stepped out of; papers strewn on the dining table; an invitation from Clara Leinhard for cocktails—<u>Brute, don't disappoint me!</u> She sorted matchboxes from nightclubs she'd never heard of, their graphics bright and bold. Had he gone out every night while she was away? <u>Brute</u>. He was out now, their first night back. Once, she'd stepped out, and he'd mooned.

She went to bed with a book. Next she knew, she felt the mattress give, and he was kissing her, tasting of whisky, lifting her nightgown—she shoved at him, but he kept pressing and finally she reached for a sheathe. The box in the nightstand was empty. She was sure he'd bought a new one before she'd left. He worked his way between her legs, avid, held her hands and pushed.

In the morning she sorted their clothes for the wash. She moved carefully, still stiff from driving, sore <u>down there</u>. Turning out the pockets of a pair of trousers left in the hamper, she felt the crackle of cellophane. Three condom packets, one torn open, empty.

She set them on his nightstand, continued to separate whites, darks, brights. She wouldn't think about them. Wouldn't think, as her stomach curdled, what her own betrayals had meant to him. *Out again.* Him. Herself. *Torn apart and stamped on.*

Writing abandoned, fabric business—what was left? Because she'd nagged, Walter had taken her to *A Doll's House* at the Little Theater, had fidgeted while she trembled, watching an ordinary woman step through a doorway into words and light. When she saw the notice in the paper—open auditions—she thought, *he has discouraged everything.* The audition would give her an evening out. *A lark.*

On their honeymoon, when they both imagined another kind of marriage, I think she believed in it. For him, their talk must always have been a form of play, a fantasy. For me, Chris imagined early tenure, books, awards—more or less what he wanted himself. When I grew impatient and began applying for teaching jobs outside Utah, knowing I might have to commute weekly to Boise or Spokane, he went into action, out of a belief in my career, yes, and to keep us together in one place. He saw a two-body problem, and Utah fixed it. Later, when Caltech, a scientist's but not a poet's Shangri-La, came knocking, willing to accommodate us both, I told Chris, "If this is what you need, we'll go." We sat down with paper and pen and made lists, joked about "maximizing joint

222

happiness." For my sake, in the end for both our sakes, we stayed.

Five weeks of rehearsals five nights a week; a week of performance. *If he objects, I'll have to stop.* Her good luck: the first Arkansas well was about to come in, and he'd staked everything on it. He couldn't sit on his hands in the office. *The new territory should develop into a tremendous new field.* All because he'd pushed, cajoled, gambled. On your head, they'd said, the New York dogs to whom Arkansas might as well have been the moon.

A feather in the Old Man's cap.

For three weeks of rehearsals, he wasn't home to miss her, and she was free. Only community theater—her ambitions trimmed— but still, the director's eye shaped her with its cool pressure. Needing to be seen, she walked on, said her one line, did it again. Watched from the wings. Then November: one more week of rehearsals, one of performance to go, and she was throwing up in the mornings. *I suppose I shall stick.* She might have got away with it, but Walter came home, tight with impatience. No oil yet. She had to get up early to see the doctor, so she was standing at the stove frying his eggs for once, about to turn them, when she looked at their quivering whites, yolks like sick, gelatinous suns. She barely made it to the kitchen sink. He sat, holding himself very still, as if he could stop time there, in the moment before she lifted her head and told him.

Miriam Joan was five; soon Miriam would have to send her to school. He longed to get back to another kind of relation with his wife, one not mediated, triangulated, by people smaller and needier than himself—a relation he imagined (trick of memory) they'd once had. A moment's undisciplined pleasure. How? One drink, another. His wife soft in silk and lace. A lapse—surely she had brought it upon him, had somehow willed it—was a symptom of his wanting, evidence of her intent. He remembered: she had spoken his name.

—Brutus, a rebuke.

—Brutus, himself, on her tongue, asking him to get a sheath, to stop.

His name in her mouth, the unrelenting lure of her. *I hope I've never forced myself on her.* She'd lain so quietly. *She still obeys.*

Goddammit, she should have been more careful.

Goddammit. For her health, for the baby's, so he could believe he had something under his control—

The body that betrays, all the burdens of being female, not even birth control in her own hands. My mother believes Miriam never tried hard at anything, that she had no fight. She couldn't fight <u>him</u>. She should have married a weakling, like her mother did—but still, Mandy had to get divorced even to spend her own money. *I must give up the play.*

<u>Biology</u>, <u>history</u>. My mother is wrong.

I'll try my luck again some time.

Are we our bodies? Recent thinking suggests not, yet our bodies are how we show ourselves to the world, how the world shows itself to us. What theory or trick of mind might slip us free?

Maybe we seek the opposite of what our parents did, not knowing our genes will rule us in the end. My grandmother romanticized adventure. My mother, having been dragged from country to country, rarely allowed to finish a term in the same school, sought settled domesticity; she has lived in the same city for sixty years.

Surrounded by scientists—father, mother, husband, brothers—I romanticized science, a set of disciplines I've loved but never wanted to practice. Instead, I made poems into vehicles to think about nature, perception, how the lenses we use to examine reality (language its own kind of lens) determine what we see: the very large or very small, the concrete, the abstract, the emotional. Not writing about myself. Writing, always, only, about myself. Still, I think more and more about how the world changes, has changed, even during my adulthood, allowing me passage into a reality they couldn't have imagined. In the sixties, my mother needed my father's signature to open a bank account, a marriage license and his permission to get the pill. Her subjugation was structural.

Even I had no female professors as an undergraduate, only

one as a Master's, one as a PhD student. Still novelties in those classrooms, some of my female friends embraced the old strategy of deploying their bodies in the service of advancement, imagining, as my grandmother had, that a charmed man could move them from where they were to where they wanted to be—an idea our professors encouraged. This also looked to be structural: power flowing as if by nature through men directly and through women by proxy.

One professor shut his office door, seated me at a typewriter, fed a piece of paper into the cartridge, and reached around my shoulders to retype my poem with his changes, his breath ruffling my hair. "That's better," he said, ripping the poem from the machine and resting his other hand lightly around my neck.

Another offered me a ride home from a party, and, when we stopped in front of my apartment building, leaned across my lap to show me the gun stashed beneath my seat, his face laid for a long moment on my tightly pressed-together knees while, again, I sat very still.

He asked, "Do you live alone?"

None of my classmates who said "yes" got far, not for long. Though at least they controlled their own fertility, they moved themselves from one position of weakness to another—if, as my nieces now say, "with benefits." Even then, I saw that my grandmother's old-fashioned model—marriage first, then honeymoon—offered more advantages than that.

Still, if this was the structure that housed us, it was already shifting. It no longer appeared immutable. It had become possible to imagine a different architecture. Already, I believed I wouldn't *need* a man to move me, not in that way.

Today, the faculty in my program is two-thirds female. In the wider department, our numbers are near half and growing. Once, I would never have imagined becoming this: a hard worker, yes, with direct deposit into my own account, not an exception.

New Year letters from Hetty, Jo, Viruly, Frits, van der Sluis. Not van Loon. She signed up for a class with a woman who sold stories to love magazines. *She said I had a very individual style, and should try for Scribners—the other two gals are to try for the Love and Confession field. What does that make me?*

The future, unknown but kicking. A baby in progress; his Arkansas field, still waiting to deliver. *Wonder what Mrs. Marth has been telling you lately.* Could the future be made visible? *A sort of test*, though she kept dropping hints to Mandy. *What would you think of a granddaughter named Darien?*

Four months, five, she kept the child to herself. Five, six, she waited for Mandy to divine her across the miles, but Mandy couldn't see what Miriam put right in front of her. Me, I have hindsight and the journal. My grandmother has taught me how to read at last—the fear and sadness she and Mandy shared but rarely talked about: lost freedom, frustrated desire, the future looming in the present as a child does in its conception. The fear Walter shared too, also not talking about it; and that I share, knowing it could have been me, but for the miracles of chemistry, a trick of history, universities and professions cracking open their doors.

Late spring, summer. What was he thinking? Walter had sought this desk job to be with her but traveled more than ever, delegating office work so he could live outside, in dust and grime. *If it isn't Arkansas it'll be Tulsa or somewhere else. He never writes any more, so I don't count on him until I see him.* She was sure when the baby came he'd still be out there, waiting for his well to come in, but he delivered first. *Brutus blew in around six o'clock, triumphantly announcing "Have we got an oil well! We've got a tremendous field!"* He brought a core sample for her to smell—heady with gasoline. She was still gravid, heavy, spinning her wheels. He was walking on air.

A few weeks before she went into labor, a letter came from *McBride's*. The editor wanted to see more of her translation, *to publish some*

chapters and perhaps some of the pictures in "Travel" magazine,
but also perhaps to publish the entire book. She packed up what
she'd finished, over half the book, and applied herself to the rest.
Maybe this time. So often, she'd come so close. *(Brutus is about as*
excited as a piece of cheese—)

His smile. His cool gaze, his all-too-legible need. Wanting
her, not anything for her. Miriam Joan watching, *lovely with her*
blonde hair and deep tan and gray eyes. Like me, mommy's girl.
Like me, like Miriam, believing if her mother could only be happy,
she could too. *You were right in wondering how I ever had such*
a beautiful kid, but she really looks a lot like Brutus. That gaze,
uncanny. *At least he shouldn't question* her *paternity!*

With his large, bouncing self, the new baby took something else
out of his mother, a force that felt essential. Immediately, Andy
was a stranger. When she came home from the hospital, the walk
from the car to the back door all but winded her. She handed the
baby to the nurse, went straight to bed. When the nurse brought
him, she fed him, then lay with her face to the wall and tried to
catch her breath. Weeks emptied themselves. She stopped writing,
even letters; the letters she wrote she couldn't bear to send.

The editor of *Travel* asked her for an article about Java, but
she would begin a paragraph and find herself staring past it. Java
and its beloved faces shimmered like mirage. The nurse ran her
bath in late afternoon, cajoled her out of bed. In the tub, she read
letters and wept. At night, to feel her mother's presence, she tuned
her radio to Mandy's favorite spiritualist plays and to Carnation's
Contented Hour:

> Won't you wait, wait, wait by the old red gate
> Won't you wait 'til the cows come home.
> *I'm really very well—and I'm contented too.*

Because of the baby, because of money, because he could,
Walter decided she should stay in Shreveport all summer. He
came home in the evening to a quiet house, the kids afraid to
make noise, Miriam's silent tears. The phone bill to Wisconsin

went through the roof. She barely managed to get the plates on the table for dinner then left the dishes for the maid, shuffling off to bed as soon as the kids were down. She sat, book on her lap, and stared into the middle distance. Where had she gone?

WHERE I'VE GONE

Following Them: Madison. Java, of course. Cuba, Singapore, Bali, Brazil, Sumatra. Eventually, Bogotá, Medellín.

Without My Husband: All of the above. Uppsala and Stockholm; Paris, too noisy and dirty for him, whenever I can; the Alsace, to visit what Miriam referred to as the family castle. Isla Mujeres, Cozumel, Akumal. Ravenna, Vinci, Vincennes, Florence, Padua, Milan, Pisa, Siena, Spello, Venice, Pompeii, Herculaneum; London, Edinburgh, Portsmouth; Istanbul; Rotterdam; cities in Germany and Switzerland I hardly remember to name. Punta Arenas, Chile. Antarctica, for the National Science Foundation—finding Shackleton, whose voice I recognized in Walter's. Canberra. All since we married. Greece, Turkey, Yugoslavia. In my chair at night, falling into sleep, at the kitchen sink, in my own mind I am also abandoning him. This is what disturbs him. He wouldn't go with me if I asked. But yes: I am happy alone, in myself. I am a traveler. *I have never been unfaithful*, only contentedly absent.

With my husband: Amsterdam, Tasmania, Okinawa, Tokyo, New Zealand, Taiwan, Hong Kong, Beijing, Shanghai, Venice, Rome, Dagstuhl, Helsinki, Berlin, Sydney, and Melbourne; on the winter solstice, Lapland, above the Arctic Circle. He prefers to bring me with him, wherever he goes. I am happy in his company as well.

And Miriam: Where did she go without her husband? To rest, fleeing the heat: The mountains. To Pladjoe with Viruly, and to Lembang. To escape him: Down the wild Magdalena, that *terrible stream*. Milwaukee, Connecticut, the future. On her couch, like me, or in bed: deep into her own mind.

How It Starts. 1939. Milwaukee, midsummer: twilight gives way to fireflies' tracings over the lawn, her cigarette their deliberate, earthbound mirror as she brings it to her mouth, inhales, lets go. Saturday nights, questions scrawled on white paper, darkened rooms where she imagines she might be seen, even while every answer misses its mark. Will she embark on an ocean journey, fall in love, succeed at anything, break free? Will this be her only life?

She's been tucking money away, five dollars here and ten there—from her short-lived textile business, gifts her mother and grandmother sent her, magazine publications and lectures. She can buy a piano. *Brutus has the herr-im-haus idea that anything I want is entirely unnecessary.* The question: who decides? She can go to Europe, with him or without; to Boulder for the writers' conference. She has the forty dollars tuition sitting in her jewelry box, and plenty for travel. *It is my own money.* He doesn't want her to have it, the little bit of power that it brings.

Chris, on the other hand, strategizes with me on negotiating raises and retention packages, reminds me how often women undervalue themselves. He is internationally famous in his field, but I'm more often featured in newspapers because of readings, a Guggenheim, my appointment as state poet laureate. He forwards the articles to our provost with notes about how often I am recognized at the farmers' market and the movies.

Once, when I am introduced to a scientist Chris has mentioned, I say, "I'm Chris Johnson's wife," just as Chris would do on meeting one of my colleagues.

The man carefully explains to me, "You're much more than someone's wife."

Who decides? Who has the right to explain what is visible or invisible?

Again that year, Walter hadn't wanted her to go to Milwaukee. *He didn't want to have to get his own dinner.* She felt as full as ever of a desire she couldn't locate, much less define. *It would interfere with my duties.* Andy's conception, the packets she'd found in Walter's pockets. *I haven't believed him at all, of course, since.* But that she would write later, in Cuba, perhaps to justify herself. For now, to think about it did no good.

Two sides. She didn't approve of the company he kept when she was gone. *He prefers being with men with whom he can revel in obscenity, and with flashy sexy women.* But if she would stay with him, he swore he would keep to her. He would stop going into the field. He wouldn't think about Clara. He was sure of it.

Only slightly foolish women like him.

Why had his own wife never been among them?

At the end of summer, he joins her. As ever avid, and she—

Feels her submission. The first few nights, he's rough, and she is tender, so when the burning starts she barely notices. She prefers not to think about anything down there. *Adjustment.* But the burning gets worse.

Back in Shreveport, home from the doctor, she goes through the children's things. Sorting, piling, packing. She's been at it for hours when she hears the car door. She has trouble facing him, as if the shame is her own. He will deny everything, but the culture says what it says. A dose of sulfa this morning, a second in the afternoon, and already the itching and discharge are better.

He tells her, *"If I'm ever unfaithful to you, it'll only be physical, & because I can't help it!"* If, if, if. What would I have done? If I hadn't wanted Chris, or he me, what then when one of us grew angry, whether or not we knew why or at what? She turns away. *Trying to justify himself, denying in the same breath, that he'd ever had any woman but me.* She shuts a suitcase. Where will she go on her hundred dollars' worth of freedom? Back to Mandy? *Your mention of the Saturday night sessions makes me homesick.* She misses the old illusion she may become legible, despite the weekly proof her secrets are safe. She misses being a child, even under Mandy's thumb. She will never be a child again.

Silent, she turns from Walter and goes up to bed. Silent through the long fall and Hitler's march into Poland; through the

230

coldest winter on record. She huddles under blankets, stares at iced-over windows, neither writes nor sews. In February, at last, a letter to Mandy. Not from Miriam, from Walter. *Maybe I can throw my hat in without having it thrown out.* Miriam writes nothing. September 1939, as Germany invades Poland, to April 1941, nineteen months, not a word. She is mute, immobile.

And I am mystified. Maybe I mistook the dates; maybe I'm missing a folder. I ransack files, imagine letters lost, burned with the others, tossed when Joan was clearing out my grandmother's house. But her letters to Mandy from Ada and Shreveport arrived boxed and complete, the documents of a shared obsession, in order, labeled in Mandy's impossible scrawl. Nineteen months, the length of their engagement. *He has made me wait too long.*

What My Mother Remembers: Their dog, Tippy. We were happy. Going late into kindergarten. Prompted over lamb chops, she barely touches on her mother's post-partum depression, then immediately repeats, We were happy. There were badminton parties and barbecues. Her memory, including the annual brief sojourn in Milwaukee, can't explain the gap. What does a child recall? To create what story, expanding or contracting events to fit? We always. We never. Happy. What could she be talking about? Perhaps only that they stayed in one place a while. My mother had friends; she went to school.

Children retain everything, imprinted. They choose what to know. To be favored, to be loved—are they the same? Who is happy? The journals tell me my mother was Miriam's favorite. Even Walter, who wrote almost nothing of Peter's infancy, raved about her.

"I could see who was important," she says. She is sure she was never loved. I have always known I was. Wasn't I?

The letters, for example, from Walter. For years, I have said Miriam burned them. Is it the truth? What she told me? A family legend? My own invention? I don't remember. You might say I'm on my own.

What My Uncle Peter Remembers: She was hospitalized.

Offhanded, as if I already knew. He can't say for what or how long. Their mother needed a rest. What was a child to make of this? And I, all these years later?

I remember my father's sabbatical in Italy, taken without us when I was ten. What were they thinking? A mood, a darkness. One winter afternoon I trudged two miles to the florist, used all the money in my piggy bank to buy my mother daisies, all I could afford—as if I, or anyone, could have filled the black hole where her happiness should have been. As if I could fill it now. Day's eyes: in summer, they grew in the yard like weeds. I left them on the doormat and rang the bell. She wept when she saw them, pretended they were her favorites. The first time she'd hugged me in weeks. He was gone six months—or was meant to be but returned early. Which? Who said he could go? Who decided he would come back?

When, during all my childhood, would I have said we were happy? When not?

Miriam reappeared, Peter remembers, speaking of herself in the third person: "Mommy needed a rest." Said the doctors "took a tuck in her muscles and sewed them back together." What rupture needed repair?

Finally, a postcard from Walter to Mandy, September 17th, 1940, San José, Costa Rica, his new base. *Hope you are all OK and that the Link tribe is not too much trouble.* In the gap, the Shreveport house has been dismantled; Miriam and the children have landed in Milwaukee. A November letter says he will fly in from Havana for the holidays. The world rumbling with war, Walter tweaking Mandy: *I want to tell you I am all for the ENGLISH.* The war still looks small from their distance, local, the sides they take still tribal, at least in Mandy's case.

Miriam's hand at last, April of 1941, on a postcard to Mandy from Missouri. Passing through. *Forgot my fountain pen. Shreveport tomorrow.* April 25th, a postcard from Miriam Joan, New Orleans. April 26th, a telegram. *Arrived Hotel Monteleone last night everything fine sail eleven tomorrow.* April 27th from the ship. *It was hard to make up my mind to come on board, but I couldn't turn back again.*

Months lost. Between Septembers, she lay in bed. Which bed? Through the coldest winter, she dreamed of being trimmed and tucked, opened and repaired. Frozen. Immobile.

Then *I couldn't disappoint him again.* Miriam sailing toward him at last. Later, she would write, *It took me many months to reassemble myself.* Months he paced empty rooms while she decided to come, changed her mind, decided again. Eight months he spent waiting until the record recommenced. He promised, when they moved to Shreveport, they would never move again. It was a promise she asked him to make but not, I think, one she wanted him to keep. She is on board a ship, moving. From here on out, every move will be the last. Stillness and stability, change and motion. What does she want? To be on the move forever, but not with him. *Chin up, Mandy—we'll be back soon.*

She will send a few stories for her final, half-hearted effort, a correspondence course she takes through *Writer's Digest*, stories reworking—or not—what she did in Shreveport. No more translations or articles, nothing meant for a stranger to see. The poems she will send me when I am in college, like the poems I find in her files, are those of a young woman, restless and yearning, which my mother uses as evidence she never grew up and I take to mean she stopped writing poems. But after that long winter and its searing cold, she sets her younger self and its ambitions aside. No more adventure. Not for now.

Where will I find her? A year here, a year there. Eight months in a hotel, some unknown number in an asylum—a word I use thinking not institution but sanctuary, refuge, shelter.

CHAPTER 19

NO MUSIC LEFT

*Never to be a foreigner again, being keenly alive with
all faculties, quick & undulled by familiarity and
sameness—the gods forbid!*
MIRIAM'S JOURNAL

IT IS ALMOST as though I had never lived anywhere else. In an
old black Ford, she rumbled through San José's muddy streets,
which had no names or numbers. *Start from some known point,
go so many blocks one way, so many another, until one reaches
a green house, then it's two doors beyond, next to the shop and
across from the church.* She hired cook, house-and-garden boy,
laundress. Applied herself to learning Spanish.

New friends Anita and Evan took her to visit the family gold
mine—more Americans pulling money from the ground, leaving,
mostly and as usual, a toxic mess, though they didn't see it that
way. It had been so long since she'd held horseflesh between her
legs. They climbed through the cloud forest, mists parting to blue
views of the Pacific, the world opening in glimpses. *Sunday we
collected the most beautiful and various ferns and little trees I
have ever seen.* Back in San José, she planted her new ferns in the

garden, their tender fronds unfolding under her windows, fated to die without their cloud bath.

Walter could feel the world rumbling into war, drawing the U.S., drawing Roosevelt, *"the big blowpot."* Japanese planes, fast-moving shadows, troubled the waves where U-boats lurked, invisible. As trade routes shut down, the drive to find oil in the Americas grew—energy independence, urgent then as now, meant the U.S. controlled its own oil and preferably everyone else's, especially in its back yard. Local governments provided natural resources, the U.S. expertise and technology to get them out of the ground.

In the office, men scoured newspapers and speculated about troop movements and munitions stockpiles. Three junior geologists enlisted. Two secretaries. *The reconnaissance falls on me.* When his confidential secretary enlisted, he wished Miriam had kept up her shorthand. He wrote her from Haiti, Havana, Santo Domingo. These letters she kept when she burned the rest, proof she may be part of history.

I imagine war scraping clumsy feet across Europe, south over Asia—the fight against fascism from this distance clearer and cleaner than the wars we fight now over oil. "Piracy," FDR said into the radio—the *Greer*, the *Sessa*, the *Steel Seafarer* torpedoed in neutral waters, flying U.S. flags—and Congress extended the draft, placed a crude-oil embargo on Japan. Walter set out under that moving shadow: Cuba, Guatemala, Honduras, Chile, Bolivia, Argentina. *There is a tremendous under cover influence going on there. There were already too many working from the inside—* the Germans and Japanese—*when the rest of the world was idle.* They had footholds in Central and South America; they wanted the Panama Canal. *It is time to kick them out of here lock stock and barrel.*

Through space and time, news arrived. She listened to American radio when she could get it, familiar accents coming in under the crackle of bad weather. *There has been plenty of Nazi activity here.* One night, late, she fiddled the knobs, ear pressed to the speaker, and heard German through the static. *An illegal station.* A call to Aryan blood. She felt a rush of guilt, just because she understood and so was fingered <u>there</u>, alone in the dark. *Marta Fassel—her new friend, German and Jewish—told a lot of stories about their escape from Europe, which was harrowing. Now the Black List has been published, which is tough on some people, but all to the good, mostly.*

August, September. Walter again did his own measuring, mapping, note-taking—a geological jack-of-all-trades. Late on their fourteenth anniversary, he wrote her from Panama. *He seems to be perfectly willing to go on with me as wheelhorse.* A warm, fragrant darkness, Walter remembering his youthful dreams. The two of them under a tent in the bush—or in the office, with her typing his letters or taking shorthand, the impossible sexiness of her working alongside him. She fell for his fantasy one last time. The morning after she got his letter, she drove downtown, found a nondescript grey building with no number, and signed up for shorthand lessons. *If he really wants me when he comes back, I'll be ready.*

But when she was there in front of him, he could hardly remember his wooing mood, the distance in which he could make her what he imagined, though when he returned home he found only her. Where does power lie? In money, in time? *Woman's place is in the home, as manager, mother, servant, and mistress—and that's all she should ask.* Then why did he keep dangling other possibilities? If he wanted to make a romantic gesture, why not just buy the diamond bracelet she wanted?

He says I'm a dissatisfied woman. Yes.

She stopped going to her German-owned music shop. *Could you call Gram's and ask them to send me <u>at once</u> Collection Letolff No. 327, Clementi, Sonatas Celebres?* She cultivated the Fassels. A Dutch couple, also escaped from Europe. Costa Ricans. Minnigerodes, Tylers, Morton Blumberg *(head of the Republic Tobacco Co., a Virginia Jew, old-family and a swell egg)*, people she loved to be around. *Swift, sparkling repartee, intellectual with a wide knowledge of literature and the arts.* She added Lane, the new American minister. *A gent told me he'd asked Frances Campbell if she had been here for cocktails, and she said, "Mrs. Link has the nicest cocktail parties in town!"*

Hilarity flared under a lengthening shadow. When he was home—rarely, briefly—Walter was tight-lipped and occupied. She worried she might not get home for the summer. *They've just taken another ship off the United Fruit run.* U-boats loaded with torpedoes crept into every sea. The U.S. government armed every boat that floated.

December 6th. Pearl Harbor. At first, in spite of the shock, daily life changed little. Then the military commandeered transport planes as well as merchant ships. Maybe she should pack up the kids, fly home while she could. *I'd sort of hate to be marooned here.* But Walter knew how things went on the docks and in the shabby little airports. She and the kids could be offloaded anywhere if someone with priority came along, could find themselves cooling their heels for days, even weeks. *Being stuck in Managua for instance would be bad.* She could guess what really worried him— not that she and the children wouldn't get home, but that she would never come back. *Sitting on my tail doesn't agree with me. I'm not so screwy as to account for my constant state of rebellion.* When he got home from the field, she knew, he wanted his wife sitting in the parlor, kids bathed and placid in pajamas, waiting to be kissed. Another fantasy. *I suppose he feels that if he's stuck here, we might as well be too.*

He wasn't stuck. In the morning, he was off again.

Hanging over everything, the sense of a hard and bloody job.

There can be only one way. In the field, Walter felt the pressure of his country's need—his own need to meet that pressure, to be seen meeting it. When he traveled north, winter seemed colder than usual, its air, day and night, darker. *We are in it very deep.* He felt, acutely, the differences between wartime and geological time. He could only work as always, day and night, with deliberate speed. He hoped someone would notice. *I hope that the U.S.A. ends up being the most imperialistic nation in the world. It is necessary for us to be the big dog with the big stick.*

The committee to organize war work.

Walter's New Year letter, Mandy's first stamped by a censor.

The shortages beginning. *Could you get me the Clementi Sonatas (not Sonatinas) in any edition? There is no music left here.*

Her sukiyaki party, Japanese food not yet untouchable, everyone sitting on the floor like in Batavia laughing and talking until well after midnight. *Then somebody got an idea.* The trails up Poás were steep and slick with mud, but the horses they borrowed from the dairy farm at the base of the mountain were working animals, rough-gaited. Miriam's curls unwound into limp strings, water streaming into her eyes. She started singing— *the old German songs* in a burst of defiance, the Fassels joining in, then Costa Rican folk songs the kids had brought home from school. By the time they reached the crater, it was nearly seven, light finally reaching the bowl below. *Infinity filled with fog.* The lake, the view—everything faded into mist. So much for seeing the sunrise.

Only the right people could change everything. New people coming in, more all the time, *military mission and other, more uniforms than I've ever seen.*

The important things: *I feel useful, and I'm not alone any more. When Brutus comes home, it will be quite complete—except I won't be independent anymore.* He would, in other words, upend everything.

241

In Haiti he was offloaded to make way for a couple of colonels and waited three days for a seat. He reread his letters from Miriam—only three in as many weeks. *There must be a flock of letters wandering around the Caribbean, entertaining the censors.* The way things were now. *But I think I've spared their modesty—they won't need to write Whew on them!*

More uniforms. In cities overrun by soldiers, on the airplane, even now, home at last, carrying his bags through San José's little airport, he was aware of his civilian clothes. He edged his tailored shoulder through knots of enlisted men to the curb, where his wife waited behind the wheel and his children bounced in the back seat. When a uniform walked by, Miriam turned her head to watch, and his sons, slack-jawed, leaned over the front seat.

How tired he was. The war created new permits and reports, censorship, customs hassles. He had of course looked into enlisting, sought advice from officers in San José, even from a major, a gallery of ribbons and brass decorating his chest, on a flight to Haiti. They all said the same thing. His work was *vital, very urgent.* Only he could do it. On his last expedition, the army had sent soldiers to help in the field. He couldn't be spared for the army; the army, then as now needing fuel, spared itself for him.

At home, he listened to the radio and chewed his cigar while Miriam emptied his pockets of the trinkets he'd stashed for her—a little carved frog and jade pendant from Peru, *very rare.* No bracelet. In his trunk, she found dresses and a suit from New York for herself and new suits for him, *one very swanky, and a dinner jacket* he would don that night when she wore her new gown. Molten gold, my mother remembers, falling in waves, so glamorous—as I remember my own mother dressing for parties in the sixties and seventies, long, brightly colored Dior and Pucci gowns, how she would let me powder her bare back, the smells of talc, hairspray, and Joy. This summer, as I help her go through the closet in the spare room, she pulls out a halter maxi with a spray of flowers down the skirt. I text a photo of it to my niece, the model, tall like Joan with a waist and hips, who immediately texts back, Yes!

Late that night, Miriam tuned the radio for news—static, more static, then, sudden and clear, a report from the Indies. *Palembang, Soengei Gerong, Pladjoe—all blasted to bits.* Stunned, she translated the Dutch for Walter. *I wonder where everybody is— Beelie, Shorty, Ed, Hetty, Frans, the refinery gang.* Her memories, bright and shimmering, gone jagged. They might have been there, she and Walter, the kids. Almost were. Where was Jons? She shivered, and he stroked her hair.

The war had never seemed so close. *If only they can hold Java!* He regretted having taken his pistol obediently to be registered. This evening, Lane had told him he wouldn't get it back. *I could account for several parachutists, anyway, with my five bullets.* This was what it meant to be a civilian—half-dressed, unarmed, sitting in the dark while your wife trembled in your arms.

The gaps in the record now are literal gaps in the letters, censors snipping travel details, flight schedules, stray remarks, giving still another way for me to read between the lines. He was on his way to—a neat excision for her mind to float through, nowhere, anywhere. But she had never worried about his going and coming back. Instead, she tried to track down her old friends in Palembang, *the refinery blown up*—who might still be there (put into a camp, into a brothel; beaten, starved—all this would come out later), who might have gotten out, scattered where. *Java and Bali—they'll never be the same.* No place would. As Walter had predicted a decade before, Java, Sumatra, Bali, Borneo, all the 17,502 islands that would become the Republic of Indonesia would go to war against the Dutch before they'd even finished with the Japanese. Once they started, they kept fighting until the dictators remaining were their own. I remember the paintings at Bali's Neka museum—intricate attention diverted from the invisible world to the visible, demons in uniform rather than sarongs blocking passage, machines instead of dragons spiraling from the air, ablaze.

Here, air-raid practice, endless bandage rolling. *There is a curious sense of waiting.* She still thought about putting their goods in storage and getting the kids onto an airplane. *I'd like to metamorphose like a grub and become someone quite different and more interesting and useful.* She dreamed alternately about Rosie the Riveter, her bed in Milwaukee, steering an ambulance across a bombed-out field, one night's sleep without fleas. *I'm getting quite expert at catching them if they just sit still for a moment.*

He'd finally been given flight priority, so unless there was a general or some useless congressman trying to get on board, Walter couldn't be bumped. He was reading a biography of Simón Bolívar, who had also traveled those mountains and deep jungle, on foot and mule. Bolívar was just another fellow, like Walter, *like millions of others. They are all humans to the core, mostly alone— bewildered and striving for that elusive thing.*

Happiness. Greatness. Love, I think, the greatest of these, but he wouldn't have agreed. From his hotel in Quito, he wrote, *Those who can do things beyond the personal desires or wants are the men who become great—there must be an ideal, dream or vision.* What, in the field, he had worked so hard to do: see beyond himself, into the underlying structure that would tell him where to find what he wanted. *They acted in a time when something was needed.*

In a time. I will never find them now.

What good would he have done as a private in the infantry? Walter knew how lucky he was, stepping every day onto an airplane or a new pavement with work to do, priority.

This probably bores you a whole lot, he wrote, so I guess I will stop.

The trip had been arduous—at every layover, he'd had to produce maps and charts and graphs as incomprehensible to the censors as they were suspect. *Then the army, navy and the marines and F.B.I. all get a shot at it and since none of them are geologists it takes a long while to get all the stuff out of hock.* In Cuba, he cleared the censors at last to learn his seat had been given to a man wearing a brown suit and a face so forgettable Walter turned his head and it vanished. The mysterious face gave him another idea. *The Germans and the Japs built up their great intelligence systems by using every citizen who left their country.* Why not him? He had experience with corporate espionage and the perfect cover: Haiti, the Dominican Republic, all of Latin America—he moved over land and sea, bearing inscrutable documents. What else could he bear? *I have offered my services.*

At last he got onto an overnight flight to New York, a plane flying dark. Walter looked out the window. Wing, air, earth—all black, except where the lights of cities and towns appeared then vanished, signs that made him feel like a shadow moving through the night, indistinguishable.

What happened? He stopped agonizing about enlisting, stopped obsessing, stopped complaining. Was never bumped again. After this trip, the letters are silent about his service. Years later, he told his children he'd been a spy during the war, but there are no records, at least no public ones, and he's not talking.

What I know: he would have kept trying. *It is like the geologist who climbs the mountain to look at another—yet something unexpected might happen at any time—and so it is here also—*

Fleas, the doctor said—male, Latin, perhaps wondering what her marriage would bear. He prescribed a powder for *down there* and three weeks in bed. *I'm just taking a rest cure.*

Out of the blasted world news trickled. Van Loon sent his Lives and news of Viruly, safe in Canada, along with two pages of Viruly's letter. *He had asked all the American consuls in Canada about me, but couldn't locate me.*

Not a rest but a change. As always she felt it coming. *I've accomplished nothing beyond producing three nice kids.* What, she wondered, would justify her existence, not to the world but to herself? *I'm going out on my own by god, and put my brain, if any, to work.* Not being a wife; not even being a mother, even now the ticket to female legitimacy, without which no woman is deemed quite adequate regardless of her accomplishments. *I should have got it out of my system before I got married.* "It" being what, herself? It was the ambulance, I think, she was made for—she could drive anything—if only she could have moved herself, if she hadn't been still Mrs. Link, Muckie, Mommy: fixed.

In the end, she didn't ask permission. She knew how to move herself. She stripped the house bare. About the crabs, she never said a word. In June, when he got back, she, the kids, and everything but his personal possessions and clothing were gone. But not for good, not yet. In August, he would join her in Milwaukee as always. Then she would pack up again, her few permanent belongings. This time, he made no promises about the last move. They were going to Havana, and they both knew now he would keep moving until he got the Chief's job in New York, however long it took.

The place looks deserted, he wrote. *There isn't enough noise and confusion around, and the chickens are also gone.*

CHAPTER 20

INTERLUDE:
CALCULATION

THEIR HOUSE IS FANCIER than the perfectly nice casa particular, a private home offering bedrooms for rent, where my mother and I will stay with a family in Mirador. My mother, who wants to see Havana again, recalls twenty-foot ceilings, servants' quarters, servants built in, all backing up on the Biltmore Yacht and Country Club, which they simply called "the beach," *very swanky*. By the time we go, the yachts are gone, but we swim in the Caribbean and lunch on the broad shaded terrace.

Walter is away, of course. She goes to a company open house in a new dress.

The men say, *"Boy, does he have a reputation in Panama!"*

"He told the guys that Havana was the lone man's paradise."

"He says he leads the perfect life—he doesn't have to stay home all the time." Where he keeps her.

"Does he have a collection of pictures! You must have seen

Hay

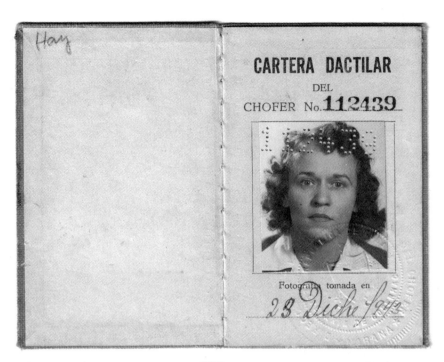

CARTERA DACTILAR
DEL
CHOFER No. **112439**

Fotografía tomada en

23 Dicbre 1949

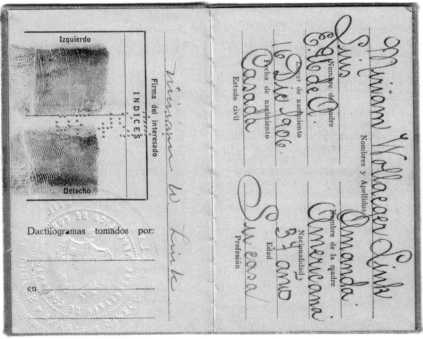

Izquierdo

INDICES

Derecho

Firma del interesado

Miriam W. Luik

Dactilogramas tomados por:

en

Nombres y Apellidos Miriam Wallaeger Luik

Nombre del Padre Luis Alde Q.

Lugar de nacimiento 16 Dic 906.

Fecha de nacimiento Casada

Estado civil

Nombre de la madre Amanda

Nacionalidad Americana.

Edad 34 años

Profesión Su casa

them!" In imagination, they see her, head bent over photographs, looking. *An avid leer and wicked gleam.* His affairs, the organisms, privilege cloaked in male necessity all astonish my mother. Her brothers refuse to credit it. They prefer to believe she made up gonorrhea, crabs, everything. She has invented for her journal before, may even have reasons now to lie about this. But for his eyes, so many times, for years?

Her bare shoulder turns; a door closes. The room is hot. The moon drags itself low over the water. Where is Walter? Shot with poison darts, electrocuted by eels, sucked dry by leeches, carried over a precipice—what does she care? For the first time, she imagines his airplane spiraling in a blaze over the ocean, plunging nose-first in front of that huge, hot moon—not with fear, but with pleasure. *I'll be damned if I know how to go on.* She thinks about changing her name. Avoiding parties. *How expert and well-known Brutus is in his line—and I don't mean geology.* And never expert with her. The plane enters the sea, Walter, his face pressed to the window, watching her watch him, the French doors blazing behind her.

We are all blown up, though in slow motion. Neither of them knows for sure. *Fool or altruist?* The simple equation: if she leaves, he will stop supporting her and the kids. *If I stay with him, I'll have to go on pretending to love him, sleeping with him.* French doors, two terraces, servants. *God, am I torn between being a dutiful, righteous mother and an honest, strong person? Between wanting to hang onto material comfort, and the honest thing to do?* Her choice in self-sacrifice. Miriam has never been able to see into anyone's heart, much less her own. Could she make her own way? *How can I know?* Remember, I tell myself, my mother, failure was built in. More for her than for me, or even for Joan. A woman's body, not her mind, was all her currency and power; when it began to go, she kept her mouth shut and hoped for the best.

—infallible signs—and I closed my eyes!

Even reading her journals, he can't see her, any more than he can see himself.

My last little bubble of synthetic contentment and pretend-happiness lasted just three weeks. I won't have any more, even such flimsy bubbles, with Brutus.

She has been waiting so long for a little luck, for Walter simply to vanish. Given his work, it always was possible.

She has spent her youth on waiting.

It's almost gone.

CHAPTER 21

WHAT A WOMAN WANTS

EVERY DRESS SHE EVER WORE. Charm, athleticism, an ability to appear beautiful whatever she looked like.

Every city she lived in, every sea she sailed, a world that appeared open and uncomplicated as if it could be hers. Entitlement, lack of awareness, heedlessness, even more than I've got. Even more than I've got, the assumption of class privilege, in her case unquestioned. The privileges of femaleness with no cost; the privileges of exception; the myth of one's own beauty.

A full tank of gas, somewhere to go. No awareness of the messes we leave behind.

I have poems, novels, essays written and published. Every morning, I open the door on a page and walk into it. In the evening, I walk out again, into my husband's arms and our life, often complicated by who we are, by what we want for ourselves and each other.

Job Seekers

Geology runs in the family of Miss Joan Link, a senior from Havana, Cuba. Her father is a petroleum geologist and her mother was one of the first women geology majors to be graduated from Wisconsin. She hopes to take graduate work in mineralogy, although she says that women geologists are under definite handicaps.

To leave home behind, as he did. To be missed, as he was not. If I'd been like her, stuck in a house and desiring, who knows what I might have got up to?

The luxury of travel for my own purposes, where I want to go, alone if I wish, anonymous. Not in staterooms and suites, with valets and deck games and staff to teach me how to dance—but on my own itinerary. Setting out, I take my own direction.

Frequent-flyer miles enough to upgrade. My husband at home fretting or not while I traipse up into the mountains of Java and the neighborhoods of Bogotá and Medellín. I phone him with whatever device is to hand, usually one he's given me. Once, in the Amazon, I call from a satellite pay phone mounted on a pole in a clearing, miles from anywhere. As I hang up, the village chief gestures me into his house, where he sits me down and gives me a blow-gun and bow-and-arrow, for reasons I will never know.

When he leaves me at the airport to begin my trip to Antarctica, which will involve crossing the Drake Passage in a small National Science Foundation research ship—on the way down, through a gale—for the first time he breaks down. We will have only the phone in my dorm room, illicit late-night Skype calls. Where I am headed, there is no air strip. If something happens to either of us (illness, injury), I can't get back. Though I haven't told him this, I know one scientist died down there, and they had to put him out on the ice until the boat returned a month later. I reassure him that nothing will go wrong, but how can I know?

All along, I've believed his fussing had to do with gender, with his perception of my female vulnerability, but now I am beginning to wonder if I'm projecting. My own relationship to gender—my embrace and rejection, my love of ambiguity—may be even more muddied and complicated than Miriam's, than my mother's. I believe in biology, in this regard more than Chris does. I also believe in culture, in projection, in my own complicity and in his.

He has never thought of me as fragile, as any more vulnerable than he is. Maybe less so. Only, I can be headlong, much more than he, and more than a little preoccupied. We both know I could walk into or off of anything.

The vulnerability that shakes him is his own. He believes he couldn't do without me.

But when I tell my canniest friend our disagreements have nothing to do with gender, she laughs and points out the obvious: he has felt entitled to object to my going, and though I've resented this and worked myself around it, I haven't complained outright. I think of my grandmother, occupying herself, *subjecting* herself again. My mother, keeping house and three children during the long, cold winter of my father's sabbatical. Myself, while Chris built his remarkable career, before he always wanted me along. This could take centuries more to sort.

When I return, he's remodeled a room, torn out and replanted the entire landscape, found a fitness regime for me to learn, bought some new device for me to master, changes I keep time by, through which he exerts himself from a distance. This may be simply who he is: a leader of men. I stop reminding him he's not my boss, and tell him instead that I'm not his employee.

Meanwhile, like the phone I carry, all this shows me I have been kept constantly in mind. In truth, every change is thoughtful, meant to make me happy if not to make me stay put. It may take a few days, but unlike her, he forgives me. We settle back in to something not quite the same as what I left.

I want everything she had and everything I have too.

Permission. What my mother tried to give me, though she, like Miriam, never had it.

I have never required permission. Chris has never let me go, but he no longer stands exactly in my way.

Miriam should have been someone's child before she was a mother. She should at least have had that.

And my mother. Whose child should she have been?

CHAPTER 22

STORMY WEATHER

TIRED OF ROLLING BANDAGES and organizing committees, Miriam still wouldn't run off to drive a battlefield ambulance. Her motherhood presented a reality she couldn't contradict or contravene. In the morning paper, she read yet another story about Havana's teacher shortage, all those young men laying down chalk and red pencils to pick up arms. The article quoted Dr. Alvarado, the principal of the kids' school, exclusive, staffed by male teachers.

She put on her sleekest suit and drove the children to Burton Academy herself. *I told Dr. Alvarado that I'd like to be of help if I could.* In her now-fluent Spanish, she told him about her degree in geology, her music and German and French, her reading, her riding, her shorthand and typing, her handiness with rock pick and surveyor's rod; they talked until the lunch bell rang and the clatter of children filled the air. She could hear Walter's voice telling her how foolish she looked, with no experience but motherhood to recommend her.

Somebody's wife, the thing I've never been, not merely. But she'd tried.

Friday. The long weekend. By Wednesday, she'd stopped hoping; Thursday, the school lost another teacher. She started reading. *250 pages in the Am. Hist. book and 100 in the Mod. Hist. book. Started Monday, nervous as a cat.*

The ground shifting. Somebody. *I'm not neglecting my children or my home, or gone off half-cocked.* It was the thing Walter feared, for good reason.

And Mandy? *Pettie dear—teaching children is the biggest & most important of jobs after that of being a mother.*

History, English for the Cuban kids. *I'm learning more every day, & loving it, & feeling, o God, useful.* In her study halls, soft breathing, pages turning. She adopted a *problem child (all the teachers commiserated with me having him).* He stayed after school and so did she, working into late afternoon, breathing together. *He's my pet, although nobody knows it. He has a quick mind & more active thought & imagination than any 20 others.* Evenings, she repaired to bed to mark papers and plan lessons. *Peter and Miriam usually sit on my bed for their last studying or reading or a game of chess.* Their yellow heads leaning into each other, pages turning. Or she went out—*spontaneous, last-minute dinners, bowling, and just sitting around drinking.* Closing the bar at the Biltmore.

Mandy: *It's getting to seem very long between your letters & I miss them.*

Miriam: *I still feel as though I were marking time.*

Mandy: *Tell me what you are thinking.*

Miriam:

Then Walter was home, talking about moving again. Lima, maybe. Bogotá? Another little bomb dropped at breakfast, not up for discussion. His right to decide, invisible, assumed. She was sure he'd asked to move because she was happy, because she was doing something that had nothing to do with him.

Dr. Alvarado asked her to continue in the fall. *I hadn't intended to go on indefinitely*—but the work, having to get up at seven and teach her classes whether or not she felt like it, brought discipline, a purpose.

Maybe, Walter said yet again, she could become his secretary. His current man was apt to be transferred or drafted. She didn't believe him, and neither do I—though he asked her in person, not mooning over a letter in some lonely hotel room. *He's sneered at me too many times before.* Right then, watching him watch her, she made up her mind. She told him the school was counting on her. Her *black sheep* had scored third highest among the seniors on his IQ test. *All the teachers had to retract—& did, by gosh!* For a moment she thought Walter had more to say—congratulations? recriminations?—but he just went back to his newspaper. Neither of them knew, yet, what she'd done.

Then it was summer. She and the kids were off for Milwaukee, he on his way to Peru. Three months in her childhood bed with the shut-up hope chest that had never traveled with her at its foot—what did it hold now, for her to *dream over?*—sailing, swimming with the kids, séances once a week, sometimes twice. Three months of freedom. And the future.

He felt her slipping away, the Indes all over—but now he was jealous of sweaty adolescents and outdated history books. Somebody else is taking my place—he couldn't get the song out of his head.

Though nothing took, in Oklahoma, Shreveport, San José, she hadn't stopped looking, had never for a moment stopped being looked at.

In September, Walter stayed in Havana for almost a month. *He seems to be profiting by it.* Every day, the five of them walked together to the beach, where they loafed and swam. She and

Walter played golf then sat on the terrace drinking rum cocktails with whomever was around. Bill Wilcox, a little man with a gleam, dapper like Bert, turned his head whenever she spoke. One night after supper, Walter handed another man's wife onto the dance floor, and Miriam stepped onto the terrace for a cigarette. Bill followed. They looked over the water at the moonrise—the sequins on her dress glimmering—but she could feel him watching her, his gaze lighting her. Behind them, the singer crooned a sleepy lagoon. She imagined being marooned, just the two of them. The moon dazzled even the black water.

Late in the season—mid-October—a hurricane gathered in the Caribbean. *There's been no plane service*—days of squalls, wind flinging rain against the house, two short blocks from the sea. *I can hear it roaring.* She telephoned to reassure Mandy she and the kids were ready to ride out the storm, even with Walter away again at last. Over the wire, Mandy could hear Miriam's voice crackling, nervy excitement, spirits high as the winds.

Bottled water, canned goods, bandages, iodine. She drove home through water crashing in sheets against the windshield. *The latest dope is that the storm is at the Isle of Pines, straight off the South coast.* The air was wild but hot. She left the French doors open and helped the servants take up rugs.

Almost midnight. Mandy gets a busy signal. *They say you shouldn't worry.* She rereads the newspaper, fiddles with the radio, finally dials Mrs. Marth. *It will be bad, but they will be safe, & she continued to say that.* Playing the odds.

Alone with the dark and weather. Miriam must have dozed, then a crash overhead—Something big hitting the house—

Just after 2:00 a.m. The wind howling and the house shifting and straining—

Mandy tries the phones again. The lines still down, only wind—

Six a.m. Full force. Rain poured in around the windows. The sea lapped the lawn, reaching the front porch before Miriam

258

sensed the wind faltering, changing, and, like that, the flood dragged itself back out to sea. Late in the afternoon, she took a break from wringing out towels and stepped outside. The worst of the storm had passed, but when she leaned against the air it held her.

That night, even under the gale, they slept. Woke to perfect quiet, a blue sky, their biggest tree leaning heavily against her bedroom windows. There were trees down all over the neighborhood, the wires with them, roads impassable, shingles and shutters strewn everywhere, broken dishes, books, table leaves. She picked up a rag doll, torn and sodden, from her front walk. Where exactly, she wondered, was Walter? Hadn't she always been going it alone? When she turned to go back into the house, she flipped the milk box open out of habit, knowing the truck could not have gotten through. Yet there were her gallon of milk and pint of cream, still cold, sweat clinging to the glass. And, picking his way down the road around and over fallen trees and pieces of house, Bill Wilcox was coming to find her.

I'm writing this by candlelight.

Mandy stays near the radio all day. Four killed, three hundred injured. *Most small wood or thatched houses down.* Still, she imagines birds' nests, crockery, shards of glass, entire trees flying through the air, what might have happened to anyone standing in any wrong place. *I hope you live in a safer place soon.*

With Christmas coming, Miriam went to parties, shopped, wrote to Mandy. *Bill Wilcox gave me a Lektrolite—it looks like a big lipstick, and you just stick your cigarro into the end and drag.* Barely contained, Miriam couldn't help revealing herself. *Had dinner with my pet Gonzalezes Thurs. night—met them through Bill Wilcox.* Did Mandy read what was in front of her, not between the lines but in them, on every page? *Yesterday good old Wilcox took me sightseeing in old Havana.* The streets where I walk with my mother under gorgeous, decaying buildings. Along the waterfront Malecón, waves crashing over the walls, where, when I walk alone, young men approach me hoping I'll trade a drink, a meal, even a bed, for a little company. The official currency is pesos, but nobody wants them. Another artifact of history and U.S. power: only dollars are worth anything outside the government stores, and inside the stores there is little worth buying.

Walter was waiting to hear about his next transfer. *I don't give a hoot where he goes.* Bogotá, Caracas, Tulsa. To him, she said nothing. For Mandy, she had questions. If they moved again, would Mandy take the two older kids? More importantly, would Mandy talk to Mrs. Marth for her? She felt foolish, as always, asking—but she couldn't see beyond her own back fence, sky glimmering through the tattered trees. Even bad intelligence, in uncertain times, was better than nothing.

Wilcox is a most useful gent to have around.

He wasn't rich. He was just a manager for the United Fruit Company—like Miriam's father, not an especially good one. But it didn't matter. *As you can gather, life is no longer lonesome here.*

She still wanted something. A sleepy lagoon. She could feel what she wanted, her heart humming with his. The question was, how to get it?

After he delivered his maps and charts to the New York office and the papers he carried secretly to an anonymous midtown building, he stood under holiday decorations at Saks. *He told the shopping advisor he wanted something for his mistress, and she said immediately, "We know just what you want!"* The saleswoman pulled out silk and ribbons and turned them under the light: a peach ensemble frothed with lace; a black corselet; a teddy in the blue he loved on her, silk chiffon. He fingered the wisps, felt them warm under his touch. Didn't even consider the diamond bracelet she'd asked for so many times. Finally, for something not so far from the price of that bracelet, bought all three. Still believing she must want what he did. Still believing his desire—singular, focused—could give them both a reason to stay.

So now I've got what the well-dressed mistress in New York is wearing. That guy has a sense of humor! Little did he know. She laughed, ran her fingers through the fabrics then lifted the garments by their delicate straps. Shutter opening, closing. The eye catching and holding. She was years past imagining his eyes on her when she unbuttoned, revealing whispers of lace against her skin. She was already looking beyond him, into next week and the next, when he would become an idea, air wafting through silk as she lifted it to dance and shimmer between them.

CHAPTER 23

INTERLUDE:
JUST ABOUT RIGHT

DRINKING MOJITOS on the terrace of the Hotel Nacional. Walking the Malecón arm in arm, waves crashing over the balustrade. Eating paella in a private paladar or flavorless rice in a State-run cafeteria with the expat son of one of my mother's friends, in Havana all these decades later to help the visibly failing revolution. Fidel is still alive and giving endless speeches. Batista has been gone a long time, but the streets are full of cars my mother might have driven back when they were new and shining, held together half a century and more with ingenuity, bits of wire.

She and I wander the old neighborhood, its huge houses, also new back then but now down at heels, looking for the one my mother remembers. Not that one, or that one. Finally, she stops at a lot vacant except for weeds and says, Here. Later, Andy tells her the house was torched in the revolution, along with the one next door where the owner, a Batista supporter, lived. James Cason, the head of the U.S. Interests Section absent an embassy, invites us for cocktails. He offers good scotch, otherwise impossible to find here, and carefully doesn't ask if we have permission to be in Cuba—which Joan, as she would have told him gleefully, does not. I have a letter from the State Department, but I will still be interrogated on my way home by a stern Marine young enough to be my son, who will treat me as if I am the child, opening and sniffing at the box of cigars James gave me as we left.

We poke through the now-abandoned beachfront apartment building, its walls and stairwells crumbling, where Miriam lived, walk the shore where she painted scenes we recognize—an island with a little ruined building on it, the point. We swim and lunch at the Biltmore, where Cubans are admitted only as guests of foreign visitors wielding dollars. There on a sofa in the upstairs alcove, a Cuban boy gave my mother her first kiss. Here, an exiled prince proposed. Like this island, which Miriam will flee in the year of my birth, barely ahead of Castro, she is suffused with memory.

Water under the bridge. All the family stories. A hurricane battering the house. A revolution building while Americans dance the night away in the Hotel Nacional. A view of the ocean—I am, you understand, making up even what she told me: how they lived in luxury, in history but caught up by personal drama, oblivious to the lives around them, to the hardships of those who made their lives there possible.

Always, people on the streets stop me. More young men hoping I seek love. Abuelas who overhear my English and draw me from under the trees, away from buildings where we might be overheard. At lunchtime, schoolgirls pour onto broken sidewalks and gesture me over to timba to their radios, their hips tracing wildly intricate patterns on the air. Every conversation I have on the cell phone I've rented, usable in Cuba and nowhere else, is being recorded. Some bored bureaucrat will hear me whispering to Chris, telling him I am fine but we may be overheard. Tenderness and rebuke. We won't shock the censors. Flyers in my hotel rooms feature near-naked girls and boys, barely pubescent: what dollars will buy.

Last picture as an entity,
Havana, 1945

Before coming, I spoke to a colleague who had visited on a state-run cultural exchange. Progressive like me, he'd been prepared to be impressed with the medical system and the country's commitment to the arts, and he was. I asked him about what I'd read—the young, even children, selling bodies; shortages of almost everything, especially decent soap.

"There was soap in my hotel," he said, taken aback. And there will be in mine too—real soap that lathers, like at home. Still, I pack an extra bag with travel-sized bars, shampoo, toothpaste. The hotels where I stay have comfortable new beds and arched hallways, redolent with polish, of history. The casas particulares tell a shabbier story, with mattresses as old as the antique cars and soap I supply myself.

Unlike my friend, we travel without guides. When we drive to Trinidad and Cienfuegos, the colonial hill town and coastal city where Miriam spent weekends in her husband's absence, we pick up hitchhikers, because outside cities hitchhiking is the transportation system and we need help finding our way where road signs deliver only slogans extolling the revolution. Unlike in Jakarta and Colombia, where the roads are choked with unruly traffic, here they are almost empty. Along the way, I give shampoo or soap to everyone I speak to. A bagful, and dollars, to the man who stops to change our flat tire. One woman we pick up on the way out of Trinidad takes my hands and weeps.

In Cienfuegos, I deliver a hundred roller pens, the kind I like best, to the writer's union. "We do not need charity," says the union officer there, and I say they are offered in friendship. Like the Indonesians, the Cubans threw out the U.S.-supported dictator, and who can blame them? Their own dictator will sicken and withdraw before the death that will bring dancing to the streets of Miami, but back then nobody predicted the Cuban flag rising over an embassy in Washington, ours in Havana, the scheduling of commercial flights anyone with dollars can take, the intricate dance of relations starting up then almost immediately thrown back into question.

I tell my mother: you were the favorite. As was her mother. Neither can believe. And me? I have a face in the mirror, the faces reflected in these pages, giving themselves up to the ever-changing present. What will my mother think of these stories I've fabricated from among possible stories? When the time comes to show her this, will she forgive the scenes I've imagined out of words?

The first time she hears me read from an early draft of the manuscript, I say to her, apologetic, I'm sorry. I know I must have gotten them wrong.

Actually, she says, her voice thoughtful, I think you got them just about right.

CHAPTER 24

MUSIC AND LYRICS

BRUTUS LEAVES THIS COMING *Sunday for Bogota, and won't come back.* Wishful thinking. January, 1945. They'd agreed, he reluctantly: she and the kids would see out the school year then go to Milwaukee for the summer.

Eight months. Why wouldn't she come with him now? He didn't know exactly what he was afraid of, only the feeling, familiar and knotted. Anything could happen. Time and space between them. Silence.

She had a laundry list of reasons to stay behind. Nothing she remembered about Bogotá was good. What she said to Mandy: *For once the kids should finish a school year, this climate is so much better for them now, it will be their last fling at this sort of life (golf, the beach, and the club so close).* She had her teaching. *I don't like the idea of walking out on my job, and I like Havana and the sunshine.*

So he vanished into damp and chilly mountains, and she stayed put. Out of sight. *Osbornes, Whites, and Bill Wilcox are waiting at the beach.* Wilcox replenishing drinks, whirling her onto the dance floor. All or nothing at all. They talked about books, philosophy, music; she felt beautiful smiling under his eyes.

Mandy still hadn't learned to read the oracles. *No letters for a long time are you all right.* Presence in absence. She refused to understand. She looked out the window at tired snow and bare trees but could not see the future. *You have slipped from the position of best correspondent among my children until you are below Constance.* But it was there, sap rising; even now buds began to swell.

Walter, too, had no word. Already March. *It is probably due to the way the mail is handled in and out of Cuba.* Longing, unease—he kept thinking he saw her on a street corner, his mind's eye composing her out of drizzle and mist. A trick. I've heard that song before. As soon as he looked, she vanished.

He wrote Mandy—a litany of complaints about his solitude, *her teaching apparently taking precedent over all else.* Though he had never set up a household before, he hoped to have everything done by August, down to furniture and dishes, so she would have no excuse to delay. *Perhaps someday I will make a good wife for some woman.* He would show her how to manage her job. *Wife, some woman.* He was always willing to work, but her work should have been beneath him, behind him. This is what being exceptional got her.

Sky-blue chiffon under her dress. *The well-dressed mistress.* Who was dreaming now? Moonlight becomes you. His lips on her ear. Bill, lighting her cigarette, touching her hand, leaning—

Miriam lying on a couch in Bill's apartment in Miramar, her head in his lap, his hands in her hair.

Walter writing her to come as soon as school ends. She must pack; she must write—what? Her lips at Bill's ear, his at hers. It can't be wrong. Question, answer. *We understand each other completely.*

She was thinking about happiness. *He is the most straightforward, honest, absolutely good and straight man I know—there isn't one single thing that I must overlook or condone.* This felt like truth. *I believe in him.* It can't be wrong.

By now, Mandy and Walter should have known better. Finally, a letter from Miriam to Mandy: one sheet. *Something terrific is brewing.* Mrs. Marth arrived a scant hour later.

What did Mandy believe? Candles guttering, no draft. Later, looking out the window as afternoon turned to evening, sleet to blizzard, she wondered, what? Buds swelled, but not to her eye. *Brutus seems uncertain of your feelings.* Did Mrs. Marth say this? He'd written, *The past eight weeks are a blank as far as my family are concerned.* Mandy wrote about the future, his and Miriam's, which she still assumed was the same.

Something terrific. Miriam was occupied, like a house or a country, shaping her interior to a new inhabitant. *Of course all Mrs. M. did was to sound off again on the subject of Brutus—and it is completely beside the point.* A question remained, *single, vital*; it had nothing, in her mind, to do with her husband. The silly woman was right about one thing only: Miriam wouldn't be going to Bogotá. *The whole picture will have changed.*

She signed her letter, drew out the checkbook. *It is all the money I will have earned to the end of June.* Less than the male teachers were making, but her own. *Will you please deposit it in your account immediately and leave it until I ask for it?* She rolled another page into the typewriter. April. Once she'd finished the year and dismantled the house, she would go to Milwaukee. And then—

Dear Brutus.

Another kind of limbo.

You will doubtless come to the same decision I've made. The whole thing can be arranged quickly and quietly, fairly and reasonably. Using carbon, making copies. Signed with her initials, *M.L.* It was her first unilateral gesture. Until now, the decisions had been his.

At the post office, she pushed the letters through the slot, out of her hands, no return. The right thing, finally done. It can't be wrong. Wartime South America. Delays, detours, evasive maneuvers, fuel shortages. Mail bags were loaded off airplanes and troops or army gear loaded on; bags sat in the corners of hangars and warehouses waiting for any plane or ship with room to take them one step farther. Her letter might wander from port to port on a slow boat, but she preferred to imagine a sleek hulk with wings, blue sky, straight lines: Havana, Panama City, Bogotá.

While she stamped the break done, Walter ordered furniture. *It is quite a responsibility to furnish a house for a woman because as a rule husbands have such obnoxious taste.* A bedroom suite, twin beds with a fashionable white wash to brighten the room. Two chairs for reading, a toy box for the playroom.

Across mountains, down a river, over the sea.

What would Mandy think? Beside Miriam on the love seat, Bill brought her fingers to his lips. *I had to be very sure indeed.* She rolled paper into the typewriter. *In case you are still wondering, it's Bill Wilcox. This is definitely not a sudden impulse, nor even—*

His mouth on the back of her neck. Bésame mucho. They went to the club for drinks; after dinner he took her dancing. Home again with the children, she realized her typewriter was at Bill's, the letter, interrupted mid-sentence, still in it. And so it went. *Writing is sort of extraneous, if you see what I mean—*

She took nearly a week to finish her letter. *I have found the man and the happiness I've been looking for since I was 15*, since she was taught she needed a man to be herself—the opposite of what I had to learn. Now, again, people told her she lit up the room. The man she'd been looking for told her every chance he got. *You wouldn't recognize me—no restlessness, no wondering what the hell it's all about, no nerves, no having to make the best of things, no making explanations and excuses for things that hurt or disgust me—no nothing that's wrong.*

Except Mary Wilcox, in Panama. *He hasn't lived with his wife for years.* Except Walter. *As soon as we can get loose from our respective entanglements, we will be married.* As long as she hadn't heard from him, she was free to hope for anything. *If Brutus is agreeable, I could even get my divorce here before I leave the end of June—.*

May already. The war in Europe, after that dark winter, suddenly finished. The airplane from Barranca skimmed between two peaks and began its precipitous drop over Bogotá's red-tiled roofs. Funny, I think as my own plane carries me over the mountains from Medellín to Bogotá, how even something as thrilling as flight becomes routine. As Miriam always said, *You can get used to anything.* Her voice in my head. The El Dorado airport lies farther out of town than the airfield Walter flew into, and we drop in gradually over a long valley, not plummeting between the peaks towering over the town. But the view thrills.

The Hotel Europa, new when they stayed there in 1927, stands in the old neighborhood in middle-class, Art Deco splendor. With no minder here, I have assured Chris I will be careful. Again, I place two fingers on my watch and send him my heartbeat, wait for his pulse to cross my wrist in return—the uncanny closeness of two people who have put no children between them: every decision, including whether to stay together or move apart, about just the two of us. Taking my key as I set out from the hotel, the clerk doesn't warn me about kidnapping. Only, I should hang tight to my bag.

I have no addresses—not for the office, not for the house, which none of his children ever saw—so I can only head hard uphill from the plaza, stretching my legs. Bogotá was already thriving and busy in the thirties, and more of it has been preserved than Medellín: the cathedral and its square; the arena where he watched bullfights, spellbound and repulsed; even the old building housing a restaurant recommended by Anthony Bourdain, where I eat a lunch my grandfather's Bogotá couldn't have dreamed of and my vegetarian husband never would—another reason to travel.

271

He walked through streets usually crowded with cars and horse carts, now empty. Everyone was at the Plaza de Bolívar celebrating—cathedral bells and a band wafted flourishes on the wind. Walking the streets of Candelaria alone, feeling loose and a little anxious after my constant supervision in Medellín, I wonder in which building he threw open heavy wooden shutters before finally picking up the small pile of envelopes on his desk and leafing through them—only one with her handwriting on it, very thin. The slightest breeze could have carried it away.

This is the logical time to face the facts and bring the break out into the open.

Walter flipped on the desk lamp, sat down.

The subject has been in your mind more than in mine.

Had it? *The break*—as if it were a given, established. *Doubtless. You haven't been happy any more than I have.*

Hadn't he? Resentment, children, drama—like her, like me, he'd threatened, more than once, to pack and go, wanting to get out from under his own anger and hers, wanting to make her think what her life would be without him. How he was her only safety. But the time was past when she couldn't afford to lose him. *I suppose that in the past 18 years I have done more things wrong than right.* Now, in the future he'd wanted her to see, he lived alone in these mountains, and she launched herself and her kids, their kids, not only out of his physical ken—he was used to that, lord knows—but beyond the reach of his authority, even his imagination. All those years he worried, as Chris does with me, that she would be removed from him by accident, misadventure, her own wayward step, and now she has removed herself decisively, on purpose.

He should never have let her take that job.

She hadn't given him a choice. *It's quite impossible for us to go on.* Already past this moment, she'd slipped the knot he'd meant to tighten, not realizing he'd lost his hold. A freedom I've always had and Chris enabled, a freedom to keep choosing, a freedom to return. This has been a luxury—not only in their time, but in ours.

The thing I wanted most I turned to Hate. A watery sunlight pulsed against the shutter, its light falling in stripes across the wooden desk, his hands capable of wielding any tool. *I don't want to plead with you or change your mind if it is so intolerable as it seems. It is wrong for us to live together if that is true.* He had to be steady, show strength, keep his pride. Poor Walter. *Whatever you say then will be final and if it is negative you will be bothered no more.* If only. Maybe if he had listened when she'd begged him not to move to Bogotá. He'd gone, as always, with his own judgment, consulted by company heads, leaders of men. Where had it left him? *I think there is a better than even chance and am willing to take it.* Back into the empty street. *p.s. If this should make any difference please wire me—thanks.*

As he approached the square, he heard speeches coming over loudspeakers, cheering and laughter. Every corner bar overflowed with the radio's jubilant voices. He was aware only of the two letters pressed together over his ribs, hers and his, heartbeat and answer. Of course, he was surprised to find the post office closed.

Around the corner, down the hill, I follow—the telegraph office door was open. The clerk sat with his feet up on the desk. Three other men lounged at the counter, talking and laughing; here, as behind every door, the radio played.

ANSWERING LETTER MAILED PERHAPS THINGS ARE NOT AS BAD AS WE THINK STOP WHY NOT RECONSIDER LOVE WALTER LINK

Love, Walter Link, as if she might mistake him for someone else. *Why not reconsider?* The clerk read his message back in halting English—*my answer, or my hope.* He paid and drove up the mountain to the almost empty house. She would not be alone there—but he'd made the same promise in Ada, Shreveport, San José. He had a good reason to break it. *I wanted to assure you and our children a proper living.* He wanted to be out.

Where they began their marriage; where it is ending. At Hotel del Salto, where they spent their vertiginous night over the falls, my driver refuses to get out of the car. In half-Spanish, half-

English, he tells me the place is infested by las fantasmas of the broken-hearted who have flung themselves into the gorge below. Una casa embrujada. I wonder if Walter remembered that place when his own heart was breaking.

She and Bill were together at his apartment, at the beach, at the bar, at the house Walter's salary still paid for. She loved to watch him talking to people, listening with interest *(he likes conversing with me!)*. She loved to dance with him, his lips beside her ear—Moonlight becomes you. What did it matter, if her hair went silver under these stars? After the children were in bed, they studied Spanish, drilling each other on the vocabularies of romance. Walter's cable came, a message from the past; she laid it aside. The break was a fact, done. She'd said her piece.

What were the children thinking? *I'm going to tell them in Milwaukee.* They liked to see their mother laughing but knew something wasn't right. Could see glances exchanged, touches light but freighted with desire.

Walter stayed that night alone in the new house, though there was hardly anything in it. *We are all blown up.* He shone a flashlight into the bedrooms he'd planned for each of the children. He lay down on one and then the other of the twin beds, imagining his long body against his wife's small one. At last, dawn broke, grey and damp. He had no razor, no food or coffee or servants. He opened the front door just in case. Of course it was too early for a telegram, and anyway she didn't have this address. Their address. He went to the office.

By noon, nothing. Nothing in early afternoon. At five, he put on his hat and walked back down the hill. The same clerk, bleary and hungover. No, nothing. He took up the pencil and tried again. YESTERDAYS LETTER SUGGESTS A TRY BECAUSE I THINK IT CAN WORK WELL STOP CABLE ME YOUR DECISION WHICH

WILL NOT BE QUESTIONED AND CONSIDERED YOUR FINAL
WISH HUMBLY AND HOPEFULLY Yet another holiday. *There is too much time to think.* The
office was deserted, but he waited until noon. STILL NO ANSWER
PLEASE LETS GO ON STOP He stopped at the apartment for his Dopp kit and a change
of clothes. The portable record player, a stack of 45s, a bottle of
whiskey. His old pistol in its box. At the house, he put on Jimmy
Dorsey. <u>Bésame mucho</u>. And if she did leave? He began to pour.
*Until something happens I can't stand it. My stomach is all full of
knots and they hurt like hell.* A matter of control. A broken coring
device or a river raging between him and his destination he knew
how to handle. *A fate I created myself.* Looking back, he could see
himself being unreasonable, ungenerous, mean, entitled. He had
seen it even in the moment, how he was pushing her, testing his
power, seeing how far he could go. *Many of the things were just
the opposite of what I really felt and wanted. If the occasion ever
arises or the chance ever again comes back, which it may not, and
I can't blame you, it won't happen again—and if it should I hope
you bash my head in with a mallet.* The gun at his elbow—in a
novel, it would have to go off, but he valued his life, and without
her watching, what was the point? *It is just you.* He was still
missing the important thing. Not what he wanted, but what she
wanted. Not to submit. To make her own decisions, even bad ones.

It was very late. He looked over his page woefully, wishing he
dared serenade her. <u>I can't begin to tell you</u>. He'd never been good
with words, so she'd always said, never been able to turn a phrase
toward sweetness. *What I would like to do is take you in my arms
and tell you what a fool I am, how wonderful you are and how
much you mean to me.* The bottle half gone. *Goodnight dearest
sweetheart.* While he is still hopeful, begging, I almost love him.
If only I could believe him. He put on a coat and walked down
the road. The rain had stopped. Moonlight silvering wet stones,
fresh air, frogs calling all around—he should have been enjoying
the night, but he only wanted to get that letter out of his hands.

275

Cuban All America Cables

ANTES

Commercial Cable Co. of Cuba

| COMUNICACIONES POR CABLE, LINEA TERRESTRE E INALAMBRICO CON LOS ESTADOS UNIDOS, CENTRO Y SUR AMERICA, CANADA, EUROPA Y TODAS PARTES DEL MUNDO | All America Cables and Radio | Cuban Commercial Cable | FECHA DE RECEPCION 8 - MAY 1945 |

CUBA 226 ESQ. A O'REILLY-HABANA **THE INTERNATIONAL SYSTEM** TELEFONOS: M-9801-M-9808

EL SIGUIENTE TELEGRAMA FUE RECIBIDO **"VIA CUBAN ALL AMERICA"**

W 89 BOGOTACOL 28 8TH

NLT MIRIAM LINK HAVANA BILTMORE
COUNTRY CLUB JAIMANITAS HAVANA

ANSWERING LETTER MAILED PERHAPS THINGS ARE NOT AS BAD AS
WE THINK STOP WHY NOT RECONSIDER LOVE

WALTER LINK

A second telegram set aside. A third. She still hoped he would stay tucked up in his mountains, almost out of mind. She hoped she might never see him again. But Walter had never been able to read nuance, much less her silences.

TERRIBLY SORRY THANKS FOR EVERYTHING I MEAN THAT STOP WRITING MORE EXPLANATIONS HOPE YOU UNDERSTAND AND FORGIVE AND ARE MUCH HAPPIER LATER ON STOP HAVE NO RESENTMENT OR ANGER ONLY REGRET ML

After four—*I had all but given up*—he saw the boy walking up the hill. He retreated to his inner office, ripped the cable open. *ONLY REGRET*. No love. No punctuation. *I MEAN THAT STOP*. Nothing to help him parse. *I MEAN THAT STOP WRITING. STOP WRITING MORE EXPLANATIONS*.

Still, how could he have misread? He saw *THANKS*. Saw *I MEAN THAT*. There was only one way for him to be *MUCH HAPPIER*. Back to the top: *TERRIBLY SORRY*. *REGRET* his own, resonant. As ever, he read his desire, not her words. At the telegraph office, he handed over his message. *THANKS A MILLION LOVE WALTER LINK*. No stop. He was too happy. This time—*Dearest Sweetheart*—he couldn't wait to get back to the house and write her at length. *The knots have been disappearing from my tummy and I am sure that tonight once again I can sleep a sleep of happiness with but one thing wrong—that you can't be here with me.* Arm's reach. *Now I can feel happy about V day.* Maybe he could still persuade her to bring the children to Bogotá in June.

He put Bing on the phonograph—Moonlight becomes you— and imagined dancing her through the rooms with a mastery and grace he'd never had. Why did he always feel most romantic when she was too far away to touch? *I intend to try and woo my wife like she has never been before (by me) and I am sure that you will like Bogota and love me at the same time.*

Pages turning, a day for every letter. He kept the cable in his breast pocket next to his heart; he obsessively reread it, never once seeing what it said. *It makes me feel good to have you tho so far away.* He wrote about the house, its refinished floors, furniture arriving from the States. *Our second honeymoon in Bogota will be a lot better than the first.* He imagined watching the plane swoop between the peaks, his heart swooping with it. *I sure was dumb. I have been away too long.*

Three days. Four. My heart, as I read, is still breaking. He dined out, collecting the sort of people she liked. How long would this attentiveness have lasted? *He is the Rockefeller foundation man working on Yellow Fever and Malaria. She is one of the Alexander G. Bell offsprings.* And what company was she keeping?

A week. Eight days. A letter from Mandy, oddly distant. She was getting older. *Muckie we must be gentle with her which I know is hard to do and easy to say.* He couldn't think too closely about anything. *She is a strong character and like a lot of other people probably has made it hard on herself when it wasn't necessary.*

Ten days. He was a fly caught on flypaper, buzzing helpless wings. *Your Lover.* Trying so hard, believing he still had time to remake himself.

AWFULLY SORRY YOU MISUNDERSTOOD MY CABLE STOP. Again, she had waited too long, wanting only to be finished, apologizing for the wrong thing. I FEEL WE MUST SEPARATE NOW STOP BELIEVE & HOPE SINCERELY YOU CAN HAVE A HAPPIER LIFE AFTERWARDS STOP YOU HAVE NOT (*True?*) LOST CHILDREN ONLY THE WRONG WOMAN M.L.

ARRIVING FIRST POSSIBLE PASSAGE PROBABLY WEDNESDAY LOVE WALTER LINK

During a two-hour layover in Barranquilla, he thought of the time he'd wasted. *I misunderstood.* He paced crowded streets, looking into shop windows still bare of goods, paying so little attention that he came around a corner into the square and almost mowed a fellow down. By the time Walter registered who he was, Wilcox's eyes were already sliding away, as if he could slip past unrecognized. But Walter stopped to shake hands. Wilcox had just come from Panama, was traveling to Havana on the evening plane.

Something funny. That old knot in his gut, a buzz in his ear. Keep your enemies closer, Walter thought, and invited Wilcox to dinner. They shared a taxi back to the airport, sat together on the plane. In Havana, Wilcox sent Link home in his car. By the time he arrived, he was no longer lovesick. Just the sight of her, standing in the open doorway, forewarned, her face carved from stone, filled him with fury. He could see it hurt her to move aside so he could walk into his own house. His.

"What does Wilcox have to do with this?" He hadn't even set down his valise.

She looked not at him but past him. Sat down on the sofa and lit a cigarette with a lighter he hadn't seen before.

She thought she would marry him sometime.

He couldn't believe the idiot had promised to marry her. Back in her presence, no longer longing for her, he felt more than ever his usual fury. He lit his pipe and she chain-smoked while they waited for Wilcox, the smoke rising blue, haloing her head. What did the chauffeur think, driving men back and forth? *Something went astray.*

When Wilcox came in, he and Miriam exchanged a look, as if love had made them invisible. His wife's lover. When had she looked at him that way, utterly complicit? How should a rational man act, a man of science? She wanted to be divorced immediately. She wasn't asking, not now, for a single other thing—only that he release her.

Her. Into another's arms. His money, his children. His power over her. He would surrender nothing. There had never been an ours, I see, not really. Can't be, when one belongs to the other by tradition and law.

Whatever else he may have believed, Chris never for a moment thought I might obey. The best we ever hoped for was what we came to: a turning, after years of meeting the world back to back, to see each other, eye to eye. A facing up to. At our moment of greatest crisis—imagine it, like that in any marriage, in no other marriage—he let go of resentment. So did I. I book tickets. He updates my phone, which I use not quite as often as he would like. He drops me off, as I do him; when he picks me up, he takes me home, makes love to me, then shows me what he's done. We are far from finished. But we make our own choices, keep choosing each other.

Wilcox sat near her, as if to protect her—touching her hand as if he had the right. For a moment, Walter wished he'd brought the pistol after all.

Florida. En route to Tulsa. Sleepless again. *It is about 4:30 AM— no I haven't been out.* He'd stayed up writing to Mandy, to his brother Alfred, to his sisters, to everyone he could think of. At last, to her, *You need not give the statement that we had words about*, in which he imagined her admitting fault, relinquishing all claims. He would give her $400 a month, for the children. Andy should stay with Mandy *until you are in a house with a yard, and the honey moon is over.* That stopped him. *(I hope it will always be a honey moon, to make up for the years there wasn't any.)*

What did he hope for himself? To behave well, if only he knew how. To win her back. To make her suffer. *This then is the SWAN SONG or the GOTTERDAMMERUNG.* He couldn't shake her off. *It is a tragedy—at least for me.* It was almost 5:30; his train left at 8:00. *Good luck, happiness and God Bless you.*

He lasted two days. From Tulsa: THERE IS STILL TIME TO GIVE OUR CHILDREN AND OURSELVES A BREAK.

She marked her cable PERSONAL. GAVE MATTER EVERY SERIOUS CONSIDERATION BEFORE WRITING LETTER TO BOGOTA DECISION REMAINS UNCHANGED.

How had Mandy not seen it at the beginning, when she held her daughter's happiness in her hands? *Darling do you think I could look at your dear face, always sad, hopeless & lonely all those years and not be completely happy to know that that loneliness is a thing of the past?* Or, later, when she had urged Miriam to stay with him, to have his children. *What kept me awake many times at night was wondering to what extent I was to blame.*

When he phoned, she said to Walter, *"You were never happy anyway."*

He had been. He was certain. Or something like it.

He told me he was going to fight for the children. For their own good. He hardly knew them. *There are no words. If you ask me it is only self love that is wounded.*

He showed up again at the house in Havana with no warning and let himself in with his key. He told her he would be staying two nights. Said *my roof.*

Miriam had the maid prepare the guest bed, checked the lock on her bedroom door.

Neither would surrender the need to be right, to be innocent. Neither would budge.

He walked through the house with pen and paper taking inventory of the accumulation of their long marriage: wedding gifts, the fragile bark of worldliness they'd launched upon; everything collected in the meantime—she remembered a sedan chair; steep, narrow streets lined with shops; how she longed for crystal and amethysts while he bought those stupid dishes.

I think of the bookshelves Chris and I had built, the dishes we chose, the couch we found to fit his large frame and my small one—it took months. In my own fantasies of flight, what would I have taken, from a life so knit? The maple bed we designed together?

Her silver platter, engraved for her by a sea captain she charmed, now ornamenting my study. Chinese rugs, vicunas he'd brought her from Ecuador, Baccarat crystal he'd given her for Christmas in '43. *He's welcome to it. I'm glad to be rid of it.* He would have taken it all, but he couldn't stand how he looked to himself. *He has allowed me to keep the wedding present silver.* She had her clothes, her jewelry, her books. *—o yes, and the love of my children. I'm*

281

coming out of the darkness into the light.

At the kitchen table, he presented papers saying neither would contest the divorce, and *neither party would ever lay any claim to anything from the other.* For the children, he offered subsistence if they lived with Mandy, not ever with Bill. *Alimony is out, of course.*

No attorney. The two of them in a room where they'd lived together as strangers, four walls that no longer exist. He was still in charge. *I told him I didn't want anything.* She had a job, but she was being a fool. She wanted to be done. To throw off her oppressor. She reached for the pen, still warm from his hand. *So, of course, we both signed it.*

But he wasn't finished. *I cant quite get through my head, you who pride yourself on honesty etc should go about a thing in the very underhanded way you did it.* She felt she was watching him from a great distance, a lab specimen on a slide. How had she thought she might get away with it—stringing him out like a kite, until he was a speck on the clear blue sky of her mind, then cutting him loose? She should have known him better, but she knew him too well. If she'd tried to sit him down and talk it out, he would only have raged. His.

You had definite leanings toward a great number of men. His brother. Murphy. Bert. Viruly. *Tho you probably never worked up passion for the man.* Viruly, her true love and heartbreak. He knew less than she'd thought, and more. My heart tells me. He'd believed it, always, and he'd been wrong. All those journal entries he'd read, like her telegram, and not understood. Anyone but him.

I have never been unfaithful. She wrote it, perhaps believed it, though I wonder how. She had struggled from the beginning, and stayed so long—a version, I guess, of being true.

In fact you have been mentally unfaithful for many years. Mind, heart, for her they were what mattered, though, in this narrow case only and for the sake of argument, they were irrelevant. Infidelity was what he had done: casual, flesh against flesh. Something left on the skin, a residue to bring home, infection. She had done what was necessary.

282

When you thought you had Bill tied and bound, which you haven't, you then decided to quit, because you recognize the security a woman of your age needs.

Of her age. How Bill looked at her. How he made her feel.

There are many things that you probably know and many that you don't know at all.

Her: *We know everything about each other.*

Everything? This was what he'd brought, this time, instead of the gun. The private detective had been worth every penny. *From Bill's history he likes affairs and a certain excitement.* It would only make things worse, but he couldn't stop himself. *You are now in a state of love that is something one would expect of a twenty year old girl or even an old man looking for romance, but not a 39 year old woman. You are not young, you are not pretty and I think now to many men not even attractive sensually.* Adding two years to her age. *You had with your vitality a good many brains, a lot of personality and a good figure.* Gone. *When your hair became thinner, and gray, the lines showed in your face, your skin became splotchy—that for me did not in the least deter me from your beauty.* The little half smile on her face. *When your breasts began to droop it was because you suckled my children. When you became flabby and soft it was for the same reason, it was my fault too.*

Despite the photos, she has spent five months feeling beautiful. Spinning under the stars with a man who never lifted his eyes from her face. <u>Moonlight becomes you.</u> Now, under her husband's eye, her husband's words, *my fault too*, she becomes what I see when I look at the photos.

I have never met a man who could really say that after many years their wives were exciting to them in bed—as they were on their wedding night. Seventeen years. *To the last I was still proud that you excited me as much as the first night.* Is she humiliated, deflated under his words—is she listening? *So with all that and the years that caused it, to me you were never compared with some 18 year old lithe girl.* He can't stop trying to convince her nobody else could love her, that she is not lovable, that he loves her, actually her. *Once he has you—and if by chance you find that it may not be all that you expected—you will have thrown away not only your only chance for happiness, but also your chance for security and that is what almost any woman 40 or over wants.*

Is it? I want so many things. I, who, like Miriam, unlike my mother, have never been beautiful, want Chris to see me, to love me not in spite of seeing but because, to please me, body against body, pulse against pulse. I could be wrong. It's not only in my hands, and things never stop moving. But I believe now that we will always be together, one bending to the other. This lets him breathe, perhaps, when I go. I have never asked him.

She is two years and a half shy of forty. Motionless before him, she is moving away so fast nothing he can say in person or on paper will reach her.

When people want something they make strange promises and say strange things. The inherent honesty about all things is what counts, not a single flaw condemns a man or a single act makes an angel out of him.

Walter never understood how, during his absences, she willfully forgot him until she had to fear his return. Click goes the latch. She rises and sweeps up the stairs to the bedroom they once shared, turns the key. She leans against the door, shaking now.

I remind myself: his heart is breaking too. Hers, mine. I belong to them both.

How could everything feel so different? Bogotá's surround of mountains, shops spilling radio music out their doors into the washed afternoon. Somebody else is taking your place. In the office waited a little pile of letters, finally the ones she really had sent in March. Such an air of innocence. *You sounded happy.* He missed, now, being deceived.

It wasn't the end. He had a twenty-year habit of telling her what to do, of being entitled to tell her. His letters came and came. She let them lie for days on the hall table, then opened them all at once. *After you get your divorce but not in our own house with the children go away with him for a week. Sleep with him—then examine the situation. This may be your last chance for the happiness you didn't have but hope to get.* He wrote niggling complaints that would bind them longer, more firmly, more rancorously than marriage. He enclosed copies of photos he'd taken in Havana, labeling the backs: *The last taken as an entity,* and *Link children in front of house in Havana—the unfortunates,* and the photo showing him and Miriam alone, *17 years 8 months 13 days 18 hours.* When he considered how long the letters would take to reach their destinations, he preempted them with telegrams.

—To Wilcox. *A 39 year old woman acting or living in a romantic heaven of a 20 year old virgin is not fully responsible.*

—To friends, family, colleagues. *Actually in my heart I was a rotten sport.*

—To Mary Wilcox, whom he'd never met. *I know that there are grounds for divorce in your family other than incompatibility but there are none in mine.* He fanned detectives out across the Caribbean. NONE OF THE LETTERS MENTIONED A CORRES-PONDENT IN THEM, *and I wonder what you know about the whole thing.* The smallest glimmer of hope: that Mary Wilcox, for love or anger, would not consent to a divorce. That she would make cause with him. But he couldn't imagine anyone else's pain, couldn't compose two lines free of insult. *If you find this a usual procedure of romance in your husband a word of warning to Miriam is in order because if this should fail her I think it would be mighty tough. I am afraid that there will be many heartaches before it is all over.*

As far as I know, Mary never answered his letters, but they weren't meant for her. He sent copies of everything to Miriam.

"Miriam, *Ain't I a heel? All the mistakes are due to my grand typing.*"

So many mistakes. The words piling up, their broken vows.

Walter wanted to understand how this could have happened. *As things drift in from the Caribbean it looks pretty bad—Be certain you know all you need to know—But birds of a feather do flock.*

There in his high mountains, in the big house he has decided to keep, to put his children in along with the wedding presents, he sits at night with his whiskey and phonograph, thinking of all the nights she lay beneath him. *It makes me shudder to think of what your mental anguish must have been to prostitute your body and your soul for me.* How has he never known the difference? *I have done things that a wise person should not do but I wasnt wise.* He pretends it's not too late. *Pack it all, ship it and then come back with me. Stop the whole thing and send me a cable that it is all a mistake. I know this is useless, but there still is Time.*

The church bell rings midnight, turning over another day. Where is she? *I guess it is better to stop now.* She used to tell him what a good dancer Wilcox was, before she stopped mentioning Wilcox at all. *Somehow you have never realized the tenacity to which I hang onto things.* He pictures the two of them wafting across the floor of the club. *I've heard that song before.* He'd thought they would be together forever, hadn't he? *His Muckie* leans back in Wilcox's arms, laughing. *There is just one angle of this whole thing you forget. That is the fact that you know, both of you do, where you are going. Your future is made as far as you are concerned, while mine isnt at all.* Wilcox bends and places his lips on Miriam's throat then spins her under one archway, another, away and away down the long gallery, receding.

Forever looked different now.

So adios to you all and good luck.

CHAPTER 25

DENOUEMENT

A YEAR OF SEPARATION passes—Miriam in Milwaukee, Walter in Bogotá, Bill in Havana waiting, everything moving at a pace Bill calls *"jicotea," meaning turtle.* The battle over children and money continues, in Cuba and Wisconsin, growing more bitter with time.

But at last Bill and Miriam are together in Havana, early evening, church bells pealing overhead. Miriam wears an off-the-shoulder frock and carries orchids. *She was the nicest looking, most attractive, and most elegant bit of feminity (hell, I can't even be calm enough to write correctly thinking how beautiful she looked) femininity.* Bill, in black tie, beams from behind his round eyeglasses. It doesn't take long to speak the vows confirming what is, to them, the destined marriage that will settle them both. *CONTRACTED FOREVER WONDERFULLY HAPPY LOVE BILL AND MIRIAM.*

What have I been waiting for if not her happiness, as if life and history could follow a simple arc and gently light, as if all struggles could end with the click of a shutter. As the bride and groom speak their vows, Andy safely beside them bearing the ring, Walter's brother Alfred rides the night train from New York to Chicago, going to pick up Peter and Joan for the long journey to Bogotá—does Walter really think Mandy will hand them over? Their bags are packed; they have their passports, as he has requested. But Mandy wakens them before dawn and puts them in the Ford with Louis to Chicago, to begin the journey to Havana and their mother. Two cars pass on the road, going opposite directions, and again Walter is wrong-footed. He has to chase after what he wants—and he will not get it.

So those two will be joined unto death by bitterness and memory acted out over their children. They will fight about custody and money, who should buy new coats and pay tuition; they will bicker through attorneys, bankers, psychologists, school principals, the children themselves, as he fulfills his own prophecies that divorce would bring them hardship and grief. If they could have come together as a "we" and still remained, each of them, an intact "I," they might as well have struggled on together. But they never found their way to each other.

Andy will stay in Havana with his mother and Bill. Joan and Pete will return each autumn to Milwaukee, to Mandy and her tender cruelties, more cruel than tender, especially for Joan. *Even if she is a girl, Mother, she needs a little affection and approval once in a while—female creatures are just as much human beings as males, oddly enough.*

Of all people, Miriam should have known better.

At last, when I make an offhand comment about my grand-mother's lack of interest in sex, my mother suggests Miriam may have found satisfaction with Bill. I remember a sweetness between them, a desire on each of their parts, even as she grew shrill in response to his deafness, and maybe vice versa, to touch each other. Perhaps this attachment enabled her, finally, to make her escape. In creating a place for herself as a teacher, in marrying Bill, she moved willfully, for the first time in her life, toward something rather than away, carried by her heart. She gave up dalliance, at last happy with one man, even while she let another make her miserable until her dying day. And her students flocked to her, my mother recalls, followed her down the hallways, angled to walk her to her car. It wasn't only the little money she earned. Teaching made her somebody, not somebody's wife. It saved her *black sheep*. Though she was angry until her dying breath, this was something. I believe it saved her.

I hadn't imagined, when I began reading their letters, I would be typing this years later. I thought I might squeeze out a few poems, an essay or two, even a short novel, but journey followed on journey; one story became another, then another; the Bush years became the Obama years. In January of 2017, I am preparing for yet another trip, one I cannot justify through work. On the night of the election in November, I was giving a reading. On the way home, I called to get the good news about the returns, and Chris answered the phone in tears.

"You're joking," I said, and again, but he clearly wasn't.

Until that moment, I believed I was going to see a female president in my lifetime. But my real surprise in the weeks since has been Chris's heartbreak. He can barely talk about the election, but—not usual for him—he forwards articles and signs petitions and shakes his head dolefully over the headlines. When on New Year's Day I tell him I am resolved to march in Washington, I brace for argument, but he just nods.

I pack as if I am heading out into a precarious journey I'm not sure how to plan for. I dig out my theft-proof shoulder bag and Gore-Tex rain hat; I order a wireless phone charger with enough power to recharge my phone three times. I lay out waterproof boots, long underwear, ponchos. On the way to the airport, I remind Chris there might not be network coverage for several hundred thousand cell phones, and not to worry if he doesn't hear from me.

As always, he gives me instructions: stay with my group, don't react to provocation, keep hydrated, wear warm clothes, don't get arrested, don't get run over. "You're small," he reminds me, as if I may have forgotten. "Don't get trampled." Be careful.

"I won't do anything to get arrested," I say, though what I do may not matter. At the curb, I take Chris's hand and say again, "Don't worry."

He says, "Stop doing worrisome things," and we both laugh.

That weekend, when I comment on Facebook ("I started early—Took my dog," though of course only the first is true), he shares my posts. Paying fierce attention, he emails articles as they come online and evolving reports about numbers; he will note over the next few days that aerial photos and on-the-ground reports suggest that the overly careful women in charge, based on a limited moment-in-time snapshot, are underreporting attendance by about half. When I return, inevitably with the flu, he takes me home and tucks me into bed. What I feel: grateful, enveloped, beloved, fully seen.

Almost in passing, my mother tells me that my grandmother worked in the late forties as an assistant for Anya Seton doing historical research and typing manuscripts. Not only does Bill allow her to work, their circumstances require her to put to use the secretarial skills she honed for Walter. Another glimmer. I go on line and order Seton's *Foxfire*, published in 1950, secondhand. Miriam may not have written a single sentence, but I imagine she drifts between—even in—the lines, a kind of haunting, an almost palpable presence. The main character is Amanda, nicknamed Andy, a young woman "delightfully compounded of emotion and romantic illusion." She travels across the west in 1932, the year of my mother's birth, in a Model T "flivver" with her new husband, a mining engineer she met on a transatlantic voyage. He is "a real man," and for this she loves and resents him. In the primitive mining town where they arrive, which might as well be on the other side of the world, she becomes a "discontented little housewife." The novel is full of geologic detail and books from Miriam's library—Charles Morgan's *The Fountain*, Ouspensky.

It could all have been coincidence, but I see in the novel not just what she might have dug up in archives and libraries but a version of her own story, in which her younger self—romantic, stubborn, wayward but finally faithful—learns to live with her silent man, even sets out into the wilderness with him and his partner. That old longing of hers to be better, to be other than she was. When the inevitable crisis comes, *she* saves *his* life. But he had, first, to let her come along.

Still imagining herself, what might she have become?

I see my grandmother in the tilt of my mother's chin and the way she looks down her nose. A series of reflections: Miriam in that old photograph twisting toward the water like a blade becomes my own face reflected in an airplane window, though, like everyone, to myself I'm always vanishing.

What is there to say that can express emotion too deep to put into words? What a liar a diary is. But she kept the diaries, and the letters too, knowing what lies and truths they held, and passed to me the chance to know her in retrospect, telling, inadequate, speculative; to make of her a reflected being, and, to my surprise, him too, and me, and mine.

Betrayal in every line.

I'll be seeing you.

ADVENTURING

MIRIAM MAGDALEN WOLLAEGER, age 16
University of Wisconsin, 1923

To plough the foaming waters of the boundless Spanish main,

To plunge amid the swelter of a pelting tropic rain,

To wade thigh-deep against the racing waters of a stream—

All these would be fulfillment of my highest, golden dream.

To hear the billows swishing as they're riven by the bow,

With their crests like smoke a-flying, lighting dark green depths below,

To feel the rush and smother of a million airy bubbles—

O, the dash and vigorous joy of life make a fellow lose his troubles!

To stand with both feet bracing 'gainst the slanting of the keel,

To make the schooner answer to my hand upon the wheel,

To feel the liquid sunshine fill my blood with golden fire—

O the joy of sailing free! What more could any man desire?

Or to climb through the blinding, stinging, pouring summer rain,

To fight a way through tropic growth, bowed to the hurricane,

To stand at last triumphant at the peak, and look to sea

Through the slowly swirling mists, with their grey lure of mystery,

To see the jungle lie below in dank, green apathy,
While sullen sea and lowering sky blend in grey unity,
To feel the sudden sharpness of a salty on-shore breeze—
O, what is worldly sordidness to artistries like these!

To make and hike through morning light before the dew is gone,
To sing and whistle with the birds a-caroling since dawn,
To sit in dreamy reverie at drowsy summer noon,
And hear the locusts singing and the golden bees' low croon,

To wander at the twilight when the world sends up a prayer,
To know that my beloved ones are watching, waiting there,
To linger with them for a while upon my glad return,
But then rise up and go again, after a brief sojourn:

For my Spirit of Adventure flies as restless as the swallow,
And so forever through the world he calls—would that I could follow!
But some day when I've won away from all the things that seem,
I'll go to find the things that are, and so fulfill my dream.

Chapters from this book have appeared in different forms in *Ascent*, *Terminus*, and *Crazyhorse*.

This book took many years to write, and while working on it I accumulated almost too many debts to enumerate. My deepest thanks go to my closest readers and dear friends, Betsy Burton, Nicole Walker, Kay Winder, and Kit Ward (whom I miss), who believed in the book even when I didn't; and most especially to Melanie Rae Thon, who believed so deeply she read and talked over many drafts, including the longest one. Melanie, your love and compassion buoy me every day. I also send thanks out to Vincent Cheng, Maeera Schreiber, Dana Luciano, Gema Guevara, Lisa Flores, Erica Bsumek, Hale Yilmaz, and Mauricio Mixco, who gave me invaluable early feedback when I was a fellow at the Tanner Humanities Center; and to Jacqueline Osherow and Julie Paegle. Thanks to W. Scott Olsen, Bret Lott, Travis Denton, and Katie Chaple, who published chapters from the book, and to Pam Wintle and Mark Matienzo, who welcomed me and Walter's films into the Human Studies Film Archives at the Smithsonian. Thanks also to all who shared memories of my grandparents with me, especially Joan, Andy, and Peter Link, Stancia Butler, and my brothers Jeff and Peter Coles, and to Tom Link, who put me up in Madison and regaled me with tales from the past. Particular thanks go to George Angel, my translator and cultural guide in Medellín; to my protector and alter-ego Jackeline Builes Gómez; and to Pamela Ospina and Ángel Arboleda Hernández, who indulged me with warmth and friendship. Last but never least, thanks to my beloved husband, Chris, who doesn't always understand what I do but loves and supports me anyway.

The travel and time required to complete this project came to me through a number of generous gifts. In addition to the Tanner Humanities Center's Aldrich Fellowship, I received support from the University of Utah Research Committee through a Faculty Research Grant, a Faculty Fellow Award, and a Distinguished Research Award. Though my Guggenheim Foundation Fellowship was awarded for another project, it gave me extra time to rework this book, an unexpected bonus for which I am grateful.

KATHARINE COLES is the author of two novels and six collections of poems, the fifth of which, *The Earth Is Not Flat*, was written under the auspices of the National Science Foundation's Antarctic Artists and Writers Program. The recipient of grants from the NEA, the NEH, and the Guggenheim Foundation, she has served as Poet Laureate of Utah, and was inaugural director of the Poetry Foundation's Harriet Monroe Poetry Institute. She is a Distinguished Professor of English at the University of Utah.